Racial Separation in South Africa

Raci

The lion and the elephant can live, but they live better apart

DR. H. F. VERWOER

*Nationalist Minister of Native Affair
in a speech before th
Native Advisory Board of Atteridgeville, Pretor*

To My Mother and Father

Preface

THE UNION OF SOUTH AFRICA IS TODAY IN THE THROES OF mounting social unrest and constitutional crisis; both are far-reaching in their implications. Since the rise of the Nationalist party to power in 1948 under the leadership of Dr. Daniel F. Malan,* South African racism has attracted an unprecedented amount of attention in the United States and throughout the world. Under the Nationalist program of racial separation—called "apartheid"—the pattern of restrictions sponsored by former governments is reinforced and, in certain aspects, replaced by a pattern of social reorganization dedicated to the proposition that the peaceful coexistence of races—white, black, and Asiatic—is dependent upon their being effectively isolated from one another. As the erection of ever higher barriers among the races proceeds, so also, claim the Malanites, will white supremacy become permanently preserved.

The course upon which the Nationalist government has embarked leaves no room for compromise; there is no turning back from the crucial issues which have emerged. The apartheid program will have such far-reaching effects that no one can tell at this stage just how drastic the changes in the system of government will ultimately be. Rising opposition to the consequences of the program has brought forth extreme circumstances from the matrix of which no South African of any race or strata can remain unaffected. In the rivalry for control of the government the major parties are engaged in a conflict the outcome of which

---

* Although obtaining the greatest number of seats in the House of Assembly, South Africa's popularly elected lower house, the Nationalists did not receive a majority of the popular vote. However, by bringing the leader of the Afrikaner party into the cabinet, the Nationalist party became the government of the Union. The distribution of seats was as follows: Nationalist party, 70 seats; United party, 65 seats; Afrikaner party, 9 seats; Labor party, 6 seats.

will determine the course of South Africa's future for many years in many ways.

Status of judicial review, status of race, status of ballot, and status of language are the more immediate issues involved in South Africa's tensions. Recent events have tended to confirm the view that these issues may culminate in civil strife before peaceful and workable solutions are arrived at.

Americans feeling the impact of rising militant nationalism in the Far East are disturbed by the rising revolt against colonialism in Africa. Dissent against British and French colonial rule north of the Sahara, already having reached the stage of destruction and violence, is being closely watched by Native peoples south of the Sahara and by the microcosm of whites in their midst. It is against this background of events elsewhere that the theory of apartheid must be critically examined and appraised.

This study approaches the apartheid program and related events primarily from the point of view of contemporary significance, combining, as much as possible, an interpretation of Nationalist racial theory and its past and present determinants. This approach is not in the spirit or sense of an apologia but rather in the spirit of a well-rounded analysis without which meaningful conclusions are impossible. The historian, the economist, the sociologist, and the political scientist will no doubt have much to ask and much to add. Each may feel that his particular field has not been dealt with on an adequate scale. I have, however, felt it necessary to forego a highly detailed analysis of the South African problem restricted within the domain of any one field in favor of approaching the topic from an over-all view and presenting the highlights of the problems posed by apartheid within the context of the several fields.

A word of grateful appreciation is expressed to Dr. Charles R. Nixon and Dr. Dean E. McHenry of the Department of Political Science, University of California at Los Angeles, and to Dr. Sol. Tax, Department of Anthropology, University of Chicago. Each has contributed much to the present manuscript through his constructive criticism and helpful advice.

Mrs. Theresa Steiner has given invaluable assistance in the typing and preparation of the manuscript. To my wife, who worked at my side throughout the later stages of writing, I can only express that which is not easily put into words but is nevertheless understood.

EUGENE P. DVORIN

LOS ANGELES, CALIFORNIA
April 1952

Table of Contents

xi

CHAPTER I

Apartheid as the Outstanding Characteristic of the Postwar Nationalist Party

THE NATIONALIST THEORY AND PRACTICE OF APARTHEID IS THE outstanding characteristic of the postwar Nationalist party in the Union of South Africa.[1] Although some writers consider the concept to be but the extension of the historical segregation policies, merely to attribute to the program a historical significance is to lose sight of its true relationship to South African politics today. Whereas the theory of apartheid may be considered as merely one form of segregation between the white and black races in the Union, its value as a potent political weapon and its contemporary role of attempting to alter the pattern of segregation already existing give to the concept an importance of the first magnitude in race relations and in the more limited sphere of practical South African politics.

With the question, "What is apartheid?" a difficulty arises, for the concept is hardly liable to one all-inclusive definition. Perhaps at the end of this book a more precise meaning of the term will emerge from the materials presented. Most definitions of the term are nebulous at best; this for two reasons. First, the application of apartheid is "something new under the sun" as far as Union politics are concerned. Second, the term has gained wide use in the Union as a sort of catchword, political slogan, or carry-all term to describe Nationalist non-European policy. It was meant to be vague in order to woo the largest possible electorate to the Nationalist camp during the last general election.

In its early days the word meant a great many things. It was used to indicate anything from partial segregation to the ultimate estab-

1

lishment of a separate Bantu state. As the general election approached, the definition was sharpened as a political weapon with which to attack the United Party. A Nationalist committee sat to define the policy and succeeded in drawing up a statement which was sufficiently vague to be used throughout the county. Somewhat to its own surprise, the Nationalist Party won the election and was then faced with the need to give practical effect to what had been the theories of a party in opposition.[2]

Although "not yet a dictionary word, it nevertheless won the last election for the Nationalists."[3] Dr. T. E. Donges, Nationalist minister of the interior, states of apartheid: "The policy of the Nationalist Party with regard to apartheid means that in their national development there shall be separation between Europeans and non-Europeans, and this will give the non-Europeans an opportunity of developing their own national character."[4]

A more elaborate definition of apartheid is provided by the prime minister of Southern Rhodesia, Sir Godfrey Huggins:

While there is yet time and space the country should be divided into separate areas for black and white. In the Native areas the black man should be allowed to rise to any position to which he is capable of climbing. Every step in the industrial and social pyramid must be open to him, excepting only—and always—the very top. The Native may be his own lawyer, doctor, builder, journalist or priest, and he must be protected from white competition in his own area. In the European area the black man will be welcomed when, tempted by wages, he offers his services as a labourer, but it will be on the understanding that he shall merely assist and not compete with the white man. . . . The interest of each race will be paramount in its own sphere.[5]

Apartheid, broadly speaking, therefore can be considered as the social, economic, political, and sexual segregation of persons on the basis of race. As shall be shown, it differs from the pattern of segregation previously enforced in the Union, which is supported by the United party, and is of a different nature. Nationalist apartheid differs from the racial policies of the United party in several vital aspects, and herein lies the key to understanding much of the contemporary political issues in the Union today.

Apartheid is an effort on the part of the Nationalists to preserve the cultural and racial unity of the Afrikaner people.[6] It is an effort to preserve and to reinforce the dominant position in all spheres of human activity of the white man over the black man or, in other words, the continued supremacy in the Union of the European over the non-European. Fundamentally, the concept of apartheid conceives the "parallel development" of two groups of people in the Union (i.e., the European and the non-European). Each group is to be strictly segregated socially, politically, and economically. The Nationalists contend that only in this manner can either group attain its fullest development.

The Afrikaner-Nationalist today is partly characterized by racial fear. This fear is not of contemporary origin but owes its life to a carefully nurtured historical root. The Afrikaner-Nationalist fears being overcome by a British culture; he lives in constant uneasiness at the threat to his way of life and thinking caused by Anglicization. This sentiment can be traced to pre-Trek days on the Cape and became imprinted upon the Boer mind by the teachings of the Dutch Reformed church and by the political forces which shaped the emergence and decline of the independent Boer republics.

The Nationalists also fear the Jew. This in itself provides an indication of the fear of the Afrikaner for non-Afrikaner peoples. Nationalist anti-Semitism, though reinforced by European persecutions of the thirties,[7] has a long history which antedates Nazi racial theory and can very easily be directly traced, in part at least, to Boer suspicion of Uitlanders or immigrants from abroad who rushed to South Africa after the gold strikes on the Rand. "It was not in order to be overrun at last by a crowd of English, Australian, and American miners, employed by capitalists, mostly of Jewish extraction, that they or their fathers had trekked out of Cape Colony, fought . . . heathen Kaffirs, founded their own Republic."[8]

Anti-Semitism remained, regardless of its historical derivation, as a prime characteristic of the Nationalist party and was evident in Nationalist legislation,[9] writings, and speeches in the decade of the thirties:

> Some members influenced by events and doctrines in Germany, were aggressively anti-Semitic. . . . The stress of new and harsh circumstances and the penetration of ideas from abroad led the Purified Nationalists, in 1938, to demand formally the exclusion of future Jewish immigrants. *To the Black Peril was added the Jewish Menace.*
> In part the bitter feeling against the financiers [mining magnates on the Rand] resulted from the general assumption that they were "foreigners" especially British and Jews.[10]

But, more than these races, the Afrikaner fears the black man and the Asiatic. It is from them that he sees the greatest threat to his self-preservation; it is to them that the policy of apartheid is directed. Before presenting a detailed analysis of the apartheid doctrine itself, it is necessary briefly to present the ethnic and population structure in the Union today. It is upon these population figures that the Nationalists have based their apartheid doctrine.

Out of a total of over thirteen million persons in the Union, only two and three-quarter million are European in origin. Of the European, approximately 60 per cent comprise the Dutch element and 40 per cent the British South Africans. Some one million are Colored and are most often referred to as "Cape Coloreds." There are three hundred thousand Asiatics, mostly East Indians. There are more than nine million Natives, mostly Bantu.[11] The Bantu, unlike the Cape Coloreds and the Indians, are spread all over the Union. Owing also to their overwhelming numbers, it is the Bantu principally who inspired the theory of apartheid.

On this basis, therefore, the Nationalist sees himself as a European outnumbered by the non-Europeans at a ratio of 4:1. He considers himself as preponderantly outnumbered by alien races, that is, alien to his culture, which have a far lower standard of living. The Boer-Nationalist therefore contends that "liberal ideas on race as a foreign importation"[12] have no place in his world. He pictures liberal concepts as basically "in conflict with the spirit of his people struggling for survival in a harsh environment."[13]

Nationalism believes that "every person can only attain his highest freedom and fullest self-realization within the unit of the nation." Liberalism believes in "the individual and his so-called rights and liberties." Liberalism stands for "equal rights for all civilized beings, for the wiping out of all boundaries, for the dumping together of all individuals, irrespective of race and colour, and their being reduced to a nondescript mass of individuals."[14]

The passage above is from Dr. Diedrichs, Nationalist M.P., and a leading intellectual of the Nationalist party. "Such a doctrine," says Dr. Diedrichs, "was totally abhorrent to Nationalism."[15] A moral justification for Nationalist racial policy is derived from the theology expounded by the Dutch Reformed church, with which the party is intimately aligned.

The entire doctrine of apartheid is based upon the allegation that to apply any other policy would eventually lead to the end of white-race dominance in the Union and inevitably lead to virtual race suicide. The Nationalist, along with the other Europeans, would thus be engulfed by the non-European races. The struggle would then be between the black races and the Asiatics for dominance over the southern portion of the continent.

To give the non-Europeans the franchise would be to give them political supremacy; to grant them economic privileges on a par with the Europeans would mean that cheap Native labor and Asiatic labor would soon replace European labor and drag the European standard of living down to that of the Native and Asiatic. Of this fundamental political and economic problem, Dr. D. F. Malan, prime minister and leader of the Nationalist party, has said:

It does not seem to be generally realised that the structure of the Union, in its political and public system, in its cultural institutions and in its economic activites, is basically and predominantly European.

In this respect the Union is unique in the world; and unless this fact is constantly borne in mind it will be difficult, if not impossible, for an outsider properly to understand the great problem facing the Union.

Agitations based on ideological concepts, with a total disregard for realities, directed towards the attainment of full political rights for non-Europeans would, if successful, inevitably lead to the ultimate political and economic suicide of the European community—a prospect which no government can view with equanimity.

Such an event would be a calamity also for the Native races, and would plunge the southern portion of the African Continent into tribal wars and chaos.[16]

The Nationalist never lets himself lose sight of the fact that, of a total population on the African continent of a hundred and fifty million, the Europeans number little more than four million.[17] Dr. Malan's passage is particularly significant because it provides the bridge by which to arrive at the central core or theme of Nationalist racial theory. An understanding of Nationalist racial theory is prerequisite to any detailed analysis of Nationalist apartheid. As Dr. Malan attempts to point out, moral justifications for the racial policies of the Nationalists and abstract ethical allusions to equal freedom and political rights are meaningless in relation to the actual realities of the situation.

It is necessary at this point to note, however, that there is a certain "morality" to Boer-Nationalist concepts of racism. As to be developed more fully later in this study, this unique Christian morality which is furnished by the Dutch Reformed church has developed into a theological schism between the Dutch Reformed church and the overwhelming preponderance of other churches in the Union. Racial inequality as an avowed tenet of Christianity is a cardinal point in the church doctrine. This is due to

the literal fact that the Boers . . . apply the Old Testament language concerning Israel literally to themselves, and its language concerning the Canaanites who were destroyed and crushed out, literally to the native tribes. . . .

. . . In their prayers the language of the heroes of the Old Testament is freely appropriated; they are God's people, and their enemies are His enemies. . . . No one who has freely and for years mingled with this people can doubt that they have persuaded themselves by some wonderful mental process that they are God's chosen people and that the blacks are the wicked and condemned . . . over whose heads the Divine anger lowers continually.[18]

These convictions are honestly held by them and must be taken into consideration in any analysis of Nationalist racial theory. "It is hard to say how much hypocrisy there is in this; it must be confessed that in a very large number of instances it is no hypocrisy, but a clear belief in which they had been trained from childhood."[19]

The prevention of race suicide and the furtherance of the white man's dominance over the black man and the Asiatic are per se, in and of themselves, the present-day justification for apartheid. For the Malanite Nationalist no other policy is politically feasible (particularly at election time), and in the actual application of apartheid, as is now being attempted, no ethical considerations are forwarded. The supremacy of white civilization in all spheres of endeavor is forwarded as the criterion for evaluating what is morally justifiable or unjustifiable in race relations. However, if pressed hard, the Dutch-Nationalist can always turn to the Scriptures for ethical justification.

Throughout the history of the Boers in South Africa, the fervent adherence to racism, at times almost approaching fanaticism, has been the dominant feature in their political thought. "His people are the Chosen race of the Bible, which is his guide; and it is part of the design of Providence that the black man should toil."[20]

Apartheid attempts to develop the non-European in his own sphere. It is based on assumptions which will be analyzed in detail in the succeeding chapters but which are relevant to any broad introduction to the concept. The most significant assumptions, upon the alleged validity of which the entire doctrine is based, are:

1. That the non-European can develop in European areas only at the expense of the European.
2. That there must be complete separation, as practiced in the Transvaal and Orange Free State republics, and complete inequality between whites and blacks in both church and state.

3. That the Native will be happiest left "to develop along his own lines."
4. That the doctrine of apartheid is feasible and capable of being carried out under the Nationalist administration.

As one writer on apartheid has pointed out, there are, under the Nationalist program, two aspects of apartheid which must be considered as inherent in its theory.[21] One is the so-called "positive" side of the theory; the other is the "negative" side.

The negative aspect seeks to restrict the Native in those endeavors by which he will compete with the European. This negative aspect has practically unlimited possibilities; for example, the reduction of political rights already attained by the non-European races; preservation of the present restrictions and additional restrictions on areas of employment open to non-Europeans; further restrictions on real property rights of the non-Europeans; increased restriction of movement of non-European races; repatriation of the South African Indian population to India in order to prevent further economic competition with the white man; and so on ad infinitum. In short, any policy which artificially holds the non-European below what he is capable of attaining in competition with the European, that is, to reduce the area of competition by applying further restrictions to those already imposed by the former government.

The positive aspect of apartheid, however, theoretically serves as a counterbalance to the restrictions which the doctrine imposes upon the non-European. For the positive aspect has as its function the replacing of these rights taken away with "something better."[22] Thus the doctrine of apartheid is composed, on the one hand, of the program to take away certain rights or to impose certain restrictions which the Nationalist administration feels necessary for the development of the Native in his own sphere; the non-European must be kept from becoming a "bad imitation of the white man."[23] On the other hand, something is given; the negative and positive would be, in a sense, in a state of crude balance to the benefit of European and non-European alike. This sets up therefore another theoretical justification to the Nationalists for restrictive measures against the non-European population which are considered necessary.

For that which is to be taken away, something "better" is conferred upon the people. The critics of the apartheid doctrine, however, have pointed out that, "since the present Government has come to power, every official statement and every official action in the sphere of non-European affairs has been of the negative, the taking away kind."[24]

The historical emergence of the philosophy underlying apartheid, of the peculiar Nationalist type, is the result of the interplaying of potent forces upon the Afrikaner environment. Though a greatly detailed study of the history of Nationalist political thought would be necessary to appreciate fully the conditions from whence has grown the modern Nationalist public policy, a few of the most important of these factors as affects racial policy should be cited in order more thoroughly to appreciate the "spirit" behind Nationalist apartheid.

CHAPTER II

Pre-apartheid Racial Policy

The Prelude to the Native Policy of the Independent Boer States*

In 1652 the dutch east india company established at table Bay a victualing station as had been recommended in consequence of the Dutch maritime route to the East being south of Madagascar. It was imperative that they have a port of supply at the turning point of the long voyage between Holland and Batavia.[1] The organization of the Dutch East India Company was on a thoroughly military system,[2] which had significant consequences in that it determined the mode of government under which the occupation took place.

The Dutch settlement advanced very slowly over a period of many years. The maladministration of the Dutch East India Company produced a discontent which served to emphasize the bold and restless character of the settlers.[3]

As early as 1658 slave labor was introduced. This labor was performed at first by West African Negroes. This step encouraged in the whites an indisposition to work and doomed that part of Africa to be dependent on the toil of slaves.[4] Later the Dutch East India Company added to its African slaves numbers of Malay convicts from Java and other Dutch East Indian territories. In 1689 three hundred Huguenots came from Holland and joined the Cape colonists. It should be noted that this was an extremely important acquisition, since it tended to offset the rapidly increasing servile element.[5] By the middle of the eight-

* The history of early settlement at the Cape and of the Boer-British contact and its consequences is perhaps of unexcelled interest. Nevertheless, it must be sketched here in the briefest possible outline as merely the prelude to the Native policy of the Trekker States.

10

eenth century the Huguenots were amalgamated with the Dutch colonists in language, religion, and politics.

The administration of the colony through a governor and council appointed by the Dutch East India Company was never popular with the colonists, and the governor was in no way held responsible to the people he governed. The colonists retained a fervent love of freedom which the company could not satisfy or control. "The distinctive Africander type of character began to appear at the time when the settlers began to move from the coast to the interior of the country. There was everything to favor the rapid development of a new type of humanity."[6] The Boers sought to increase their distance from the center of authority.

England captured the Cape during the great war with Napoleon (1806). The Dutchmen of South Africa had lost their attachment to Holland in the meanwhile, as had also the Huguenots for France. Their fatherland was no longer in Europe, but their true home and destiny was to be in Africa. They did not become attached to England either, however. "England . . . managed things ill."[7] She altered the existing system of courts and local government, thereby reducing the rights which the people previously enjoyed. She insisted on the exclusion of the Dutch language and the use of English.[8] She also inherited the situation which Macmillan describes as

the contact of advanced and backward peoples . . . inside the old Cape Colony, where European colonists met with hardly any opposition from the aboriginal Hottentots—nomadic tribes, with little or no organization, no skill in agriculture, and no power of military resistance—and gradually ousted them from their grazing lands, reducing them before the eighteenth century was out to abject dependence, economic, legal and political.[9]

In the first generation after the British occupation of the Cape the legal status of these people was thrashed out, with the year 1828 marking the freeing of the Hottentots owing to the efforts of the Emancipationists.[10] This was but the local manifestation of a world-wide movement "in whose current the Cape, tiny . . . remote . . . became engulfed."[11] The complete emancipation of slaves, an exotic element of the population, in 1833 reinforced the ranks of the newly freed people of color. Hottentots, former slaves, and a strong admixture of Europeans were becoming merged into what is now known as the "Cape Colored people."

In addition to this new irritant in Boer-British relations,[12] there were other factors—alleged undercompensation of slave-owners and failure of the British government to prosecute the troublesome and costly wars against the south-coast Kaffirs, who often made livestock raids and burned property of the Dutch frontier farmers. "He [the Boer] became determined to found in the north a community remote from an unsympathetic government with liberal ideas, hated rights for the black man, and novel administrative methods."[13]

The emigration of 1837, known as the Great Trek, resulted in Natal being established as the first Boer or Trekker independent state. This was followed by the founding of the Orange Free State and the Transvaal (or South African Republic). "Thus it was that the Great Trek . . . or secession . . . of the Dutch Boers began . . . twenty-five years before another question of color and slavery brought about a still greater secession on the other side of the Atlantic."[14]

RACIAL POLICY OF THE INDEPENDENT BOER STATES

The Nationalists today, as always, look backward to the era and racial policies of the independent Boer states of Natal, the Orange Free State, and the Transvaal. That is their "Golden Age."

NATIVE POLICY IN NATAL

The Boer victory over Dingaan, the Zulu king, on December 16, 1838, established in the Republic of Natal the settled government of approximately six thousand Europeans over approximately twenty-five thousand Natives.[15] "What is of even greater interest is that here for the first time we have a body of South Africans in a position to frame their own Native policy."[16]

Generally speaking, the policy of the Voortrekkers prior to British annexation of Natal in 1843 was (1) to mark off an area for predominantly white occupation; (2) to retain sufficient Natives therein for agricultural labor purposes; (3) to secure an equitable distribution of this labor supply; (4) to segregate the remaining part of the Native population; and (5) to rule such Natives as remained in the white area paternally, justly, and kindly, but retaining them in a position of entire subordination— social, religious, political, and economic.[17]

Mackenzie reaches different conclusions as to the "paternal" treatment of the Natal Natives. He explains the Boer exodus from Natal upon British annexation in the following terms:

It is probable that not mere prejudices against goverment by Great Britain led to their fresh emigration. The fact is that they were once more brought into contact with the fundamental principle upon which Great Britain deals with native races. That principle . . . had driven them from Cape Colony, and the prospect of its application drove them from Natal. . . . First, there should not be any discrimination founded upon distinction of color or language or creed. Second, no attacks should be made by private persons or bodies of men upon natives residing beyond the limits of the colony without direct authority of the government and, thirdly, slavery in any form and under any name must be considered as unlawful within the Queen's dominions.[18]

Macmillan points out one of the major difficulties in early Natal native policy—the gross underestimation of the native population not only in Natal but in the Trekker States generally.[19] He refutes the contention, such as Hooker[20] and Mackenzie[21] forward, that the Chaka Wars had almost denuded the region, which was destined to become Natal, of native inhabitants. The consequences of this underestimation of the native population had a wide significance, for it resulted in inducing the emigrants from Cape Colony to move toward these regions and establish themselves there.[22]

The numbers of the natives in Natal were an unlooked for embarrassment, and imposed on the Boers a task of government for which they were unprepared and indeed unfitted.[23]

The statistics of slaughter in the Chaka Wars are little more scientific than Herodotus' fabulous estimate of the size of Xerxes' army. The native troubles in which all the Trekker States were at once involved are proof positive that in the 'thirties the natives were far more numerous than is commonly believed.[24]

The significant point is this: on the "assumption" that the Natal area was supposed to be "empty" of Natives in the early days of the republic, the Volksraad[25] had promised land to the Natal burghers accordingly. The Volksraad had promised burghers two farms each, their leaders claiming not merely two but ten and in one instance forty farms each, the standard Boer farm being 6,000 acres.[26]

As a result the Native "Reserves" to provide for the actual surplus of Natives, and marked off by a land commission under the British administration, inevitably included in the Native areas farms claimed by Boers. A majority of the Boers withdrew rather than abate their full claims.[27]

Macmillan observes that the Reserves later became a device for leaving perhaps more than a fair share of the acreage of Natal open for the "occupation and speculations" of Europeans.[28] Here therefore is part of the contemporary Native problem in the making.

The early settlers in the Transvaal were at once faced with the same problems of surplus Natives that were at the moment confronting the Republic of Natal.[29] It is important to note that at this time[30] a *Plakkers Wet*, or Squatters' Law, was passed by the Natal Volksraad to the effect that no more than five Native families should be permitted on a farm (excepting that of the commandant-general, who was permitted to have more than five).[31] This was but the first of a series of squatters' laws restricting the number of families on a farm. Though justified on the grounds of securing an equitable distribution of the Native labor supply, it was nevertheless passed in the face of inadequate Reserves for the surplus Native population. A Transvaal law of 1885 adopted this same five-family limitation on any one farm. "The limitation has never been enforced. It could not be, for the reason that the

'reserves' have never been adequate for the 'surplus' native population of any of the republics."[32]

This points out one of the principal characteristics of Boer
administration of Native affairs in the Trekker States. The members of the Volksraads were suiting a practical policy to practical
ends. They were not concerned with the problem of the Bantu
tribes eighty years ahead and deliberately shirked the problem of
how to govern an overwhelming Native population at the time.[33]

They did not attempt to solve the land problem. Though the
demarcation of Reserves made little provision for the natural
expansion of the Native population, an outlet was at first found
by allowing the Natives to become rightless squatters on Boer
farms. As shown, the later squatters' laws necessarily became in-
effectual as the Reserves could not absorb these Natives. The
Dutch seemed merely to put off the "evil" day when the land
problem would have to be solved—a problem which has now
grown to almost insoluble proportions.

ORANGE FREE STATE NATIVE POLICY

The Native population of the Orange Free State is really an
overflow from adjacent territories, and it has no large surplus
population to rule aside from Natives in European employ.[34]
After 1854 almost the first action of the newly established republic was to bar any Colored person from holding land or
acquiring rights as a free burgher.[35]

The Free State had already shown its conception of "Native
Policy" by parcelling out as Boer farms the whole of the "Conquered
Territory." . . . The British Protectorate of 1868 saved what was left
of Basutoland from a similar fate, and by so doing "solved" the Free
State Native problem—at once guaranteeing a highly necessary
Native Reserve and relieving the Republic of the onerous task of
governing a huge dependent Native population . . . therefore gave
the Free State that comparatively homogeneous character which was
long its pride, its strength and its safety.[36]

Even after having won the Anglo-Boer war, the British government appeased the majority of Europeans, both Afrikaans- and

English-speaking, by not living up to its previous insistence of rectification of disabilities against the Coloreds and Indians and accorded to the Orange Free State and the Transvaal constitutions wherein the franchise was restricted to Europeans.[37] The Colored people remained in the same position as before the war.

The Orange Free State has been, for all intents and purposes, the home of many prominent Nationalist party leaders, and it seems to represent, in its characteristic rural life, the essence of Voortrekker views on non-European affairs. It remains today the only province which has since republican days consistently maintained a complete exclusion of all non-Europeans from the voters' rolls. In the industrialized Transvaal and in Natal there had been a much greater contact of Boer and Briton than in the Free State. The Free State played a significant role in pre-Union non-European policy, and it perpetuates today the Voortrekker doctrine of race relations.

TRANSVAAL NATIVE POLICY

The Transvaal Republic, called later the South African Republic, dated its independence from the Sand River Convention of 1852. This convention was concluded between the British government and the commandant and delegates of the Afrikaners living north of the Vaal River.

According to the fourth article of the Sand River Convention, "it is agreed that no slavery is or shall be permitted in the country to the north of the Vaal River by the Emigrant Farmers." Under the terms of this agreement, therefore, the Transvaal Republic was bound to have no slavery.[38] But in the *Grondwet*, or fundamental constitution, of the republic, drafted in 1855 and adopted in 1858, which was the basis of the South African Republic, it was determined that "the people [the Boers] will suffer no equality of whites and blacks, either in state or in church."[39] "No coloured persons nor half-castes," it continues, are admitted to meetings of the Volksraad or to any civic privileges.[40] On the other hand, the *Krijgsmagt*, or army, comprises "if necessary all the coloured people in this country whose chiefs are subject to it."[41]

It is essential to note that, in the *Grondwet*, Native administration comes very significantly under the heading "over de Krijgsmagt en den Krijgsraad" ("about the army forces and the court-martial").[42] The preservation of order is intrusted to the field cornets and assistant field cornets[43] and, in the case of internal insurrection of the colored population, to the commandants and commandos.[44] However, disaffection on the part of Europeans was reserved for the higher dignity of the commandant-general.[45] "By *commandos* in case of internal insurrections of the Coloured population is understood, *keeping the Kafir chiefs to the performance of their duty*."[46]

Macmillan draws the conclusion that "the problem of the Native consists, in fact, in keeping him in order, and forcing him to do his 'duty,' that is to say, to come out and labour as and when required."[47] He also observes that this obligation carried with it no corresponding right even to security of land tenure.[48] "The 'Kafir' question ended, so far as any chief or tribe was concerned, when the tribe's power was broken and the chief 'finally crushed.' "[49] In short, the Transvaalers, as far as they safely could, ignored their Native population, satisfied if only, in the words of their own *Grondwet*, they could "keep the Kafir chiefs to the performance of their duty" and "suppress vagrancy and vagabondage."[50]

In the Transvaal the black man possessed practically no status in the eyes of the law, except in relation to such laws as limited his freedom of movement and his possession of property.[51] The people who gave the blacks no equality in state or church could not allow Natives to own land even when they had enough money to purchase it. It therefore became the custom for blacks who desired to own land to register it in the name of a missionary or other white man in whose honesty they had confidence. "This was all that the black man could possibly attain."[52] Together with restrictions of Natives' freedom of movement, this

resulted in the Native adults of the Transvaal being "wholly dependent for their work, rate of wages and opportunities for purchase, upon the Boer farms on whose land they happened to
live."[53] Article 19 of the London Convention of 1884 states:

> The Government of the South African Republic will engage faith-
> fully to fulfil the assurances given in accordance with the laws of the
> South African Republic to the Natives at the Pretoria Pitso by the
> Royal Commission in the presence of the triumvirate and with their
> entire assent:
> (1) as to the freedom of the Natives to buy and otherwise acquire
>   land under certain conditions;
> (2) as to the appointment of a Commission to work out Native
>   locations;
> (3) as to the access of the Natives to the Courts of law; and
> (4) as to their being allowed to move freely within the country, or to
>   leave it for any legal purpose, under a pass system.[54]

Bovill in his work *Natives under the Transvaal Flag*[55] contends
that these four points were the minimum that any "humane
Government" could insist upon being carried out and that the
Boers did not faithfully fulfil the assurances.[56] Macmillan seems
to confirm this view of Transvaal Native policy. He shows that
land was the first objective of the Transvaal Boers and a plentiful labor supply the second, with "proper" relations between
master and servant.[57] "The possibility that the primitive Natives
amongst whom they found themselves could ever attain to civilized status, or become a political problem, never entered into
their calculations."[58]

The great majority of Natives paid a "labor tax," which was
variable and indefinite in amount.[59] A few weak tribes volun-
tarily surrendered their independence for the privilege of settling
within the republic and remaining under its protection and became for the most part rightless squatters; they received scanty
return.[60]

> The Boers took . . . the responsibilities of a governing race. . . . Boer
> government, however, meant control by a close oligarchy of farmers,
> and masters, nervous for and jealous of their own exclusive interests,
> highly sensitive to farmer opinion, but quite unchecked by a strong
> independent bench.[61]

The labor conditions were what masters chose to make them, and there was some "actual physical ill-treatment by field cornets and Landdrosts."[62]

Such service, uncertain and variable in quantity, with no effective appeal against lord and master, was of the very essence of the unfree tenures of the Middle Ages.[63]

Whatever outward appearances there may have been of ceasing to enforce servitude from the blacks, there is indubitable evidence that little more than a change of name for it was effected—the thing went on. A new system of virtual slavery was invented and prevailed under the plausible name of "apprenticeship.". . .[64]

"Apprenticeship" has been treated both as a characteristic of the Transvaal[65] and as a characteristic of Natal as well.[66] It should be noted first of all that the supply of Native labor was maintained by the importation of captives, mostly young women and children taken in Boer raids upon Native tribes beyond the borders,[67] and that during the first twelve years of the Transvaal Republic the apprentice system flourished and was hardly distinguishable from slavery.[68]

In principle it was a method whereby the children brought from Native tribes, whose parents had been slain in tribal wars, were apprenticed to Afrikaner masters for a limited period. In many cases, however, the children had been orphaned by Afrikaner bullets; therefore, "the benevolence of the institution becomes a vanishing quantity."[69] This apprenticeship lasted until they were twenty-one or twenty-two years of age. Since the ignorant Kaffir apprentices had no means of knowing their own age,[70] "some of the poor creatures took far longer than the rest of mankind to reach their twenty-first birthday."[71]

Nor was there any one to speak and act for them when the proper time for their release from bondage came. The new system was slavery under a less repulsive name, and was so regarded by its victims.[72]

In 1866 the British high commissioner stated in a letter to President Pretorius of the Transvaal Republic:

I am informed, native children and youths, called orphans, or perhaps made so by the murder of their parents, can be registered as apprentices for a term of 21 years, and can, during that term be sold as a *marketable commodity*. I must plainly state that such arrangements, no matter under what name they may be disguised, can only be regarded as sanctioning practical slavery, and as being therefore the greatest violation of one of the most important stipulations of the convention between the Government and that of her Majesty.[73]

NATIVE POLICY SINCE THE UNION

Much of the post-Union Native policy was foreshadowed by the majority report of the Native Affairs Commission of 1903–5.[74] The report represented largely the views of well-to-do land and mine owners, "representatives of an acquisitive society hardened by pioneering experience."[75] They had a five-year plan which looked to the development of mines, roads, railways, and farms in order that South Africa would be raised to a higher economic plane than previously. It advocated communal parliamentary representation (if any) for the Bantu, checks on Native land purchases, and an end to Native squatting on European farms in order to stimulate the Native labor supply. Little or no action on the report was taken at the time, and the National Convention avoided its discussion in order to escape the "disruptive Native question."[76]

The general effect of the South Africa Act, as far as Native policy was concerned, was to maintain the status quo.[77] It was decided that the qualifications for the franchise should remain the same in each province as before Union.[78] The Cape Native vote was maintained, and certain restrictions were placed on the parliamentary power to remove it, while not extending it to the other provinces. Although the Natives had, theoretically, in the Cape a right to be elected as members of the Union Parliament, this right was withdrawn under the South Africa Act. This new restriction was the product of compromise in the National Convention rather than part of a harmonious system.[79]

The rights of the Colored voters in the Cape Province were protected by a clause stating that the Colored franchise could be altered only by the agreement of at least two-thirds of the members of both houses of Parliament. Like the Natives in the Cape, the Coloreds lost their right to stand for Parliament. The color bar which existed in the Transvaal, the Orange Free State, and, in practice, Natal was maintained. As a return for the slight loss of political power, the act provided that four of the eight nominated senators should be elected "on the ground mainly of their thorough acquaintance by reason of their official experience or otherwise, with the reasonable wants and wishes of the coloured races in South Africa."[80]

Thus, under the constitution, the divergent racial policies of the provinces were perpetuated, and, while one realizes there is no advantage in a dull uniformity per se, there was much scope in the Union for consolidating legislation, the output of which was disappointingly small.[81] At the time of Union, Native rights of occupation (i.e., Native land policy) had been by no means clearly defined.[82] In addition, Native land policy in the four colonies had followed divergent and contradictory lines.[83]

With the passage of the South Africa Act, another contradiction immediately became apparent. Section 147 provided that the control and administration of Native affairs throughout the Union are vested in the governor-general-in-council. Section 85 of the act vested control of municipal legislation and administration in the provincial councils. However, the view of the Union's Native Affairs Department, that it be recognized as the controlling and supervising authority in matters affecting Natives, prevailed. The power of the central government was affirmed by the courts, which ruled that all regulations affecting Natives required approval of the central government in order to be valid. At the time, however, the central government lacked authority to insist that its recommendations be carried out.[84]

In the field of Native policy nothing notable was done during the first few years of Union beyond the enactment of the Mines and Works Act (1911), which sought to regularize, in the Transvaal and Free State only, the practice of excluding non-Europeans from skilled and semiskilled employment by the color bar.[85]

The Botha government's Land Act of 1913 was mainly in response to pressure by the Free State, where the Bantu's right to acquire land was already more limited than elsewhere.[86] It aimed at a uniform and stable land policy.[87] The fundamental idea underlying that law was the territorial segregation of white and black[88] on the basis not of residence but of ownership.[89] It clearly demarcated the Reserves and forbade the transfer by sale or lease of such lands to Europeans. This portion of the act was welcomed by Africans;[90] however, a further provision forbidding Natives (except in the Cape Province) to purchase land outside the Reserves was regarded as discriminatory, in view of the over-crowded nature of the Reserves and the small area of land allowed for Native occupation. The act was designed only as a temporary measure, however, to maintain the status quo "until Parliament should make other provision." It was conceded that the Natives were entitled to further areas of land, and the appointment of a commission was provided to determine what additional land should be set aside for Native occupation.

General Louis Botha's act operated in those provisions which stopped non–Cape Natives from getting any more land and remained suspended in those provisions which contemplated the release of additional land from the ban against Native purchase.[91] The 1913 Land Act remained unaltered until 1936, when the Native Trust and Land Act of 1936 was introduced as an integral part of General Hertzog's segregation policy. Thus twenty-three years passed before European legislators "released" a single acre of ground.[92]

In 1918 the white miners of the Rand extracted a status quo agreement which checked their employers' attempts to admit non-Europeans to semiskilled occupations. The Natives were subject, in case of Native strikes, to the penal clauses of the masters and servants law, which served to remind Natives everywhere that they had not the same freedom in the labor market as their European competitors.[93]

In 1920 General Jan C. Smuts endeavored to put the administrative side of the Native question upon a sounder basis, and a

Native commission of three experienced Europeans was set up to advise the premier, but the local councils of magistrates and Bantu on the Transkeian (Cape) model, then prescribed for general application, did not benefit the Natives scattered upon the European farms. According to the Land Act of 1913, it was they who constituted the real problem.[94]

Early in 1922 a serious European revolt took place on the Rand. Though in some aspects it was revolutionary, in other aspects it was a republican movement; it was, however, primarily a determination of European workers to maintain the color bar despite the fact that the courts had recently declared regulations framed under the Mines and Works Act of 1911 *ultra vires*.[95]

After much bloodshed the color bar was relaxed somewhat, the mines reorganized, and the Labor party driven to an alliance with the Nationalists. This alliance of urban socialists and rural Tories was held together by a determination to make South Africa safe for the white man. This determination was strengthened by erroneous conclusions drawn from the 1921 census that the blacks were increasing at such rapid rate that within a comparatively short time they would "swamp" the whites.[96]

In 1923 the Smuts government attempted to regulate the flow of uprooted Natives into the towns by means of the Urban Areas Bill, which embodied the views of many of the Natives who had been consulted. Wide powers were given to municipalities to segregate Natives into separate townships, and Natives were offered only leasehold and not the expected freehold in such townships. Thus European opinion in the mass would not tolerate any extension of Native landownership. The towns were to be European, and the Bantu were merely to be a temporary encumbrance.[97]

In 1924 the Nationalist-Labor government took office and immediately introduced a color-bar bill which restored in more explicit form the restrictions on non-Europeans in the north which had been declared *ultra vires*.[98]

As far back as the end of 1925 General J. B. M. Hertzog had

outlined his main segregation proposals. His interest in Native matters was no new or sudden one evoked by his call to the premiership. Long before he was minister of Native affairs in the Botha cabinet of 1912, Hertzog had been a careful student of race and color problems in South Africa.[99] Brookes asserts that prior to 1925, when Hertzog began expounding his views on racial policy, there was no such thing as a distinct Union Native policy—as against the politics of the various colonies before Union—and that Hertzog introduced the first really constructive attempt to provide a genuine Union Native policy.[100] The government previously had simply maintained and administered divergent and irreconcilable provincial policies.[101]

One of Hertzog's fundamental racial principles was his distinction between "Colored" and "Native." Earlier legislation in the old republics and to some extent in Natal followed the American precedent of treating as non-Europeans all citizens who were not unequivocally of pure European descent. The distinction was thus between Europeans and non-Europeans. However, since Union, a process had been going on the logical culmination of which was the Hertzog policy of making the distinction one between Natives and non-Natives. In other words, men of mixed race were to fall, generally speaking, on the European side of the color line. This was to affect the parliamentary franchise, the right to purchase land, the pass laws, and other points. There still remained, nevertheless, considerable discriminating legislation against Colored persons.[102]

As regards land purchase and segregation, the differentiation between Native and non-Native had already been made by the Botha government in the Natives Land Act of 1913 and by the Smuts government in the Natives Urban Areas Act of 1923. What was new in Hertzog's policy was the partial application of this principle to the parliamentary franchise.[103]

Hertzog's policy of "parallel institutions" for white and Colored on the one side and for Natives on the other was another basic tenet of his racial program. The supporters of his policy argued that the place of the educated Natives is as leaders of their own special institutions rather than as exceptionally favored individual voters among the European and Colored electorates.[104]

General Hertzog's proposals affecting the political development of the Natives may, broadly speaking, be summed up by saying that he wished to disentangle Native interests as far as possible from European interests, to set up institutions for local and national government parallel to the provincial and parliamentary institutions of the European, and, finally, to grant the Natives limited representation in Parliament. The limited representation would afford the opportunity for speaking and voting on subjects still common to black and white, and the representatives of the Natives would act as liaison officers between the purely Native institutions and Parliament. Representation of the Natives was the less important part of his scheme.[105] Hertzog wanted to establish a new Union Native Council, largely elective, whose members would be chosen by an indirect electoral method, which he considered would become the normal legislative body for Native areas.

In the matter of the relationship of the Natives to Parliament, Hertzog's policies looked to the abolition of the Cape Native franchise and in place thereof the provision for seven European representatives of Native interests in Parliament chosen by a system of indirect election similar to that of the proposed Union Native Council.[106] This, it should be noted, would act as a compensation to Union Natives as a whole though not to Cape Natives in particular.[107] The powers of the representatives of the Natives were to be limited, such as their being debarred from voting on questions affecting their own status and on questions of confidence.

The success of the system of parallel institutions can be permanent only if some large measure of territorial separation between white and black is attained.[108] General Hertzog's proposals affecting the economic development of the Natives were in the form of land legislation. Since the principle of partial separation, based on rights to land, was approved in 1913, the utmost difficulty was experienced in finding adequate land for the Native population. In desperation he fell back on the plan of declaring certain areas "released" from the operation of the Act of 1913 (i.e., open competition between white and black), Crown lands, however, being reserved in these areas for Natives only.[109]

The second portion of Hertzog's land bill attempted to encourage Natives living in white areas as squatters or tenants to move to the released areas or engage themselves as farm laborers. Smuts attacked the land bill from the standpoint of Native rights, while many of his rural supporters criticized it as unduly liberal to the Natives. They demanded that Native Reserves should be more fully developed agriculturally by administrative assistance and capital expenditure prior to being enlarged or before Natives overflow into lands in European occupation.[110]

In 1926 Hertzog, as prime minister, presented four bills to Parliament. These were the Native Land Bill, above described, and three other bills which incorporated Hertzog's principles of Native policy—the Representation of Natives Bill, the Native Council Bill, and the Coloured Persons Rights Bill. They were referred to a select committee. Smuts attacked the franchise bill, which looked to the abolition of the Native franchise. The bill was supported, however, by country members of Smuts's party, the South African party. A large English element remained silent, however, in deference to party wishes.[111]

The Colour Bar Act (1926), under the Hertzog government, virtually amounted to a government declaration that Natives might not in the future aspire to skilled posts in industries and works where certificates of competence are required. The Trade Unions—the South African labor movement—wholly allied itself at the date of the Colour Bar Act with General Hertzog's party.[112]

In 1929 Hertzog at a joint session of the Senate and Assembly introduced the Native Franchise Bill and the Coloured Persons Rights Bill. The franchise bill did not receive the requisite two-thirds majority prescribed by the South Africa Act, however, and the allied bill was also withdrawn.

In 1930 Hertzog referred his four bills to a select committee of both houses which did not report until 1935. Their report at this time made no mention of the Cape Colored people and reduced the other three bills to two, namely, the Native Trust and Lands Bill and the Representation Bill. No changes were made on the principles of the original bills.

As far back as 1903 the Inter-Colonial Commission had recommended:

(a) That the time had arrived when the lands dedicated and set apart, as locations, reserves, or otherwise, should be defined, delimited, and reserved for the Natives by legislative enactment.

(b) That this should be done with a view to finality in the provision of land for the Native population and that thereafter no more land should be reserved for Native occupation.[113]

The 1936 Land Act of Hertzog claimed to do exactly this.[114] It was introduced as an integral part of General Hertzog's segregation policy and was carried through Parliament without difficulty. The trust, mainly dependent upon parliamentary grants, was given authority to acquire up to 7,250,000 morgen[115] to be added to the 10,000,000 in the areas scheduled in the 1913 Natives Land Act. Among other provisions the right of Natives in the Cape to purchase land outside the reserved areas was abolished. Their status was thus reduced to that of Natives in the other three provinces.

The Representation Bill, which also carried, abolished the franchise hitherto allowed to educated Cape and Natal Natives, except in the case of individual Natives then living and already exercising it. In Natal the Native franchise had been more in theory than fact and was actually applied to only a handful of Natives.[116] In the Cape, however, although the representatives elected were exclusively European, the Natives actually constituted a majority in some constituencies. As compensation for loss of the franchise, a Natives Representative Council was set up to discuss Native needs and grievances for representation and to elect four European senators to represent their views to the Union Parliament. The franchise bill aroused a great deal of opposition from a significant segment of the Cape white population which had prided itself on having enfranchised educated Natives. The principle of communal representation of different races in place of the cherished individual vote was also attacked as emphasizing the cleavage between white and black and as counter to the thought of the South African community as a whole. The ideal had been a common franchise open to all irrespective of color, whereas the bill implied a difference of interest and even hostility between the races.[117]

Smuts, speaking on this bill, emphasized the importance of the proposed Natives Representative Council as providing for the first time a platform for expression of genuine Native opinion and wants. Smuts himself went to preside over the first meeting of the Natives Representative Council in December, 1937.[118]

In 1937 Hertzog carried his third major Native measure, the Natives (Urban Areas) Amendment Act, through Parliament. The act provided that urban Natives could be sent to Reserves and could be refused passes to seek work in towns, thus making more effective the Urban Areas Act of 1923 and a similar act in 1930 which curtailed the right of the Bantu to enter urban areas.[119]

One of the most continuing problems of Native policy since union and one which has raised much controversy has been the issue over the supplying of alcoholic drinks in the Native locations.[120] The control and supply of kaffir beer, regarded by the Bantu as an essential food, has been the most contentious issue of the entire problem.

Under the Natives (Urban Areas) Amendment Act of 1937 three systems of supplying kaffir beer are recognized. The first is domestic brewing, the second is the sale by individual Natives under license, and the third is municipal monopoly. The act provides that, in the event the local authorities do not undertake to supply kaffir beer or to arrange for its sale by means of licensing, domestic brewing automatically becomes lawful. There is also provision, under the act, for domestic brewing to be carried out in conjunction with municipal supply or sale by license.

Natives have always been opposed to any municipal monopoly system and have demanded the right of domestic brewing. Nevertheless, forty-one municipalities by 1940 had adopted the municipal monopoly system. The individual license system has not been adopted, and local authorities have not availed themselves generally of the permissive simultaneous operation of domestic brewing and municipal supply. The issue has spilled over into the political sphere, for all Native political organizations have forwarded demands for domestic brewing.

The beer issue is no longer regarded primarily as a liquor problem but, because of the large profits realized from municipal sale of beer, is intimately tied in with the wider problem of municipal finance. The Natives allege, among other things, that kaffir beer is their national beverage, that it is a part of their social and religious life, that it has nutritional value (recognized authorities have confirmed the value of the vitamin content), and that they are compelled to purchase beer at much higher prices than the cost of home brewing.

The 1923 Urban Areas Act required the formation of a Native Revenue Account by those municipalities conducting locations, hostels, or the supply of kaffir beer. Municipal beer-hall profits were unfortunately exploited by meeting recurring expenditures on ordinary municipal services, which, one commission pointed out, should more properly be financed by the General Accounts of the municipalities.

In 1944 an act was passed setting up a Kaffir Beer Account (as a separate part of the Native Revenue Account) where the municipal supply system was in force. Proceeds from this fund were to be used only for expenses in the manufacture, sale, and supply of kaffir beer and those purposes certified by the minister of Native affairs to improve social or recreational facilities for the Natives or in other ways to improve their welfare.[121]

CHAPTER III

Forces Shaping Racial Policy

The Interaction of Liberalism, Antiliberalism, and the Physical, Economic, and Social Realities of South Africa

WHILE CERTAIN ASPECTS OF UNION RACIAL POLICY SINCE 1910 and the heritage of the racial policy of the independent Boer states in particular are significant factors in the development of the philosophy underlying apartheid, another approach to the complex race problem in the Union today will bring to light a new aspect of the problem which is requisite to an understanding of the contemporary issues involved in apartheid.

Three potent factors have been at work in the Union: liberalism, antiliberalism, and the physical, economic, and social realities of South Africa. It is from their interaction and conflict with one another that the apartheid doctrine might well be explained in part.[1] One is the force of European liberalism which has had its champions within South Africa. The more liberal South Africans do not come from the Nationalist party, which has traditionally been a conservative party and is closely linked to the Dutch Reformed church at its most vital points.

European liberalism is certainly not a dominant characteristic of contemporary South African society, though it had begun to emerge in the Cape following the abolition of slavery in 1834. As will be developed more fully in a later portion of this chapter, the Christian missions in the Union have played a contributing role in relation to European liberalism as regards Native policy.

The United party, however, certainly will not go as far as the missionaries advocate in liberalizing segregation and providing the full franchise for all qualified non-Europeans. Although the

30

United party is on many significant points, as later to be shown, more liberal in respect to Native policy than the Nationalist party, in other aspects of Native policy there is little to choose between the two. Nationalist apartheid is but the grafting, by a rising generation of young Nationalists, of a new theory onto the older concept of paternalism which has characterized the practiced racial policy in the Union thus far.[2] Thus liberalism in the Union, though not extinct, is becoming weak and flabby from lack of exercise. "In Native policy the mild accents of liberalism have long been rendered inaudible by the clamour which ceaselessly clangs through the three northern provinces for a white South Africa at any price."[3]

It is difficult to explain liberalism in South Africa in terms of groups. This is primarily because English or Continental liberalism in South Africa has never succeeded in winning mass support.[4] Liberalism as a doctrine in the Union does not satisfy the more fundamental expectations or needs of large groups of individuals; it has failed as a really effective force in politics. As a result, liberalism in South Africa "has been an affair of individuals rather than political parties."[5]

When Liberalism was first transplanted to the Cape more than a century ago, it did seem that it might secure in time a popular basis of support among the politically conscious. Unfortunately . . . a Liberalism that was suited to conditions in England was not necessarily suited to conditions at the Cape, and the attempt to apply it regardless of local conditions was bound to end in failure or in a phenomenon like the Great Trek. The old Cape Liberalism even in a later, more South Africanized form, remained suspect to large sections of the European population and although it has added an invaluable tradition to our South African heritage, as an effective force it came to an end not long after the formation of the Union in 1910.[6]

There is another facet of the antiliberal tradition. Professor MacCrone points out that the historical prejudice against the color-blind liberalism derived from English sources has been reinforced by a similar prejudice against another type of liberalism derived mainly from Continental sources.[7] The opposition to the former was due to its attitude on matters of race and color; the opposition to the latter is due to its attitude on matters of religion. He writes that Continental liberalism has been greatly influenced by anticlericalism and that anticlericalism has been closely associated with free thought, irreligion, and hostility toward the role of any kind of church.

The Dutch Reformed church in South Africa, therefore, has discouraged attempts to introduce more liberal ideas into the church and has unceasingly tried to preserve the original form of Calvinistic doctrine which was seriously threatened during the ascendancy of liberalism in the Cape during the nineteenth century.

> It is no wonder, then, that the path of the Liberal in South Africa winds uphill all the way and that not a few liberals have either taken a path of lesser resistance or decamped and shaken the dust of the country off their feet by departing for "fresh woods and pastures new." It takes plenty of grit as well as a determined conviction that the cause of Liberalism . . . is worth fighting . . . not to give up the struggle in despair.[8]

Liberalism and its counterpart antiliberalism not only conflict and interact upon each other but take place within and are affected by the environment which South Africa provides. The physical characteristics of the country have influenced to a significant degree the Boer philosophy of life and likewise must be considered in the examination of contemporary South African society. The physical, economic, and social characteristics of modern South Africa act for purposes of this approach as more or less a unit since they form, however loosely that may be, a third force which sets, so to speak, the boundaries within which the racial struggle has emerged.

The primary physical feature of the present Union is that it comprises an area of 472,120 square miles, which is increased by 317,725 square miles if the former mandated territory of German South-West Africa is included as an integral part of the Union's territory. The Union proper, that is, excluding South-West Africa, consists of four provinces: the Cape of Good Hope, Natal, the Orange Free State, and the Transvaal.

The distinctive topographical feature, lending peculiar physical unity and which has deeply influenced its history, is the gradual rise of the land near the coast to the flat and rolling plains of the interior, the altitude ranging between 4,000 and 6,000 feet. Latitude,[9] altitude,[10] and narrow shape endow South Africa with a climate approximating that of the Mediterranean. The altitude moderates the temperature northward toward the interior of the continent. Although the climate is favorable to the vitality of the white race, the extent of white settlement has been greatly affected by the relatively light rainfall.[11] The rainfall varies greatly in different parts of South Africa and gradually increases from west to east.[12] Half the Union receives less than 20 inches of rain, and nearly 44 per cent of the Cape Province receives less than 10 inches. The annual mean precipitation is about 19 inches, and evaporation is high; in addition, the rainfall is irregular throughout the year in most regions.

One of the peculiarities of rainfall in South Africa is that over most of the country the rain comes mainly in the spring and in the summer months. When it comes, it is usually in thunderstorms and "torrential downpours which cut new gullies in the land, flow off quickly, magnify the erosion of soil, and involve loss of water in areas where it is urgently needed."[13] This fact has an ever increasing significance today, for, as will be shown in the chapter concerned with rehabilitation of the Reserve areas, the erosion of the soil is a major factor in the present land problem.

One of the most remarkable things about South Africa is the fact that there are few natural harbors and no significant rivers navigable for any distance inland. Just prior to the turn of the century Mackenzie wrote:

This fact has undoubtedly much to do with the slow development of this region for travelers and explorers have been compelled to make their land journey from the coast by ox wagons. Until within a few years only three or four ports have been much used, and from these ports nearly all the development of the entire region has taken place.[14]

South African development was retarded until the railroad became possible and profitable, and until this time also the inland Boers were practically isolated from the thoughts and progress of the outer world.[15]

The amount and erratic distribution of rain together with physiographic limitations made the country in great part unsuitable for intensive cultivation and forest growth. A more or less continuous belt of mountain ranges stretching from the eastern Transvaal through Natal and the southern and western Cape Province divides the country into two broad regions. The first is the coastal range which fringes the country between the mountains and the sea in a rough V shape. The second region is the interior plateau with few mountains but, as pointed out, with rolling plains and also numerous low hills, isolated or in ranges.

This tableland is South Africa itself, since it consists of seven-eighths of the entire region so named. In the north it descends slightly to the channel of the Zambesi; to the west it slopes down gradually and less abruptly to the sea level than on the eastern coast. Colonization and the prospects of development in South Africa cannot be understood unless one clearly realizes the peculiar characteristics which result from the extension of this plateau region.[16]

The Drakensburg Mountains form the only watershed determining the direction of South African rivers. Many of what are known as rivers in South Africa are merely dry channels and contain water only during the rainy season. This can be said only of the rivers which flow from the Drakensburg westward, but it is not true of the rivers flowing the shorter course eastward to the Indian Ocean. This is due to the fact that the serried mountain ridges which fringe the tableland on the east coast intercept the moisture-laden winds blowing inland from the Indian Ocean, allowing only dry air to proceed into the interior.[17] Thus most of the extensive inland country (veld) with meager and uncer-

tain precipitation is best suited for pastoralism rather than cultivation. More than 80 per cent of the country is never likely to be
used for more than grazing.[18] "On the dry uplands pastoralism
dominated the South African past, created the Boer and his peculiar culture, and to contemporary times deeply influenced the
political life of the Union."[19]

Because of the pastoralism the great plateau is, aside from the
mining areas, sparsely populated and, prior to the establishment
of the mining areas about Johannesburg and Pretoria, helped to
account, in part, for the isolation of the Boers. They were isolated not only from the liberalizing influence of the Cape but
from their fellow-Boers as well. Most of them were "semi-nomad
ranchmen."[20]

Prior to 1870 the inhabitants lived by a traditional self-sustaining agriculture on the bare veld or in isolated valleys, and their
economy was neither intimately linked with the external world
nor greatly sensitive to the changing currents of modern capi-
talism.[21]

The discovery of diamonds at Kimberley in 1870 and the development of gold-mining on the Witwatersrand in the southern
Transvaal in 1885 introduced the "new aggressive mining era."[22]
It introduced the capitalistic industrial revolution to which the
Boers had to adjust themselves within a few decades as compared with the people of western Europe, who had gradually adjusted themselves to it for more than a century. The development
of mining on a vast commercial scale, besides quickening the
pace of South African economic development, had the consequence of drawing the Natives from their inadequate Reserves
in order to seek employment, a movement of great importance
in the present South African economy and a focal point of the
present apartheid program.

The rivers of South Africa, though largely unnavigable and thus
noncontributory to interior development, have helped, nevertheless, to shape the history of the country. One of the first instances
of attempts at territorial segregation in South Africa was the use

of rivers as the boundary lines between white and black races.[23] The greatest river system of South Africa is that of the Orange River, whose chief tributaries are the Caledon and the Vaal, the Vaal being a large river with tributaries of its own. The Orange River with its tributaries drains about 300,000 square miles. The Limpopo River has its source in the hills near Pretoria and flows northward and then eastward, forming the northern boundary of the Transvaal, to join the Indian Ocean north of Delagoa Bay in Portuguese East Africa.

Such rivers as the Orange, Limpopo, Vaal, and Blood have played leading roles in the settlement of the Trekker States. More often than not they were the gateway to the "Promised Land" of the Boer. It was in fact the Boer trekkers who opened up the interior of South Africa when in the case of the First and Second Treks there was little known of the territories beyond the Orange and Vaal rivers which flowed under the wheels of their Trek carts or ox wagons. The Battle of Blood River,[24] so aptly named, is recalled to Afrikaners each year as Dingaan's Day—a day of mourning as well as rejoicing when a mere handful of Afrikaners put to rout and decimated overwhelmingly numerically superior forces under their Zulu king, Dingaan. This avenged the previous massacre of a Dutch trekker party and opened the way for Boer emigration into Natal. It is an official national holiday for the Dutch South Africans and serves to remind them of the nearness and dangerous potentialities of the Native hordes.

The economic factors which today affect Nationalist racial policy and, in fact, determine the heart and core of the doctrine of apartheid are dealt with in later chapters, particularly those relating to the Natives and Indians in the Union. It is germane at this point, however, to state them succinctly.

First is the realization that the economic system of South Africa appears to rest on a very insecure and unsound base,[25] owing to the fact that the entire economy is dependent upon the gold-mining industry. This industry is one of the most important purchasers of farm products, its Native and white workers constituting a formidable market. A large portion of South African coal is utilized by the gold industry, and the transportation industry derives much of its revenue from it. The gold industry requires goods and services of the manufacturing industry, and nearly one-fourth of the government revenue is derived from taxing the mining industry. Should the mining industry decline, the whole domestic economy of South Africa will collapse.[26]

Second, the Union is capable of mining low-grade ore, as is mined in the Union today, owing in part to the availability of cheap semicivilized labor.

Third, the large number of Natives in the Union present a lucrative market for products for which both European and Indian are competing with each other to provide.

The ethnic division of the population as described earlier is the outstanding social reality of the South African scene. Like the physical environment, it too has set the stage upon which the drama of the conflict between liberalism and ultraconservatism in racial policy has taken place. The ethnic division of the population was thrust upon the Boers and numerically has placed them in a precarious position. The apartheid doctrine and its implementation is an attempt to maintain European supremacy in all fields of endeavor in spite of this unique ethnic division.

At any rate, having an appreciation of this "eternal triangle"[27] (i.e., liberalism, antiliberalism, and the physical, economic, and social realities of South Africa), one can better appreciate the gradual emergence of conditions which allow the Nationalists at present to attempt to recast South African society into a new mold. It is extremely difficult to maintain that any of these forces operate exclusively by themselves; they each have influenced, do influence, and will continue to influence South Africans of both Dutch and British descent. In addition, they have significant consequences for one another. The economic characteristics of the Union today are the direct concomitant of the ethnic division of the population as well as the physical characteristics of the country. Likewise the harsh physical environment, the peculiar economic structure of the Union, and the ethnic division of the population have interacted upon one another and upon the South African Nationalists to produce an aggressive conservatism in racial policy, the antiliberalism of which we have been speaking.

It is significant to note that liberalism in the Union, which was nurtured primarily in the Cape, was born of a seed introduced from foreign sources and did not emerge from the South African milieu. The factors which have helped shape the early Dutch frame of mind and the present Nationalist political and racial philosophy produced a "vector" force which, when pitted against the principles of a more enlightened liberalism, forced it to be isolated in the Cape and, since Union in 1910, has kept it in a state of defensive exhaustion. These same historical forces which have produced the Afrikaner-Nationalist outlook must be taken into consideration in any attempt at appraising the course of South Africa's future. For any discussion of the present their significance is hardly capable of exaggeration. "The emotions and ideas behind the concept [of apartheid] have a historical emergence."[28] This is the point to be made.

THE DUTCH REFORMED CHURCH

Any description of those forces which have greatly affected the historical emergence of Nationalist political thought or racial theory would be incomplete without reference to the unique role played by the Dutch Reformed church, the most influential unofficial organization in the Union. It has played a singular and vigorous role in shaping Afrikaner nationalism and racial doctrine. Today "the peculiarities of the Dutch outlook set the dominant tone of South African society."[29] In much the same manner the conservatism of the Dutch Reformed church has set the tone of Nationalist aspiration and politics.

There are three main branches of Dutch Calvinism in South Africa. The three branches together total nearly 1,500,000 European adherents; they form the largest Christian community in the Union. On questions of relations between the white and black races they forward similar doctrine and act as a unit in Native policy.

The smallest of the three main branches of Dutch Calvinism in South Africa is the Nederduitsch Hervormde Kerk, which served as the state church of the Boers' independent South African Republic (Transvaal). The second branch of Dutch Calvinism is the Reformed Church of South Africa (Die Gereformeerde Kerk van Suid Afrika). The oldest and largest church of Dutch Calvinism in the country is the Dutch Reformed Church of South Africa (Nederduitsch Gereformeerde Kerk van Suid Afrika).

The Dutch Reformed church "for generations has exhorted its members to hold fast to their cultural identity, and to let the past die hard."[30] Historically, it has been the chief agency by which the Afrikaans language has been preserved. In the nineteenth and twentieth centuries the church has served as a great social influence in the daily lives of the Dutch South Africans. The church came closer to the individual lives of the rural Dutch than did the state. It was often their only agency for social life or gatherings. The church "invigorated the social cohesion of the group, whence grew a national spirit."[31] And today "on all matters of national concern its predikants freely transform their pulpits into political platforms."[32]

Barnes, in the following passage, has seemed to catch the essence of the significant relationship between the party, the church, and racial theory:

This church represents the Dutch mind's one triumph in self-expression—the only considerable example of collective art which the Afrikaner has yet produced. Its presbyterian system of government has kept it continuously in close touch with the more benighted laity, whose unschooled prejudices it reflects with the obedient automatism of a mirror; the same factor has made its clergy inveterate *politiques*, wielding an influence no less powerful than the Irish priests over the opinion of the faithful on all affairs of state. Thus for the Dutch, religious feeling and national feeling are mixed beyond disentangling.[33]

"Based doctrinally on the narrowest and most uncompromising Calvinism,"[34] the church provides a close link between the pulpit and the practical Union politics as practiced by the Nationalists. The church today occupies the dominant position among the churches in the Union. Being a dominant factor in keeping alive the spirit of nationalism and aggressive conservatism, the church therefore takes on increased significance in any historical or contemporary view of Nationalist party principles. From the ranks of the church have come the most vigorous leaders of the party. Dr. Malan, the prime minister and leader of the party, is himself a former pastor of the church; his pulpit was in the Cape.

The state controls the church, and, conversely, the church controls the state, for it is necessary for a man to become a factor in religious affairs before he can become of any political importance. As a result of this custom the politicians are necessarily the most active church members.[35]

Ironically enough, this passage was written before the turn of the century, but a more accurate and concise statement could hardly be made of today's party-church unity. This intimate relationship is not characteristic of the other political parties in the Union, whose leaders are selected on the basis of other attainments.

In April, 1950, a congress of the Dutch Reformed churches was held in Bloemfontein. The four federated Dutch Reformed churches, the three Dutch Reformed mission churches (for non-Europeans) of the Cape, the Orange Free State, and the Transvaal,[36] as well as the Hervormde and the Gereformeerde churches were represented. The conference was under preparation for more than two years, and its purpose was to discuss the Native problem from the Christian point of view.

The majority findings were in support of total separation between white and black—social, residential, industrial, ecclesiastical, and political. Apartheid was the declared policy of the government, and the congress was convinced that there are basic principles in God's Word which support it. Only along this road of total apartheid would there be any future for white civilization in Africa or any real justice for the Native.[37] (It is interesting to note that the congress passed a resolution stating that "it is the considered opinion of the congress that the Native question should be kept above party politics.") The main purpose of the Dutch Reformed church is dissemination of God's Word. God's Word is now "total apartheid."

Even Dr. Malan, however, finds that he cannot go along at the present time with the full implications of absolute separation. He has declared during parliamentary debate that total territorial separation was not a practical policy. "It was an ideal but not the policy of the Nationalist Party."[38] He has always stated clearly that, owing to the fact the whole economic structure was based to a great extent on Native labor, total territorial separation was not in accordance with the realities of the situation.[39] The party was not in conflict with the final aim of the church. The government would, on the contrary, further the aim of the church, but there was a great deal of work to be done before that aim could be achieved.[40]

Although the Bloemfontein congress of the Dutch Reformed churches supported the policy of total apartheid and accepted the interpretation of the Scriptures which allowed such a pronouncement, the church has never presented unanimity of thought on this topic. Vigorous dissentient voices have let themselves be heard from the Dutch Reformed church's own theological seminary at Stellenbosch.

In 1949 *Die Kerbode*, official organ of the Dutch Reformed church in South Africa, published a series of articles entitled "The Holy Scriptures and Apartheid" dealing with the scriptural basis for apartheid. The articles, the result of a report of the Cape Dutch Reformed church's Synodal Commission on Race Relations, presented a defense of apartheid from the Dutch Reformed church's point of view.

Dr. B. B. Keet, prominent scholar of the Dutch Reformed church and also a member of the faculty of theology at Stellenbosch University, writing in Die Kerbode dealt with the scriptural grounds quoted by the Synodal Commission. In his article condemning the findings of the commission, Dr. Keet stated:

> When we come to the second part of the Commission's report, viz., the scriptural grounds of apartheid, we must remember that the pronouncements of the Scriptures are used to support the political as well as the religious policy of apartheid. . . . Considered by themselves, the interpretations given to the texts are not untrue—they say only that the Bible recognizes the existence of different races and peoples and declare it to be the will of God that there be a variety of races and peoples—but in this connection, as justification for a policy of apartheid (both political and religious), the whole reasoning is false and unscriptural. One can only ask: "How does the Commission arrive at such an interpretation and declaration of the Scripture?" I notice that some of the members of the Commission were old students of mine. I can but declare solemnly here that they did not learn such an interpretation of the Scriptures at the Theological Seminary, and they will find it nowhere else in the Christian Church. It has been declared that we know we stand alone in the world—this would not have seemed so bad to me, but the tragic fact is that we stand alone in the Christian Church. And then I mean not only, as so many people think, the liberal and modernistic part of the Church, but also the strict Reformed part. Even though it is for this fact alone, that we stand alone in the Christian Church, we must be very careful in pursuing the chosen path. One cannot help thinking of the mother of the soldier, proudly pointing out her son and saying: "Look, Jan is the only one in step!" Or does the Commission think that our Dutch Reformed Church has really discovered a new theological point? I am afraid that it is a very old and to Christianity, a foreign conception which was defeated in the days of the Old Christian Church.[41]

Dealing with the matter further, Dr. Keet says that it is dangerous to attempt to start at the policy of apartheid and then go to the Scriptures for justification. He remarks that if one goes to the Bible with a preconceived idea for justification one will in all probability find it but will not in this manner arrive at the teaching of God. Thus, he declared, "Satan on occasions also used the word of God for his own purposes."[42] Dr. Keet points out that the Scriptures do not lend themselves to direct judgments on national, biological, cultural, economic, or other natural phenomena.

The commission says that they find nothing in the letter or spirit of the Old and New Testaments in conflict with this policy of separate, autonomous development to independence. It all depends what is meant by separate development. If it means separated, divided from as it must be read in the whole context, then it is opposed to everything for which the evangelical message, both in the New and Old Testaments, stands.[43]

This declaration, coming as it does from one of the Dutch Reformed church's own theologians, reveals a significant rift in the ranks of Afrikaner Calvinism. Dr. Malan has declared that the Nationalist government acknowledged God's guidance in governing South Africa.[44] If the theological schism widens, however, Dr. Malan may have to revise his statement. Apartheid as defined by the Dutch Reformed church, although not attainable under present conditions, and faced with dissent at Stellenbosch, nevertheless has become the *idée fixe* of Afrikanerdom.

The relations between the English-speaking Christian churches and missions in the Union and the Dutch Reformed church present another aspect of the apartheid program of the Nationalist party—an aspect which is taking on increased domestic and international importance. Reports coming out of the Union reveal the vehement and concerted attack on the part of Anglo-American missionary societies in the Union against the assertion by the Nationalists and their church that Christian and ethical grounds are not transgressed by Nationalist apartheid. It is from reports of those agencies who make the welfare of the Native population their primary concern (i.e., the Christian missions in the Union) that such contemporary material can be gathered and analyzed on the effect of Nationalist apartheid:

Reports from South Africa show a steady increase in the number of church protests against the government's policies of racial discrimination and segregation. A recent dispatch from Johannesburg to Religious News Service tells of three national denominational confer-

ences just held, in each of which the condemnation of apartheid
(segregation) measures occupied the top spot on the agenda. The
Synod of the Church of the Province of South Africa—which is to
say, the Anglicans voted that Christians could never be satisfied with
any social policy which did not envisage extension to members of all
races of an adequate standard of education and an effective share in
government. The Methodists and Congregationalists are equally con-
demnatory of the present policy. Moreover, a meeting in Capetown
attended by 80 ministers has set under way preparations for a day of
prayer . . . which is to be followed by a general conference of church-
men to frame a declaration against the Malan Government's discriminatory measures. One of the most revealing developments in this
growing tension between church and state came when *Die Kerbode*,
official organ of the Dutch Reformed Church, devoted its main editorial . . . to a defense of that denomination for supporting apartheid.
The Dutch Reformed Church, though the largest in South Africa,
is almost alone in this stand. The *Kerbode* after listing the churches
lined upon the other side declared that it recognized "the voice
of Communism" in the condemnation which these churches have
leveled against the Malan racial policies. When a Christian church
is reduced to charging that other churches are Communist dupes or
agents, that's a sign that it has about run out of valid arguments by
which to support its position.[45]

The Foreign Missions Conference of North America has already
"vigorously urged the U.N. to take appropriate steps to curb the racial
policies of the present Nationalist South African Government." It
has called such policies "anywhere and under all circumstances, un-
christian."[46]

These assertions that the Nationalist apartheid program vio-
lates the fundamental tenets of Christianity, however, could as
well be leveled against the United party and its traditional policy
of "paternalism" in non-European affairs, especially if the missions envisage eventual political, educational, and economic
equality between Europeans and non-Europeans. There are two
fundamental differences, however, in the United and Nationalist
racial programs as they affect the missions in particular. First
is the difference in degree or intensity of segregation to be carried
out. The Nationalists envisage a much stricter segregation program in all its aspects than hitherto attempted. Second, the
mission societies fear the power of the Dutch Reformed church
itself. They have an apprehension, steadily increasing, that their

position in the Union under the Nationalist government and its alter ego in the form of the Dutch Reformed church will be undermined.

Dr. Malan's refusal so much as to discuss his policies with delegations from the Anglo-American churches has communicated alarm to London church headquarters. It is plain that one result of a continuation of the Nationalist policy will be establishment of the Dutch Reformed Church as the dominant Christian body in the whole southern part of the African continent. The Dutch Reformed Church does not permit natives to become full members. The implication for the future of Christian missions in Africa is too clear to be mistaken.[47]

This fissure between the two widely variant views of what constitutes the true moral spirit of Christianity in relation to the nonwhite races is a schism whose role in the historical environment of the Afrikaner people is of primary significance. This same moral antipathy on the part of the Dutch South Africans and the missionary societies for each other was, as previously touched upon, not only evident but intensive in the pre-Trek history of the Cape Colony. At this point the rise of early liberalism in England and its impact in abolishing slavery in 1834 in British territories must again be mentioned.

Slavery was one of the legacies of the Dutch East India Company, which had introduced negroes from West Africa and "Malays" from Java.[48]

The crowning injustice came in the shape of the emancipation of slaves. . . .[49]

. . . Carried out, as regards details with a maximum of injustice to slave holders.[50]

The slave owners were compensated; but those at the Cape received only a million and a quarter for slaves valued by the Commissioners at three millions sterling.[51]

It [the British government] was determined to put away the evil thing, and Dutch farmers were ruined that the British philanthropists might sleep more easily.[52]

Another element served also at this period to provide the conditions of which the present controversy is but one manifestation:

The missionaries . . . set to work about this time in South Africa and became for many years the censors of the Dutch. The missionaries saw black men in the light of the Kingdom of Heaven as potential angels or saints. They therefore resented the practical treatment of the blacks as inferior beings, and the standard of humanity which they set up was an offence and stumbling block to the Dutch Boers.[53]

This was one of the most directly contributing factors leading to the Great Trek. Thousands of Boers emigrated, since their slaves had been taken away and they had been forbidden to treat the blacks as inferior beings.[54] From this arose the ideological conflict and a resentment carefully nurtured between the English-speaking Christian missionaries and the Boer people on the basic principles of Native policy. The conflict goes on today scarcely unabated.

The Dutch-Nationalist finds his succor and his moral sustenance in the Dutch Reformed church; within it he can isolate himself against the outer world and its foreign ideas. He finds his most enhanced role within the unique Christian theology which the church expounds and turns to it when seeking confirmation that he is a member of a master-race, the *Afrikanervolk*. From the pulpit the Nationalists derive their political and social theories, and from the confirmed disciples and hierarchy of the church they draw vigorous and devoted leadership; and upon the floors of Parliament in Cape Town they combine the two.

The suspicions and foreboding experienced by the Anglo-American Christian missions in the Union today are certainly not an innovation and cannot be laid exclusively to the Malanites. Another Christian missionary, Dr. Livingstone, also had his views on the role of the Dutch Reformed church. Indeed, it was not without foundation that

Livingstone himself . . . could not understand how the Boers could reconcile their practice of slave-raiding with their profession of Christianity. To his amazement as he wrote to a friend at home, "their church is, and always has been, the great bulwark of slavery, cattle-lifting and Kaffir Marauding."[55]

THE MISSIONARIES

King John II of Portugal, when he sent Diogo Cão on two memorable voyages (1482–84 and 1485–86) along the western coast of Africa, paved the way for later European explorers to the area around the mouth of the Congo River. John II and his successors in the early sixteenth century not only were in quest of trading profits but, being devout Catholics, also aimed to evangelize the Natives. It was indeed for this very purpose that successive popes granted them exclusive rights over the newly discovered territories.[56]

In 1560 Father Gonzalo da Silveira landed at Sofala and thus became the first Christian missionary to southern Africa. It was nearly two hundred years later when, in 1737, Georg Schmidt landed at Cape Town to establish a mission station on behalf of the Moravian Missionary Society.[57] By the end of the eighteenth century the Roman Catholics under the Portuguese had established a few stations near the Zambesi.[58] It was not, however, until the nineteenth century that mission societies began to play a really important role in the carrying of European civilization into Africa.[59]

To the present time the influence of missionaries has been uninterrupted and immense. An ever increasing stream of missionaries, all inspired by the same ideal of conquering for Christ the Dark Continent of Africa, "poured in from England, France, America, Germany and other European countries."[60]

It must be remembered that at this time the Bible also accompanied those devout Christians, the Voortrekkers, on their Great Trek through Bantu country, from the Cape to the Limpopo. The Bantu religion was thus assailed from two quarters.[61]

The resultant impact of Christianity through its harbingers in the form of the mission societies have made the missions "the greatest conscious force for change operating upon Bantu life."[62] Bantu thought and practice have been deeply influenced, and today the missions very largely control Bantu education.[63] With no important tribe lacking its resident missionary, with the Bible, in its entirety or extracts, available in seven South African Bantu languages, and with the hundreds of mission churches and schools, European civilization has, in one form or another, "reached the darkest parts of the Dark Continent."[64]

Mere statistics pertaining to the number of Christian Bantu, the number of missionaries at work in the Union today, or the annual financial outlays for mission work are not a true measure of the effective influence exerted by mission societies.[65] To appraise the full consequences of missionary efforts on behalf of the Natives, the scope of the task facing the missions must be appreciated and the interaction of the divergent civilizations must be understood.

The paths of the early missionaries were smoothed by what were numerous points of contact between the religion of the Africans and Christianity. The African found no difficulty in trusting in God or envisaging the supernatural or invisible. "The idea of God was not new to him."[66] Indeed, there is abundant testimony that "there is a true relation between what the missionaries teach and what the heathen fathers believed."[67] Thus, even with the marked absence of temples, images, and "holy men," that the Africans had a religion is beyond doubt.[68]

Although there was some common ground between the two religious systems, the missionaries brought with them not only a new religion but a new social order.[69] "The universe for the African is centred in his group. It is a small universe moulded by the actions of a few men—himself and his fellow tribesmen. The phenomenon of nature awaits their cooperation."[70]

The God of the Africans was too remote to be concerned with the individual member of a clan.[71] The African conceived of himself as primarily a member of the group. Any philosophy of individualism would have been untenable, as the old chiefs feared any deviation from time-honored tribal practices and lore. They viewed with suspicion, as a threat to their own power, any sudden or rapid rise in prestige by the younger men within the tribe who might introduce new ideas or methods. African sta-

bility depended on the group life. The African learned to fear
and even to hate that which lay outside his tribal group.[72] "The
clan or tribe was the world."[73]

On the other hand, it was the evangelical revival in England
which set the tone for early missionary efforts among the Bantu.

There was an intense pre-occupation with the work of *individual
salvation*. This was not only regarded as the *primary* object of missionary activity, but was so interpreted as almost to crowd out the secondary objects.[74]

Christianity insisted on conversion as a personal matter, an affair
between God and man. A man could draw his family with him, but
the decision became, in the last analysis, a personal step for each
one.[75]

It was inevitable that this intense individualism, which was
Christian, partly Protestant, and early Victorian, smacking of the
age of radicalism and laissez faire, would come into conflict with
the Bantu social organization.[76] There was, in short, an "anti-
tribal bias of mission teaching."[77] Those Natives who became
Christians were lost to the tribe. As a result, "the Christian gospel
was during the nineteenth century the most powerful agency in
the disintegration of South African tribes."[78]

Tribal solidarity was always like a stone wall. . . . For one member
of the family to hive off and cast away the beliefs of the family and
tribal tradition in response to the call of a new faith seemed prepos-
terous. Many an individual must have been torn in the conflict. . . .[79]

Thus, in the face of the impact of Western civilization and its
Christian message of repentance and renewal, tribal life could
not remain unchanged. This remaking of African man is summed
up in the following pasage:

African society must change. There is much in it which is contrary
to what is best and highest in human life, and these fetters on man's
true development must be struck off. Christianity teaches the personal responsibility of the individual before God, and the progress of
society depends on the acknowledgement by individuals of this responsibility, even when it brings them into conflict with the customs
and conventions of existing society.[80]

Obviously with the weakening of the traditional bonds of African society there had to be a growth of new social groupings. The individual who was called upon to break with traditional authority did not become emancipated from social obligation but merely owed his loyalty to a different community. Social obligation could not be discarded but had to be reawakened. "Christ came not to destroy but to fulfil."[81] The missionaries came to Africa for the same purpose.

These early missionary efforts have been criticized because of missionary preoccupation with "otherworldliness" (what Brookes terms "the escape from harsh reality to dreams of a heavenly future where all God's chillun got shoes"), contempt for Bantu custom, and denominationalism.[82] Granting to a certain degree the validity of these criticisms, the missionaries, nevertheless, realized the enormity of the task before them and the very essence of its nature.

What had come about was a stage of transition in which the African, owing to the increasing deterioration of tribal life, stood between two civilizations. At the rear of him was the centuries-old tribal communal life; at his front and beckoning him, at the behest of the missionaries and irresistible economic forces, was the Christianized Western civilization with its emphasis upon the value of the individual per se.

A bridge between the two civilizations was needed; a medium was required which would connect the old with the new. Those Africans who, by dint of newly Christianized conscience or otherwise, desired association with, or ultimately membership in, the Western civilization had to be oriented to the prerequisites for conversion to a new life. Those who did not desire separation from the lore and life of their ancestors, nevertheless, had to be the recipients of that which Western civilization had to offer as a supplement to, and not a substitute for, tribal life. Thus, for example, elementary rules of sanitation and hygiene, erosion-preventing agricultural practices, the best operations of animal husbandry, and other Western methods and processes would mean a more healthful and productive life within the traditional tribal framework.

The medium which was seen to serve as this bridge across the otherwise virtually uncrossable chasm was education. It softened the impact of the transition upon the individual African. Little wonder is it therefore that, apart from the teaching of religion, the most important aspect of mission work has been education.[83]

The early governments were not prone to spend money for Native education and evidenced little interest in the subject. Hence, the mission societies became the greatest body of social influence upon the Africans. Education became a key tool in the attempted remaking of African man.

The transitional stage or phase has not yet passed. That this is so is evidenced by the emergence of Nationalist apartheid itself. It is only in such a phase where the situation is yet in flux, dynamic, and capable of change that the revitalization of Native tribal life and the reversal of the urban flow of Natives could be visualized. To admit that the time is now too late to reorient the bulk of Union Natives to a geographical and cultural isolation, as speakers for the Opposition allege, would completely undermine the Nationalist party program. For the Nationalists the situation has not, as yet, become so static or permanent that it cannot be vastly altered. It is this Nationalist contention that there is yet time to act which gives to apartheid theory its present sociopolitical significance. If that contention be valid, and the Nationalists were brought into power by those who believe so, the transitional phase is the period in which apartheid must be carried into actual practice, that is, the implementation of the doctrine.

The question inevitably arises whether the Nationalists can afford to direct all their energy and zeal toward fulfilment of the idealized apartheid community when Native education, predominantly under missionary auspices, espouses that doctrine which by its very nature has led to a breakdown of tribal organization. The full implementation of apartheid will undermine the whole concept of missionary education; the two are in essence incompatible. The missionary view is best expressed by J. H. Oldham and B. D. Gibson of the International Missionary Council:

> The school cannot be separated from the total life of the community. . . . Western civilization has immensely enlarged the possibilities of man's life. . . . It has been in many directions a movement of expanding life—an expression of the creative activity of God.
> In these good things the African is entitled to share. . . . He must have the opportunity of broadening his intelligence through acquaintance with the ideas and activities of the wider world of which he is made a part . . . he must be free to assimilate the learning and culture of the West, in order, that he may not be permanently enslaved by his ignorance to a class possessing a monopoly of knowledge. The African will certainly demand that the road to western knowledge should remain wide open to him, and in making this claim he will only be uttering the demand of all living things to grow in accordance with their divinely given nature.[84]

The Reverend Seth Mokitimi, in his article "Apartheid and the Christian Spirit," reviews similar considerations and observes that under apartheid "the aim of the education given the Africans will be to 'anchor them to their way of life.' "[85] This, he concludes, would merely mean a denial to them of the fundamental human right of attaining in the land of their birth and domicile the highest of which they are capable.[86] No longer would Natives or other non-Europeans be practically trained or spiritually oriented to a life in common with other South African races.

In this regard a portent of things to come was bared in debate in the Union Senate by Dr. E. G. Jansen, former Nationalist minister of Native affairs, as he indicated Nationalist Native education policy. The question was whether the £5,000,000 or so being spent on Native education annually was being used to the best advantage.

> He [the Minister] was afraid that very largely that education was calculated merely to Europeanise the Native, with the result that every Native who had had a modicum of education did not want to do manual work. For many years to come the bulk of the Native population would have to do manual work. *But now they wanted*

to be clerks or teachers, or work in an office. People were asking to-day whether public money should be used to educate Natives and to train people who became Communists.[87]

The Dutch Reformed church in its support of apartheid must accept its share of the responsibility for the fullest implications inherent in that theory. One of the most significant of these implications is this requisite reorientation of Native education. This is an impressive responsibility to undertake. Is the Dutch Reformed church ready for such a task? While the Dutch Reformed church has been the very soul of educational effort among the Europeans, it has been the English-speaking denominations which have made the greatest contributions in the realm of denominational Native education.[88] In addition, Blaxall writes that, though the Dutch Reformed church has always been liberal in support of missionary work and of such organizations as the British and Foreign Bible Society, in the main the fields of mission work have lain *outside* the Union of South Africa.[89] Thus Dutch Reformed ministers and lay workers of unquestionable devotion have left homes next door to unevangelized Africans in the Union to labor in the Sudan, Nyasaland, and the Rhodesias.[90]

The Christian Council of South Africa (officially defined as "an Association of Churches and Missionary Societies for the Advancement of the Kingdom of God"), in which the other churches are associated together[91] and in which there is neither an explicit nor an implicit color bar, is the body most representative of those churches which have dealt primarily with Native education in the Union. This council has openly expressed opposition to the principle of apartheid. At the inception of the Christian Council it was hoped that all non–Roman Catholic Christian forces would be represented, but, of the federated Dutch Reformed churches, only two joined. These have since withdrawn.[92]

The Christian Council of South Africa represents more than thirty churches and missions. These include four of the principal English-speaking churches with large European communities, namely, the Church of the Province of South Africa (Anglican) and the Congregational, the Methodist, and the Presbyterian churches. Each of these churches has its missions among the Africans and Colored people, and there are small missions to the Indian community in South Africa.[93]

Although at the inaugural meeting of the council the president elected was a minister of the Dutch Reformed church (Rev. William Nicol) and the secretary appointed was a licentiate of the Dutch Reformed church (Rev. J. M. de Toit), significant divergences between the member Dutch Reformed churches and the other churches on the council became increasingly evident. Although Afrikaans, the language used in the Dutch Reformed churches, was recognized as equal in status to English, in actual practice English predominated. The president complained that those who spoke Afrikaans were listened to "with tolerant and admirable deafness."[94] Other obstacles were even more formidable, however. The divergences of viewpoint reflected the differing traditions of the churches and resulted in conflicts among the membership. Fundamental schisms appeared on almost all questions dealing with the Natives. They appeared on the issues of evangelism, education, social service, economics, social contact and equality, and politics.[95] After three years the president revealed that the advisability of setting up a parallel or counterpart organization in which Afrikaans would be the prevailing medium of deliberation and in which "the other viewpoint of the social application of the Gospel to South African conditions could be adequately represented"[96] was under consideration by "some of our fellow-Christians."[97]

Thus South Africa, which could already point to two official languages, two capitals, two flags, and two seminational anthems owing to the traditional rift between "Englisher" and Afrikaner, was to be able to point also to two Christian councils, each representing to the bewildered Native widely variant interpretations of the Christian message.

Mr. Nicol in what has been described as a "historic state-ment" reveals the point of view of his church:

The last reason for the failure was the deepest of all: our conflict-ing views on the right relations between White and Black. The Eng-lish-speaking missionary, especially the one born overseas, wishes to see as little difference as possible between the white man and the Native. He does not hesitate to welcome the civilized Native to his dining table. In many cases the Native finds lodging for the night as an honoured guest among such White people. *For us, on the other hand, the thought that we should use the same bathrooms and bath-room conveniences as even the most highly civilized Native is re-volting. These principles run through all our conduct.*[98]

Thus the new Afrikaner-oriented (in language and policy) or-ganization came into being. Known as the Federal Mission Coun-cil of the Dutch Reformed Churches, it is a powerful Afrikaner missionary bloc.

CHAPTER IV

Apartheid and Political Theory

As a theory of social, political, and economic organization within a future community, apartheid has unique and significant contributions to make to the field of political theory. Regardless of present attempts within South Africa to put the doctrine into practice, apartheid still remains essentially in the theoretical stage.

Although the state under apartheid is founded upon racial concepts, the theory does not deny the value of democratic theory and practice per se. For instance, the Grondwets, or constitutions, the representative Volksraads, or legislatures, and the elected public officials played vital roles in the political history of the Boer states. A love of independence and a well-defined freedom of spirit and movement were, in part, characteristic of the early Dutch South Africans. They resented arbitrary authority and were disposed to recognize no higher authority than their own free wills and their Scripture. Apartheid theory does not reject this same spirit of independence and faith in the parliamentary form of government. It merely, like Boer racial policy of the pre-Union era, does not hold these as applicable to non-white races in South Africa.

Thus in the idealized community which apartheid envisages racial derivation is the sine qua non which determines the role of the individual in the community and the benefits to be conferred to the members of this multiracial society. The organization of the community is to be determined by racial principles arrived at and applied by the white element of the population. Natural law is replaced by racial law.

The implication of such a theory is that the existence of a

"natural," "common," or "universal" man is denied and that men are conceived as only members of different races. The destiny of entire peoples is to be governed by racial law. The "good" in life thus becomes associated with that which is to be preserved at all costs, that is, the white race and its European culture.

The Dutch South African spirit of the *Afrikanervolk* bears a striking similarity to the European idea of the *Volk* which arose in Europe at the end of the eighteenth and in the nineteenth centuries. The ideal of the *Herrenvolk*, or "master-race," a people with a common past, common language, and biological superiority, required a common future. This in turn required that a common political unity should develop. In Europe this political unity did develop and led eventually by means of fervent nationalism and Aryan racism to the National Socialism of Nazi Germany.

In South Africa political unity, racial cohesion, and the sense of integral nationality on the part of the Dutch South Africans developed as a result not of contact with the European scene, from which the Dutch South Africans were effectively isolated, but of contact with overwhelming large numbers of hostile Natives and the Native wars which served to reinforce the Boer belief in the inequality of races. Today the theory of apartheid bears considerable resemblance to the avowed doctrine of racial inequality of National Socialism which aggressively denied the "cosmopolitanism" of European liberalism.

Under both apartheid and National Socialism, standards common to all men are rejected. Both seek to perpetuate and magnify differences between men. Yet there is a significant difference between the two doctrines. The racially pure Aryans, under National Socialism, were given no choice in determining their own destiny. The individual was allowed no free will as the basis for political responsibility, and as a result the individual remained passive in political affairs.

Apartheid theory provides instead for exercise of the will on the part of the European. Thus the rational nature of non-Europeans only is attacked, and they alone are considered to be unable to control their own destinies. The Aryan under apartheid therefore, unlike National Socialism, is a man responsible for his own destiny; he is more than a mere product of society, for he helps create it by his own free will. The Dutch South African is a member of the *Afrikanervolk*, a race destined by physical and mental superiority to dominance over other races, and he prides himself on the fact that he is also a rational creature determined to create his own opportunities and to lead life in his own way.

Under National Socialism there was little or no private association or group life aside from the party. There was complete control of all phases of community life by the party elite. The totality of life came under the state, and behind the state was the party. The control of the party was thus totalitarian control. The state controlled the community and the party controlled the state.

Under apartheid the emphasis is more upon the aristocracy of race rather than of party. The Nationalist party does not demand the control of the state in all phases of community life. It looks to a state based upon democratic-aristocratic concepts, that is, of democratic processes within the fold of the white race. The organization of the state therefore is not akin to National Socialism. Apartheid conceives of aristocracy founded upon the principles of self-determination, whereas National Socialism conceived of an aristocracy based upon unswerving obedience to the state-party and a complete negation of democratic precepts.

The powers of the state under apartheid are, in short, limited by the will of its white citizens. The powers of the state under National Socialism were subject to no limitation save that prescribed by the party hierarchy.

In India the Hindu caste system played a determining role in allocating to each individual his niche within the community. The many castes and even the hierarchies within the castes stratified the population into a hierarchy of privilege and right. An essential feature of the system, however, was the lack of a spatial concept of racism, that is, of territorial separation between the castes. Hindu society was thus characterized by a vertical segregation. A spatial or horizontal separation was not conceived.

Apartheid is unique in racial and political theory in that it is an attempt on a wide scale, certainly larger than any heretofore attempted, to combine both the vertical segregation of races and the horizontal separation of races. The state patterned on apartheid theory would therefore be an extremely static community. The vertical hierarchy of races would allot to each individual his role in the community and permanently limit his rights and duties. The territorial separation of races, so greatly stressed in apartheid theory, would in addition limit the individual to specific territorial boundaries within the state itself.

Such an organization of the South African multiracial society implies that the benefits of European civilization and culture are to be, to all intents and purposes, denied to the Native population and, more than heretofore, to the Colored population. This is a refutation of the standard of liberalism which is unique to South Africa alone. As shown, English and Continental liberalism have not made much headway in South Africa. Nevertheless, the existence of a "South African liberalism" is not to be denied because of this. There has been, as perhaps best exemplified by the policies of the United party, a movement which must be considered as "liberal" in relation to South African standards.

This is the movement which looks to bestowing upon the non-European the best which a European culture has to offer and looking to the ultimate "uplifting" of the Native from his primitive tribal culture. It accepts the present non-European population in the urban industrialized areas as a necessary condition of economic well-being on the belief that the non-European is already permanently integrated into the Union's economic structure and knows only the environment of the towns and European farms. Racial harmony is to be furthered rather than undercut by contact between the various races, though this does not imply abolition of present social and residential separation. Avoidance of race mixture is a fundamental tenet.

The European culture is the "good" life, a life from which the non-European races can profit and progress. This can be accomplished not by isolating them in their own spheres but only by harmonious co-operative endeavor in industry and the community itself. The ideal of permanent white supremacy remains intact, and, as will be elaborated in the concluding chapter, this may lead to a contradiction within United party theory.[1]

Apartheid theory, however, maintains that the "good" life for the Native is found in his racial, cultural, and territorial isolation. Apartheid theory is a complete denial of English and Continental liberalism and "South African liberalism" as well. It becomes therefore the standard for South African conservatism.

All the widely divergent threads which have served to make up the main fabric of Nationalist racial policy have woven themselves into a distinctive pattern. From this pattern one conclusion is overwhelming: "The Dutch have swung themselves to power on a racial wave,"[2] and they intend to stay. It is the purpose of the succeeding chapters to show how that is to be accomplished.

CHAPTER V

The Colored Population under Apartheid

THE COLORED POPULATION OF THE UNION, THE THIRD LARGEST racial group, is a distinct social entity with unique problems before it. Though historically the Coloreds have not developed a group consciousness, owing in part to the diverse racial strains which compose the group, the Coloreds, nevertheless, consider themselves apart from the Native population. Though the Coloreds recognize themselves also as distinct from the Europeans, they "have always tended to identify their interests as closely as possible with that of the European."[1]

The bulk of the Colored people are descended from three main sources. There are the descendants of European-slave unions, European-Hottentot unions, and the later slave-Hottentot unions. The European-slave admixture is the numerically larger and most progressive group.[2]

It is not possible to state exactly in general terms how large an infusion of European blood has taken place into the Cape Coloured. It is however an important constituent of their descent. Individuals range from those who obviously have little or no European blood to those who approximate so closely to pure European descent that they are able to "pass" as such, and there is often uncertainty and difficulty in distinguishing such "Coloured" from Europeans.[3]

Descended as they are from the union of white and black blood, they form a mixture which is socially between the blood-proud Bantus and the equally blood-proud Europeans. Owing to the European quest for racial purity and the endeavor on the part of the Europeans to preserve their culture and traditions, the Coloreds are kept in a socially and economically inferior position. They are included in the traditional color bar imposed by the term "non-European." On the other hand, the Coloreds are regarded by the Bantu as socially apart and are likewise excluded from Native social functions unless they are willing to consider themselves as Native without any qualifications.[4]

This, of course, few of them are willing to do, and, as a result, they are caught in a social pincers between two blood-proud and numerically superior groups, each of which regards the Colored "as something apart." The Coloreds, on their part, have developed a prejudice against the Native population and have traditionally been characterized by efforts to keep themselves separated as much as possible from the Natives. This is evidenced by the exclusion of Natives from Colored social functions and by the separate housing schemes in the Cape Province.[5]

As a consequence of their being socially, and to a great extent economically, between two mutually exclusive social barriers, the Coloreds have developed an acute sensitivity as regards their status within the community. In recent years their group-consciousness has increased, though there is, generally speaking, a wide gap between the urban Colored people and those of the rural areas. Of the 905,000 Coloreds in South Africa at the 1946 census, 813,000 lived in the Cape Province.[6] Thus in a study of the Coloreds under apartheid the Cape Coloreds may be taken as most representative of their group.

The Cape Coloreds have not been subject to the severe social, political, and economic restrictions of the Native and in the Cape Province, at least, have achieved a status which is more closely aligned to that of the European than the Native. Residential segregation is not compulsory, and in many cases the Coloreds live alongside Europeans; they can also own property, but few do. They are entitled, in the Cape, to the franchise. Until recently, males over twenty-one had been placed upon the common roll along with European electors, provided, of course, that they met certain minimum qualifications. The qualications which must be met before the Colored is allowed to exercise his right of franchise are: all voters (1) must be able to read and write and

(2) must earn a minimum wage of £50 per year or (3) must own property valued at not less than £75.

Having met such qualifications, however, the Coloreds may enjoy the franchise in parliamentary, provincial, and municipal elections. The Coloreds also may become candidates for municipal or provincial offices, but they are excluded from sitting in Parliament. The Coloreds, until recently, could travel on Cape suburban trains with Europeans.[7]

In the three northern provinces the Coloreds are regarded merely as part of the Native population and usually suffer the same restrictions as the Natives. They do not enjoy the franchise (except in Natal, where the property qualification is £96), they are more strictly segregated from the Europeans, and they are subject to a much more conservative racial policy. The number of Coloreds outside the Cape Province, however, as shown, is relatively small, and the Cape is regarded as their traditional home. There was until 1948 no ban against mixed marriage in the Union, that is, between Europeans and non-Europeans.

This was the social environment which, previous to the Nationalist victory at the last general election, had produced the accepted status of the Coloreds. The affiliation of the Cape Coloreds with the European interests was the result of social practice antedating the union of the four former colonies. Custom, tradition, and usage had produced in the Cape Province a unique Colored status which differed from that of the other three provinces and which caused the Cape to become an outpost of liberalism, as regards the Coloreds, in comparison with the northern provinces. Though economically, in certain types of employment and apprenticeship, they were discriminated against in favor of the "poor whites"[8] and socially, by practice, excluded from the European sphere, the Cape Coloreds were, nevertheless, under the former government and by long practice considered as an integral part of the sphere of interest of the European community. The late General Smuts, former leader of the Opposition to the Nationalist party and prime minister under the former government, declared in rejecting a Nationalist motion for more rigid segregation of non-Europeans, including Coloreds:

As far as the Coloured peoples are concerned, I want to say that I feel we are treating the Coloureds quite sensibly and wisely. That is to say, more or less as an appendix of the European population. That is to say, more or less as an appendix of the European population.

I cannot see any other solution. These people are different from the Natives and the Indians. They represent an intermediate nation. They are related to a certain degree or rather their interests are more closely allied to our interests than those of any other section of the population. We must keep them as we have done in the past. Let the position remain as it is.[9]

After the Nationalist victory in 1948, however, the Nationalists were obligated to carry out the apartheid program which had been their most significant political weapon against the United party in the political campaign. It was requisite, for them, if apartheid were ever to become anything more than a theoretical concept of race development and segregation, that the first politically strategic move would have to be made against the most liberal of the Union's provinces, the Cape. In the Cape the Coloreds had been most closely aligned with the Europeans. Their position as regarded the parliamentary franchise had to be stripped away, more rigid residential segregation had to be enforced, a ban on mixed marriages had to be instituted, apartheid had to be applied to the municipal transportation system of the Cape (as had long been the practice in the other provinces), and, in short, the position of the Cape Coloreds had to be reversed. Their interests would be linked no longer with those of the European but with those of the Native and the Asiatic. The Colored people would hold a privileged position over Natives in urban areas, however.

In Cape Town on June 12, 1948, Dr. Malan said in an address:

The days when people . . . [speak] . . . of racialism are past. We will get the co-operation of the various races. There will be no discrimination against any section. We have a policy in regard to non-Europeans, but this involves no oppression or removal of any of their rights. We shall protect them against oppression and bring about good relationships between them and the European population.[10]

One of Dr. Malan's most cherished objectives in promoting this "co-operation of the various races" and the policy of "no oppression or removal of their [non-European] rights" has been the effort to take long-existent franchise privileges from the Colored population of the Cape.

The Cape Coloreds have been granted the franchise for parliamentary, provincial, and municipal elections since 1909. Previous to the South Africa Act of 1909 the Coloreds in the Cape were given the right to vote, under the British colonial administration, when elections were held in the Cape Colony. Then, as now, the Cape was much more liberal in its non-European policy than the Transvaal, the Orange Free State, and Natal. It was, in part, in order to preserve this franchise for the Coloreds that the British government insisted, at the drafting of the South Africa Act, upon the inclusion of the so-called entrenched clauses.[11] The Cape and British authorities vehemently refused to pattern their non-European policy after that of the three northern territories. The heated and spirited controversy concerning the retention of the Colored vote in the Cape was finally compromised, the compromise being that the Cape Coloreds would have their voting privileges kept intact by a constitutional clause with the stipulation, however, that non-Europeans would be disqualified from sitting in either house of the Union Parliament. The Colored population, at the time of union, was further assured of the respect to be accorded to these provisions by the insertion in the South Africa Act itself of the entrenched clauses. The effect of these clauses is to assure that, in order to amend certain sections of the act, including those safeguarding the Colored Cape vote, certain procedures would have to be followed. Such procedures have been the Coloreds' most effective assurance that their rights, solemnly agreed at the time of the union of the former colonies, will be respected.

The South Africa Act, the constitution of the Union, provides that unless a repealing bill or altering bill passes at the third reading by a two-thirds majority of the total members of both houses sitting together, it shall be invalid. The exact wording of this provision in the act is as follows:

(1) Parliament may by law prescribe the qualifications which shall be necessary to entitle persons to vote at the election of members of the House of Assembly, but no such law shall disqualify any person (other than a native, as defined in section one of the Representation of Natives Act, 1936) in the Province of the Cape of Good Hope who, under the laws existing in the Colony of the Cape of Good Hope at the establishment of the Union, is or may become capable of being registered as a voter from being so registered in the Province of the Cape of Good Hope by reason of his race or colour only or disqualify any native, as so defined, who under the said Act would be or might become capable of being registered in the Cape native voter's roll instituted under that Act from being so registered, or alter the number of the members of the House of Assembly who in terms of the said Act may be elected by the persons registered in the said roll, unless the Bill embodying such disqualification or alteration be passed by both Houses of Parliament sitting together, and at the third reading be agreed to by not less than two-thirds of the total number of members of both Houses. A Bill so passed at such joint sitting shall be taken to have been duly passed by both Houses of Parliament.

(2) No person (other than a native as so defined) who at the passing of any such law is registered as a voter in any Province shall be removed from the register by reason only of any disqualification based on race or colour.[12]

This section of the South Africa Act makes no attempt to settle the franchise problems of South Africa.[13] It merely gives Parliament the power, if it desires, of amending the franchise laws. The Colored electors, however, cannot be removed from the common roll of the Cape unless the requisite procedure in respect to repeal or amendment of this section is followed. In addition, the procedure itself cannot be amended save by the same two-thirds majority at third reading, of the total membership of both houses, required of the removal of the Colored vote. Section 152 of the act sets this requirement for the repeal or amendment of the procedure itself, and Section 35, previously quoted, is specifically included. It is also of importance to note that Section 36 of the act states, in effect, that the qualifications for voting are to be those in existence "in the several colonies at the establishment of the Union."[14] This section also comes under the two-thirds proviso.

The Nationalist government lacks the necessary two-thirds majority of the total membership of both houses. At the same time, as part of its apartheid program, the government seeks to raise the qualifications for Cape Colored voters so as to exclude them from the common roll of the Cape. The government also seeks to abolish Native representation in the House of Assembly and transfer it to the politically weak and secondary upper house. The Coloreds, in place of the franchise which they have been exercising in common with Europeans, would, according to the Nationalists, be given a form of communal representation. Thus the Coloreds would no longer vote for the same candidates for the lower house as the Europeans or be represented, as in the past, by the same representatives as the Europeans. The form of communal representation originally envisaged for them consisted of three representatives in the House of Assembly, chosen by the Coloreds themselves but being, as before, Europeans. In addition, the Coloreds would have one European senator to represent them.[15] The theory of this form of communal representation is that the Europeans thus chosen would be completely independent of the existing political parties in Parliament.[16]

Politically this is a tactical move which in the long-range party strategy of the Nationalists would practically invalidate the effect of the Colored vote in Parliament. It would completely negate the Colored support of the United party, which has traditionally been more liberal in its Colored policy than the Nationalist party. (It has been predicted that the United party will thus lose six seats.) For regardless of the sentiments of the third largest racial group in the Union at election time as between United party or Nationalist candidates, the Coloreds would only be able to vote for their three representatives, who would be independent of any political party. This is to replace their past right of voicing their wishes in regard to the entire representation of the Cape Province in the House. Colored opinion in the House of Assembly would thus be reduced to a feeble imitation of its former self, and no longer would the Nationalists have to fear the Colored votes at the polls.

The manner in which the Nationalists are attempting to bring this about has touched off one of the most controversial disputes since union in 1910. It has raised vital constitutional issues upon the solution of which depends the future status of the Cape Colored people. As shown, the South Africa Act requires a two-thirds majority of both houses, which the Nationalists do not have, in order to amend the voting qualifications for Colored voters. Also, as pointed out, in accordance with Section 36 these voting qualifications are the same as existed at the establishment of the Union. Had the Nationalists the requisite two-thirds majority in Parliament, the establishment of new voting qualifications for the Coloreds, which they would be unable to meet, and their consequent removal from the common roll of the Cape would be in accordance with the long-accepted and specified procedure of constitutional amendment as set forth in the South Africa Act itself.

Such is not the case, however, for Dr. Malan asserts that the entrenched clauses can be amended by "adequate" majority.[17] The Nationalist government bases its contention upon the opinion of the law advisers of the Union government that Parliament may, with a bare majority, pass legislation removing Colored voters from the joint voters' roll and place them on a separate voters' roll and abolish Native representation in the House of Assembly.[18] A memorandum of the law advisers to the government states:

The contemplated legislation can be introduced and passed by Parliament in the ordinary way without first repealing or amending the so-called entrenched sections of the S.A. Act, the existence of which would not affect the validity of the legislation so passed.

The Parliament of the Union has sovereign legislative powers and may have regard to the limitations imposed upon its legislative competence by the entrenched section for as long only as it pleases.[19]

Dr. Malan has stated:

All doubt has been removed authoritatively. The sovereignty which previously was vested in the British Parliament to maintain the South Africa Act, with its restricted clauses, or to amend or repeal by a simple majority, is now vested without restriction in the Union Parliament, as our Appellate Division has had occasion to confirm. This justifies, from the juridicial point of view . . . acceptance of an "adequate" majority instead of a two-thirds majority.[20]

The United party and another school of constitutional lawyers have a different view of the matter because of the high esteem with which they regard established custom and usage. It is important to point out that on

April 22, 1931, it was stated from the Government benches that Parliament had a moral obligation to respect the entrenched clauses of the South Africa Act, and a resolution was passed by the House acknowledging that these clauses would be respected both in spirit and in the letter of the South Africa Act, as passed in 1909.[21] . . . The point of amendment of the "entrenched" clauses was not actually before the House, but the Speaker said that it was "desirable to state my views for the guidance of honourable members. . . . If it is desired to amend or repeal any of the entrenched clauses, then the procedure laid down in the South Africa Act must be followed" . . . they constitute a solemn undertaking not only by the national convention but also by the successive parliaments . . . a constitutional convention based upon a sense of public honour. It appears to be a definite and living force in the constitution, and as such merits cognizance by students of constitutional law.[22]

The opponents of Nationalist policies point out that twenty years later this same interpretation of the entrenched clauses is still valid and that nothing has happened since union to change this long-accepted view. They also contend that in 1936, when the Cape Native common franchise was removed, it was by the requisite two-thirds of a joint sitting on both houses and that the same requirement must be met in any alteration of the Cape Colored vote.

Dr. Malan has stated that "the Government would have to take steps to halt the rapidly deteriorating position regarding the

Coloured vote."[23] He has indicated that the rate at which Coloreds are being placed on the voters' rolls is increasing rapidly; 48,000 Coloreds are now upon them. He also stated that the ability to read and write is no longer a bar to obtaining the vote for the Coloreds because of the compulsory education for children. In addition, the residential qualification that the voter's residence should be worth at least £75 has also lost its force, since it is today but the cost of a "poor shack." And as far as the third qualification is concerned, few Coloreds are now earning less than £50 per annum. Taking these facts into consideration, the prime minister said that the government would have to take steps to find a solution.[24]

It is interesting to note the "surprising apathy" on the part of the Colored population in exercising the privileges of the parliamentary franchise.[25] Contrary to Dr. Malan's statements, a drop in the number of Colored registered voters followed a new registration in 1946.[26] Registration for the voters' roll is compulsory for Europeans but voluntary for non-Europeans. According to census statistics, only 40,000 Colored voters were registered shortly before the rolls were closed in 1947 out of a total of about 80,000 eligible Coloreds, and "this was attributed in part to apathy amongst the Coloured Community."[27]

The proposed curtailment of the Colored franchise as part of the Nationalist apartheid program has been bitterly criticized not only in the circumvention of the two-thirds proviso for repeal or amendment of the entrenched clauses but in the principle and theory of the apartheid program in relation to the Coloreds. This represents one of the cardinal differences between the United party and the Nationalists on the question of the permanent status of the Coloreds in the Union. The late leader of the Opposition, General Smuts, moved the following motion after the formal opening of Parliament on January 21, 1949:

This House, deeply conscious of the sacred and binding character of the obligations toward the Native and Coloured peoples on which the constitution of the Union was founded by the National convention and agreed to by the Parliaments of the constituent Colonies, and confirmed by the practice of Parliament and by solemn assurances of the House,

Disapproves of the policy of the Government to abrogate and alter the existing Parliamentary rights of these peoples without a direct and unmistakable mandate from the people of the Union, and by a two-thirds Parliamentary majority, as provided by the entrenched clauses of the constitution;

Disapproves of the verdict of the people in the forthcoming provincial elections being taken as an approval of this policy, as such a misuse of the provincial system would in itself be a violation of the spirit and purposes of the constitution;

Disapproves of any Government which, like the present Government, is not truly representative of the broad national will, adopting a policy of tampering with fundamental political rights and obligations, in conflict with the spirit and intention of the constitution, and damaging to our vital interests; and "Expresses its want of confidence in the Government."[28]

Thus the Nationalist government, in order to carry out its apartheid program, intends to interpret the constitution "in narrow legal, rather than in moral terms."[29]

The circumvention of the entrenched clauses not only has been contested by the Opposition but has also brought into the open what at one time appeared to be a very real difference of opinion between the two parties forming the present coalition government.[30] The Afrikaner party, with Mr. N. C. Havenga as its leader and minister of finance in the Malan cabinet, took issue with the Nationalists in 1948 and 1949 over the method by which the Coloreds' franchise arrangement was to be altered.

In a speech of the greatest political significance before the Afrikaner Party Congress at Brakpan in December, 1948, Mr. Havenga stated that "there was the heartiest cooperation amongst the Ministers" and that "White South Africa would never subscribe to a policy, no matter how it might be camouflaged, in which there was a danger that the White man might one day lose his position of supremacy."[31] Pointing out that it was the necessity for a clear-cut expression of the will of the people on fundamental color problems that, at the drafting of the constitution, certain matters were made subject to the entrenched clauses, Mr. Havenga continued:

I am convinced that we will not serve the national interest and, in particular, the interests of the Whites if, in our zeal and impatience to find an early solution of certain aspects of our colour problem, we ... follow a road without due regard to the explicit will of the people.[32]

Editorial review of Mr. Havenga's address emphasized the strategic position of the Afrikaner party in Union politics. Thus the *Cape Times* commented:

The Nationalist Government is dependent for its Parliamentary existence upon Mr. Havenga and his nine followers and it is to be hoped that Dr. Malan will speedily take steps to set finally at rest, the grave disquiet created by his and his colleagues' irresponsible threats against the Coloured and Native franchise.[33]

The *Star* stated editorially:

Mr. Havenga's speech ... has done much to clear the air. Even if the Prime Minister abandons his plan ... a fundamental difference remains. Is the Afrikaner Party, after all, on the wrong side?[34]

The *Natal Witness* observed:

It will be surprising if Mr. Havenga's stand does not produce a Cabinet crises. The Nationalists must either break with their embarrassing ally or retain his indispensable cooperation. Mr. Havenga holds all the trumps.[35]

Die Transvaler remarked:

If Mr. Havenga insists on a two-thirds majority to abolish Native Representation, he differs on a point of principle with the National Party. If he merely means a larger majority than the Government presently commands, it is a difference of degree, not of principle. Dr. Malan should speedily make an official statement.[36]

Dr. Malan in a statement replying to Mr. Havenga's declared stand revealed the impact of this development upon the Nationalist program:

Mr. Havenga's statement on Wednesday concerning the entrenched clauses in the South Africa Act has caused considerable deal of confusion and concern among the Nationalists. The question now arises to what extent, in the circumstances, we can proceed with our colour policy about which we have received a mandate from the nation. ...

With a view to future actions, there are certain facts which we must face four-square. The first is that separate representation of the Coloureds, and coupled with that, the elimination of Native representation in the House of Assembly, although this does not by any means embrace our entire colour policy, still forms an essential part of it. . . .

Whether in actual fact we have the will of the people behind us to his [Mr. Havenga's] satisfaction will appear from the results of the forthcoming provincial elections where our colour policy in its entirety, including the positive side, will again be put to the electorate.[37]

The United party in its refusal to consider the ensuing provincial elections as the crucial test of the mandate of the people on The Colored issue maintained that only a dissolution of Parliament and another general election could serve such a purpose.

On December 12, 1949, approximately one year after Mr. Havenga's well-known Brakpan speech, a joint statement was issued in Pretoria by Dr. Malan and Mr. Havenga on the further application of apartheid and, more particularly, separate parliamentary representation of the Coloreds. This statement revealed that the bill on separate representation of Coloreds applied not only to Parliament but to the Cape Provincial Council as well.[38]

The provincial councils of South Africa are original legislative bodies whose positive, defined, precise, and limited powers were drawn originally from the South Africa Act and were not delegated from the Union Parliament. They serve as subordinate legislatures to the Union Parliament only in the sense that to the extent their powers are limited they may not tread on subject matter beyond such powers. But within the limits of their granted powers they are as plenary, absolute, and discretionary as the Union Parliament.[39] Heretofore Cape and Natal Coloreds have elected members on the common roll along with Europeans. As the non-Europeans of the Transvaal and Orange Free State do not return members to the House of Assembly, they are not represented on their respective provincial councils because the electoral qualifications for returning members to the House of Assembly also apply to the provincial councils of each province.[40]

The joint statement concerning separate representation of Coloreds in Parliament and the Cape Provincial Council revealed that the bill would be published for general information and consideration without the Afrikaner party having to assume responsibility for it. It was also stated that, although Dr. Malan and Mr. Havenga both agree, and accept, the principle of separate representation for the Cape Coloreds on both legislative bodies, as regards the necessity for a restriction on the number of representatives of the Coloreds as advocated by the Nationalist party they differ. They also differ on the necessity for consideration of the entrenched clauses.

Dr. Malan and Mr. Havenga further declared, however, that on all other points of their apartheid policy no disagreement existed between them and that, for the continued existence of the white race and civilization, it is absolutely necessary to proceed with the enforcement of apartheid. As a result, the cooperation between the Nationalist party and the Afrikaner party must be maintained.[41]

The position of the Afrikaner party was shifted in June, 1950, when Mr. Havenga took part in parliamentary debate on the rights of Colored persons. As before, the leader of the Afrikaner party declared that, in regard to the Colored franchise, he was at one with the prime minister as to the desirability of a separate voters' list. However, he was now of the opinion that it was not a fundamental question concerning their race relationships. He was not prepared to support any legislation which would mean the taking-away of political rights possesed today by the Coloreds.

Mr. Havenga declared that where fundamental questions had to be dealt with they dare not be solved on a party political basis alone unless the overwhelming majority of the people supported them. If this is observed, he stated, there was no danger of actions of the present government being reversed by a subsequent government. He then added:

Our position in this country and in the world is difficult enough. We must take up an attitude which will consolidate our position, and in order to do that we are obliged to oppose claims to rights on the part of the non-European, but we are also obliged to maintain the existing position. Otherwise I despair whether the European can maintain his position.[42]

The Nationalist party was working behind the scenes step by step toward a solution of the Colored question with the Afrikaner party. This was brought out in the announcement of October, 1950, which revealed that, after consultations on the question of separate representation of the Coloreds in Parliament and the Cape Provincial Council, both of the cabinet parties had reached an agreement on the following terms:

1. There shall be separate representation of the Coloreds who shall vote for European representatives from separate constituencies to be set up.

2. The quota per constituency (i.e., the number of electors returning a single member to the House of Assembly) will be determined on the basis of the average number of European voters per constituency contained in the 150 seats as laid down in the South Africa Act for the whole Union.

3. As long as the South Africa Act pegs the number of seats at 150, the number of Colored constituencies determined will remain unaltered regardless of changes in the number of European or Colored voters. Should this total for the Union be altered, however, at a later date, the number of Colored constituencies will be altered accordingly but always in the same ratio as the number of European and Colored constituencies originally determined.

4. The Coloreds on the foregoing basis are to be allocated four seats in the House, one in the Senate, and two to the Cape Provincial Council. These seats are to be in addition to the existing number.

5. An elected Colored Representative Council is to be set up, on which appointed representatives from the northern provinces will serve, a special subdepartment for the promotion of Colored affairs is to be established, and the Coloreds are to gain representation in the Senate where previously they had none.

6. Both political parties are convinced that this arrangement will in no way conflict with the entrenched clauses.[43]

The actual terms of agreement constitute little in the way of a revision of the Nationalists' original plan for Colored representation. The *Star* termed the whole agreement "a worthless substitute" for the loss of the common franchise.[44]

The Coloreds are still not represented by the same persons as the Europeans. The proportion of Europeans representing the Coloreds to Europeans representing the Europeans is fixed at 4:156 (one hundred and fifty seats for the Union and six seats for South-West Africa). The four seats are representative of a Colored population of over one million; the one hundred and fifty-six seats are representative of a European population of only two and three-quarter million. By the act of fixing this proportion, consequent increases in the Colored population are not followed by increased representation. Also, regardless of any improvement of the educational and economic position of the Coloreds, their political position would be unaffected.

The proposed Coloreds Representative Council must be examined in the light of the fact the Nationalists are proposing to abolish the Natives Representative Council, as to be shown later in this study, because of an independent attitude and opposition to apartheid and to racial discrimination generally.[45] The creation of a subdepartment of Colored affairs, already an established fact, was bitterly opposed by the Coloreds, because, by providing a separate administrative structure to deal with Colored matters, it symbolizes for them a differentiation in status and permanently sets their interests more apart from those of the Europeans.

Under the above provisions, the entrenched clauses have been respected only in so far as the specific literacy, salary, and property qualifications for the Coloreds have not been raised. Beyond this, however, a violation of the "spirit" of the constitutional convention is clearly evident.

Mr. Havenga has not brought about the cabinet crisis which potentially existed at one time. His eventual regard of the Colored franchise issue as not being so fundamental a question as to require the explicit will of the people (a will nevertheless which he seems to have been very prone to stress in his public statements) merely set the stage for his agreement with Malan.

It must be realized, however, that a cabinet stalemate induced by a Nationalist party—Afrikaner party split on this issue could have led to a cabinet crisis and, if the United party took full advantage of the breach, to a dissolution of Parliament and a general election. This is exactly what the United party wants and what the parties in power do not want.

A general election at this time would hardly serve the interests of the Afrikaner party. If the United party were returned to power, the Afrikaner party, whose policies on several vital issues are opposed to United party principles, would be removed from the cabinet and from the position which it now enjoys. The Afrikaner party could not hope for a victory over the two major parties and must be content with the role of coalition partner with the more powerful Nationalist party. If, on the other hand, the Nationalists increased their strength and were thus given a more clear-cut mandate by the people, the Afrikaner party would in the same proportion lose its present significance in Union politics.

In the background of this entire issue are the elections held in South-West Africa in August, 1950. That this election came two months before the October announcement is significant. For the first time South-West Africa returned representatives to the Union Parliament. The major political parties of the Union conducted vigorous pre-election campaigns in that territory, and the Nationalists won a resounding victory by winning all six seats allotted to South-West Africa. The Nationalists greatly strengthened their parliamentary position, and Mr. Havenga, seemingly taking great cognizance of their new strength and the consequent decrease in Nationalist dependence upon him, declined to hold the Nationalists back. He would not be sacrificed on the altar of the entrenched clauses, and the Nationalists in all probability did not have to point twice to the handwriting on the wall.

The Afrikaner party, formed in 1941, was ostensibly dedi-

cated to the late General Hertzog's principles. Mr. Havenga
reiterated his intention to honor the policies of Hertzog when
he opened the Afrikaner Party Congress in November, 1948. Mr.
Havenga declared before this gathering: "Our accepted and declared policy of apartheid and the supremacy of the white man
is nothing else than the segregation policy enunciated (by General Hertzog) from 1912 to 1936."[46]

Hertzog, however, placed great stress on the differences between the Natives and the Coloreds. He insisted that the interests of the Coloreds were tied up with those of the European
community rather than with the Natives. The General had been
opposed to Dr. Malan's proposed removal of the Colored voters
from the common roll. They had been solemnly promised they
would never be treated in the same way as the Natives. They
were to be aligned with the Europeans, and Hertzog regarded
them as almost white.[47]

When Dr. Malan first suggested removal of the Coloreds from
the common roll, Hertzog described this policy as assuring that
"disloyalty and faithlessness shall be the guiding line of the white
man in South Africa in determining and fulfilling his duties as a
guardian of the non-European."[48] On this major issue Mr. Havenga has departed from the avowed ideals of the man whose
policies the Afrikaner party, at its inception, had pledged itself
to continue.

Shortly after the publication of the Nationalist-Afrikaner agreement the South African Institute of Race Relations attacked the
proposals.[49] The council of the institute in a resolution passed
in January, 1951, showed that the earlier issues of the controversy
were not circumvented and that Nationalist Colored policy had
not been modified. The resolution stated, in part:

The framers of the proposals express their conviction "that the
arrangement will in no way constitute a reduction of the existing
political rights of the Coloured people." The Institute takes the contrary view that the arrangement constitutes a crippling diminution
of the existing and potential rights of the Coloured people . . . who

at no time have been consulted as to their desires in respect of an "arrangement" which affects them so intimately. . . .[50]

The Malan-Havenga agreement was the underlying basis of the bill concerning the Colored franchise which was placed before Parliament. The terms of the bill showed, however, that Nationalist pressure upon Mr. Havenga was not to be let up in the foreseeable future.

This volatile political situation was adroitly described by the political correspondent of the *Star*, who wrote in an article in February, 1951:

> The terms of the Coloured Franchise Bill, as now published, place Mr. Havenga and his party in a compromising position and may compel him either to break with the Nationalists or to throw in his lot with them. When the Malan-Havenga agreement was published last October, Mr. Havenga and the Afrikaner Party took the view that the terms when disclosed constituted a change but not a diminution of the Coloured peoples' political rights. But at that time the question of the Coloured people in Natal had not been mentioned in the agreement or in subsequent discussions and *it was tacitly understood that Natal would be left alone.* The Government referred specifically to the Coloured votes of the Cape.
> Now Mr. Havenga and his Party were confronted with a Bill which, in at least one respect—that of Coloured representation on the Natal Provincial Council—directly challenged his former pledges. *It was widely believed that the Nationalists had insisted on the inclusion of this clause in the Bill as a final test for Mr. Havenga.* If he protested against it, as his honour had to compel him to, his alliance with the Nationalists would be broken. If he acquiesced to it after all he had said, he would brand himself as the willing tool of the Nationalists prepared to put cooperation with them before his own pledges.[51]

Die Transvaler, in supporting the Nationalists' tactics, noted that the Colored voters of Natal were included, "with the result that the absurdity of Coloured voters in one Province still being registered on the European voters' roll would now be removed."[52] In addition, *Die Transvaler* commented that the Coloreds would also be removed from "the contaminated atmosphere of opportunist politics" for which they had been used by "unscrupulous Europeans."[53] As a result of their voting on the common roll they had never returned their own representatives in Parliament but had simply played one section of the European population against the other.

The same newspaper in another editorial even attacked the provision for representation of Coloreds on the Cape Provincial Council under any arrangement. That such a clause was included in the bill at all was due, Die Transvaler said, to the fact that a coalition government was in power and that this legislation was the result of a compromise between the two cabinet parties.[54]

The Star looked to the future with misgivings and, after terming the whole affair "a disgraceful episode in our political history,"[55] declared that with Mr. Havenga's timid connivance the government was ready "to embark upon a course that white South Africa would have cause to rue."[56]

Few people were surprised when by August the Nationalist and Afrikaner parties were united to form one party. Mr. Havenga thereupon accepted leadership of the Nationalist party in Natal, and the Afrikaner party became relegated to history.[57]

On May 14, 1951, the amended Separate Representation of Voters Bill to take the Cape Coloreds from the common roll and give them communal representation passed its third reading in the House of Assembly by 74 votes to 64. Its passage through the lower house had taken eighty-six hours of discussion; one of the longest debates in the history of the Union Parliament. The minister of the interior, Dr. T. E. Donges, in charge of the bill, in his final speech answered the Opposition's challenge to Nationalist Colored policy. Before packed bays and public galleries he declared that, in regard to the bill, co-operation with the Colored community would not be lacking when "once it had been enacted and the shouting died down."[58] There were welcome indications, Dr. Donges stated, that the Coloreds would accept it as something better than the sham they had had for all these years. Every bill brought before the House was, he added, made the subject of emotional and racial appeals, and non-Europeans were being incited against the Europeans by mischievous and inflammatory speeches, thereby playing into the hands of the Communists. Dr. Donges warned his audience: "If we continue a policy of l'aissez faire it will be difficult to avoid a collapse of white civilization in South Africa and its frightening consequences."[59]

On May 24 the president of the Senate, Mr. C. A. van Niekerk, ruled that the entrenched clauses of the South Africa Act were no longer of full force and effect in the sense of precluding the Senate from considering the bill. This was in answer to the challenge of the Opposition that the Senate was not competent to consider the bill unless at a joint sitting of both houses, as laid down in Sections 35 and 152 of the South Africa Act. The ruling of the Senate's president removed the last obstacle before the bill became law.[60] As in the House, the bill passed the Senate by a simple majority.

That the judiciary might eventually be drawn into the controversy, together with the possibility of the act's being set aside by the courts, was announced by eminent legal authority. That the courts were competent to review this piece of legislation was the opinion of Mr. A. J. Piennaar, K.C., parliamentary draftsman.[61] This opinion is based upon the theory that, although Parliament is no longer subject to restrictions from outside or from the courts in order to function as Parliament and make effective laws, it must be constituted and function according to the law from which it derives its authority, that is, the South Africa Act. Thus, while the constitution provides that Parliament may make its own rules of procedure, this does not mean that by making such rules it can alter or ignore the South Africa Act itself. The question of sitting jointly or bicamerally is assumed, under this interpretation, to be not merely a question of procedure but a fundamental part of the constitution. The courts therefore are not precluded from determining whether this legislation passed in the ordinary way (bicamerally) is an enactment of Parliament. The courts would, of necessity, have to inquire into and decide what is meant by "Parliament" and what is an "Act."[62]

There were no references to this opinion of the parliamentary draftsman in the later ruling given by the president of the Senate concerning the Senate's competency to consider the pending bill.

During successive readings of the bill in the Senate the Nationalists met opposition to their Colored policy from an unexpected source. A group of Europeans under the label of the "War Veterans' Action Committee" and organized by South Africa's Battle-of-Britain veteran, Adolph Gysbert Malan, a distant cousin of Prime Minister Daniel Malan, announced their resistance not only to abolition of the Coloreds' common franchise but also to the Nationalists' increasingly severe racial policies in general. The WVAC, subsequently known as the War Veterans' Torch Commando, seeks to attract all former soldiers, sailors, and airmen, irrespective of rank, color, political party, or other affiliation, who wish to voice their protest against the "undermining" of the South African constitution. This group is as yet nonpolitical in character, having no official connection with any political party. The War Veterans' Torch Commando protest is thus not a United party protest, although the veterans' organization is aligned with the United party on the constitutional issues.

The evening of May 28, 1951, saw one of the greatest political demonstrations in the history of South Africa. Ex-servicemen of the Torch Commando, displaying the orange flame-torch emblem symbolic of their protest against the pending government bill, converged by motor convoy upon Cape Town from all parts of the country. Approximately ten thousand ex-servicemen and ex-servicewomen, European and non-European, marched by torchlight through the streets of the city, while fifty thousand persons lined their way. The protest march culminated upon the steps leading to the Parliament Building.

The peculiar temporary character of the War Veterans' Torch Commando is illustrated by the predemonstration manifesto, which declared in part: "Within one hundred hours of the achievements of our objects, we pledge ourselves to dissolve our movement. Until that moment the cause of all free men becomes our cause."[63]

Afrikaners, making speeches in the Afrikaans language, as well as trucks, autos, and marchers bearing placards and banners painted with slogans in Afrikaans, gave ample notice that the ranks of South Africa's Dutch were by no means unanimously behind the Nationalist program.

Boasting some half-million supporters, the War Veterans' Torch Commando held its first national congress in Johannesburg in July. Air Force Ace Adolph Malan declared on this occasion: "Despite our spectacular beginning, we have only succeeded in focusing attention on the dangers besetting South Africa. The battle has yet to commence in earnest."[64]

Nearly nine months later, on March 20, 1952, the Appellate Division of the Supreme Court of South Africa, sitting in Bloemfontein, declared the Separate Representation of Voters Act invalid. This ruling was based upon an application by four Cape Colored voters, directed against the Nationalist minister of the interior and the electoral officer of the Cape, contesting the validity of this Act. Chief Justice A. van der Sandt Centlivres delivered the decision with a full bench of four associate justices concurring.

For six days previous to the announced decision the court heard arguments. The government's main case was the contention that by the Statute of Westminster the South African Parliament became a sovereign legislature and therefore could legislate for the removal of the entrenched clauses in the ordinary manner. Government counsel quoted an important judgment of the Supreme Court in 1937 (*Ndlwana v. Hofmeyr*),[65] in which it was held that, inasmuch as the Union Parliament, since the passing of the Statute of Westminster, was the supreme and sovereign lawmaking body in the Union, the Supreme Court had no power to pronounce upon the validity of an act of Parliament duly promulgated, printed, and published by proper authority. In addition, the government contended that no Dominion, having evolved within the framework of the British constitution, can be a sovereign state unless it has a sovereign Parliament functioning bicamerally in the same manner as the British Parliament.

The Supreme Court now ruled, however, that the decision in the *Ndlwana* case was wrong in law. It then went on to decide that the Statute of Westminster had not resulted in any modification of the entrenched clauses of the South Africa Act. On the contrary, the Court pointed out, a joint resolution of the two houses of Parliament at the time made it abundantly clear that the Union did not desire any amendment of its constitution and had, in fact, emphasized that the proposed Statute of Westminster should in no way derogate from the entrenched provisions of the South Africa Act. In short, they were still valid.

In dealing with arguments about the South African Parliament's sovereignty, the chief justice said:

The conclusion at which I have arrived in no way affects the Sovereignty of the Union. . . . [T]he only legislature which is competent to pass laws binding in the Union is the Union legislature. There is no other legislature in the world that can pass laws which are enforceable by courts of law in the Union. . . . Consequently the Union is an autonomous state in no way subordinate to any other country in the world. To say that the Union is not a sovereign state, simply because its Parliament functioning bicamerally has not the power to amend certain sections of the South Africa Act is to state a manifest absurdity. Those sections can be amended by Parliament sitting unicamerally. . . . [I]t would be surprising to a constitutional lawyer to be told that that great and powerful country, the United States of America, is not a sovereign independent country simply because its Congress cannot pass any legislation which it pleases.[66]

The cabinet received the news while in usual morning session, and the reaction of Dr. Malan was not long in coming. Later the same day he made the following statement in Parliament:

The judgement of the Appeal Court . . . which reverses its previous judgement of 1937 has created a constitutional position which cannot be accepted. Neither Parliament nor the people of South Africa will be prepared to acquiesce in a position where the legislative sovereignty of lawfully and democratically elected representatives of the people is denied, and where an appointed judicial authority assumes the testing right, namely, the right to pass judgement on the exercise of its legislative powers by the elected representatives of the people—particularly since that judicial authority does not, or is it obliged to, act consistently.

The situation which has now arisen, creates uncertainty and chaos, where certainty and order should exist. There are now two conflicting judgements of the Appeal Court in regard to constitutional issue which is of the very greatest importance. So also, there is also no certainty that a subsequent Court of Appeal may not perhaps reverse the latest decision just as the present Appeal Court has reversed its previous decision of 1937. We will continue to drift on a sea of uncertainty, in connection with a matter in regard to which there should be certainty and finality. It is most undesirable that decisions of this kind should vary with changes in the composition of the Court, because this would certainly bring with it a danger of a "packed" bench, as has happened in other countries.

There is a further danger—which is no longer imaginary—that the prestige and authority of the highest Court is bound to suffer if it is called upon to adjudicate on a political-constitutional issue of fundamental importance. No matter how carefully such a Court comports itself, which sometimes demands an almost superhuman effort, it will be difficult for it to avoid altogether the appearance of prejudice, one way or another.

It is not fair and right towards the Court to expose it to such a danger, particularly since its authority in general must necessarily be undermined thereby. It is thus clear that the situation which has now arisen is an intolerable one, and the Government would be grossly neglecting its duty towards the people and towards a democratically elected Parliament if steps are not taken to put an end to this confusing and dangerous situation. It is imperative that the legislative sovereignty of Parliament should be placed beyond any doubt, in order to ensure order and certainty. The Government will take the necessary steps to do its duty and will, at an appropriate time, announce such steps after the reasons for the judgement have been studied and considered.[67]

The "appropriate time" to which Dr. Malan referred was the evening of the following day, when he announced that the government would introduce legislation insuring

(A) that the sovereignty of Parliament as representing the will of the people will be placed beyond all doubt;

(B) that in view of the conflicting judgements of the Appeal Court

there should be clarity and finality by establishing that the
courts of the country do not have the testing right;

(C) that, consequently, the courts of the country should be protected against the danger of being involved in constitutional
issues of a political nature and the proposed legislation would
be in accordance with the 1937 judgement of the Appeal
Court in *Ndlwana versus Hofmeyr* and the Nationalists' own
Separate Representation of Voters Act. The proposed legislation would be of effect as from the date of coming into operation of the Statute of Westminster, namely December 11,
1931.[68]

Upon learning of the government's plans, protest groups conducted mass meetings at which a "return to the rule of law" was
demanded. Within a month a formal alliance was formed between the United party, the Torch Commando, and the small
Labor party. These groups pledged themselves to "act as one
until the fears that now beset the people are removed by the
restoration of a democratic government." Nationalist speakers
in the House denounced the united front and, in particular, the
Torch Commando. Nationalist newspapers charged the Torchmen with secretly plotting a *Putsch* and secretly stockpiling
arms. The Torchmen in denial asserted, "We are determined
to preserve our democratic way of life and rule of law—come
what may."[69]

Paradoxically, the Nationalists are now in the position of ap-
pealing to that which they ordinarily dislike: the tradition of
Britain, where, owing to the absence of a written constitution,
there is no question of Parliament's supremacy over the courts.
The United party, traditionally sympathetic to British culture
and institutions, is now placed in the position of looking instead
to the United States, where since *Marbury* v. *Madison* in 1803
the tradition has been unfettered power of the Supreme Court.

The non-Europeans and Opposition whites are increasingly
being attracted to passive resistance movements against the Nationalist government during this period of constitutional crisis.
Such resistance, originally passive in nature, might well erupt

into violence if a prolonged split in white leadership, especially in its present tension-charged state, continues within the European community. While South Africa has always had more than her fair share of "portenders of doom," the situation, unfortunately, seems conducive only to an increase in their numbers.

Without attempting to look too far into the direction which future events might take, it seems obvious that the Cape Coloreds in this month of April, 1952, are effectively deprived of their common franchise. Though in the theory of law their previous rights have been sustained, it must be borne in mind that the government of the day does not even recognize the jurisdiction of the courts in such matters. The courts have no enforcing agencies of their own aside from those provided by the executive branch of the government. The judiciary does not administer the electoral laws. This is the task of the executive branch (the electoral officers are permanent members of the public service) according to the broad lines of policy emanating from the houses of Parliament. At the moment it appears virtually inevitable that the bill restricting the power of the courts and reinstituting the doctrine of *Ndlwana* v. *Hofmeyr*, already past its first reading, will be successfully pushed through Parliament, where Nationalist members are dominant.

The Supreme Court might conceivably invalidate this legislation restricting its own powers, as the Nationalists still do not have the required two-thirds majority of both houses (sitting unicamerally or bicamerally). In such an event the next election may well be fought on this fundamental constitutional issue, and the electorate would become the final arbiter. Until that time the effective power necessary to keep the Coloreds from voting on the common roll remains in the hands of the executive and legislative branches.

Obviously the issue of the Cape Colored franchise is far from settled. This is just one aspect of the total apartheid program about which Dr. Malan has said: "The policy of the Government does not mean neglect of the Coloured people. Rather does it mean more interest in the Coloured people on the part of Europeans; and more progress for the Coloured people."[70]

One of the most prominent spokesmen of the Cape Coloreds, Mr. G. J. Goldring, chairman of the Coloured Advisory Council and president of the Coloured Peoples National Union, declared, "If the Government deprives us of our entrenched rights we shall have no other course but to appeal to the United Nations."[71] However, under Article II, Section 7, of the United Nations Charter this issue would without doubt be treated as strictly a domestic problem and, as such, not within the jurisdiction of the UN.[72]

In order to further the apartheid principle of racial development in two separate spheres, Dr. Malan has announced that he wants "effective residential segregation, which meant abolition of mixed residential areas anywhere in the country"[73] and the establishment of separate villages for Coloreds. These villages are to have Colored officials as far as possible and Colored police. Dr. Malan has declared that the residential segregation of the former government had only "scratched the surface."[74] The Nationalist government also opposes Europeans and non-Europeans mixing on equal terms at the universities. The number of non-Europeans at European universities, however, has been exceedingly small. The government maintains that there should be separate institutions for non-Europeans.

The Nationalists also propose to effectuate a much more vigorous segregation policy in industry, where it sometimes occurred that European women worked under the supervision of non-Europeans.[75] In the industrial field the Nationalists do not want the trade-unions to be mixed unions. Thus, they contend, conditions, as in the Cape and other centers, where the majority of the members of the executive committee of the trade-union were non-Europeans while a non-European presided in the chair, would be prevented. Dr. Malan characterized this as "pernicious and demoralizing."[76]

Another aspect of the apartheid doctrine of the Nationalists as it affects the Coloreds in particular is contained in the ban on mixed marriages, such a ban being previously nonexistent except by custom and practice. A bill banning mixed marriages was introduced by the Nationalist government in the House of Assembly in 1949 and became law the same year.[77] The Nationalist minister of the interior, Dr. T. E. Donges, said that the bill was based on the desire of the population to maintain their racial purity. He pointed out that there were social problems arising out of mixed marriages and that the position of innocent children born of such unions had to be considered. The government also alleged that the number of mixed marriages was slowly increasing. The bill did not prohibit mixed marirages; all it did was to remove the provisions under which mixed marriages could be solemnized. Such people who married after the passing of the bill would, therefore, not be guilty of an offense, but their marriage would be void.[78] General Smuts argued that the question should be dealt with through the sanctions of ethics and religion,[79] as in the past.

Dr. Malan told the Transvaal Nationalist Party Congress in Pretoria in November, 1948, that the cabinet had decided on the compilation of a national register for every person living in South Africa. Each inhabitant of the Union would be registered, giving details of his or her race, and identity cards would be issued to the entire population. (At the present time only Natives are required to carry identification papers, and these "passes" are consequently most unpopular among the Native community.)[80]

In March, 1950, the Population Registration Bill was before the House of Assembly. Dr. T. E. Donges, in outlining its main provisions, said the basic principle was that the population register should be actually the life-story of every individual whose name appeared on it. The minister went on to explain that the proposed national register is to be centrally maintained. The purpose of the identity card is to show that the individual who carried it was the person referred to in the Book of Life held in the national register.

Thus a person could show he was twenty-one years old in order to establish his right to vote. Date of birth, it was explained, is also important in connection with military service. Another important fact is one's race. To obtain transfer of land in certain areas, it is necessary for the individual to establish that he is not of an excluded race. In the application of such legislation as the Immorality Act[81] the national register would be of assistance. It would also assist marriage officers. Dr. Donges also pointed out that the register would be of great assistance in apartheid legislation. The national register, he stated, existed in Canada, Holland, Belgium, France, Italy, Sweden, Denmark, Britain, Kenya, and Israel.

General Smuts showed at the second reading of the bill in the House of Assembly, however, that it would not have an easy passage. "We are going to contest it from stage to stage," he declared.[82] The bill had implications which, although not perhaps evident on the surface, might have very far-reaching consequences.[83] He then added:

> It is the question of national classification which is really the object, intent and essence of the Bill. It purports to be an attempt simply to institute a national register, and to supply identity cards to persons registered. It is made clear from the Bill itself, and from what has fallen from the Minister that it is not a national register.
>
> Much of the work of registration is already being done under existing legislation. . . . It is clear that the object of the Bill is to give expression to that policy of apartheid which is the essence and underlying motive of the Bill. I do not think that the Government is really interested in the registration of the white people. . . . This is not a national register; it is a Nationalist register to carry out the policy of apartheid as far as the Coloured people are concerned.[84]

General Smuts's remarks sparked the Opposition to attack the bill as merely the weapon, through registration, to provide for the segregation and elimination of the Colored people from the common voters' roll. Opposition forces pointed out that, if this bill became law, a vast new administrative machine would have to be set up and added to the administration of the country, which was already lacking manpower. Further, the door was being opened to "all sorts of mischief makers, people with racial prejudice and poisoned minds."[85] The results of these inquiries would be published in the register, and no privacy would be left. The Opposition thus held the bill to be "an invasion into the rights of every proper citizen in the country, of whatever colour and these should remain inviolate."[86]

Mr. M. C. deWet Nel, Nationalist M.P., raised an interesting aspect of the proposed legislation when he stated that the bill, despite allegations of the Opposition, would "unite the European sections in one solid community, with a common pride in their descent and nationhood," and that this same pride will work through to the non-Europeans.[87]

Mr. L. Lovell, Labor M.P., asked that thinking members of the House should consider carefully what they were doing by this bill. If the object was apartheid, that was the very thing that would be defeated by this legislation. He pointed out that

just as the arrogance of King John had united all the barons, the Church and the vassals so this Bill would unite White, Black and Coloured against the Minister. It would drive together persons who did not usually act together, and the Government would find that, so far from apartheid being furthered, the whole policy would be destroyed.[88]

The Nationalists maintain, however, that the Population Registration Bill is but a logical step in the effort to realize the ideal of true apartheid. Their zeal to maintain racial purity has caused Hoernlé to write:

There was developed in South Africa a race-attitude, or, better, group attitude, of which the objection to race-mixture is the strongest expression. "Dit is die trots van die Afrikanervolk, dat hy die enigate Europese volk is wat in 'n vreemde land, te middle van oorheersende getalle inboorlings, sy bloedsuiwerheid bewaar het . . . ("It is the pride of the Afrikaner people that it is the only European people which in a foreign land, in the midst of overwhelming numbers of Natives, has preserved its blood purity. . . ").[89]

Hoernlé holds that the Afrikaans-speaking South Africans (Dutch South Africans), especially in the two northern provinces, do maintain both in theory and in practice a more rigid barrier against race mixture than do other sections of the South African population,[90] although "there are no doubt plenty of individual exceptions, as may be seen both from the court records of rape and seduction."[91]

The Nationalists, for the first time in Union history, have applied apartheid to Cape trains. Segregation between Europeans and non-Europeans has been in force in the other provinces since the introduction of rail transportation in South Africa but was not extended to the Cape Peninsula when the systems were amalgamated under the South African State Railways in 1910, in deference to what was known as the Cape tradition. Speaking in reference to the application of apartheid to the Cape trains, which went into effect by means of an administrative order in August, 1948, the Nationalist minister of transport, Mr. Paul Sauer, stated:

> It is a beginning and not the final scheme. Somewhere a start had to be made, and that is now done. . . . Experience showed that the best way of avoiding friction between the races was to keep them apart where possible, and this experiment on the Cape suburban railways . . . is . . . a start.[92]

The reaction of the Cape Coloreds to their new status under Nationalist apartheid shows an overwhelming feeling of bitterness and hostility. There were demonstrations in September, 1948, at Cape Town station by non-Europeans who had entered coaches reserved for Europeans.[93] The Coloreds are being confronted more and more with "For Europeans Only" signs, many of which, like the Cape Peninsula Railways signs, had not existed before. The customs and traditions, which have been acknowledged by Europeans and non-Europeans alike, originating in the pre-Union Cape Colony are today being replaced by Nationalist apartheid. This is, of course, done under the pretense that the Coloreds will immeasurably benefit—that they will have more freedom by the process of isolating them more and more from the European population. In this manner they are supposed to reach or attain their fullest self-development in their own sphere.

The full implication of this aspect of apartheid, however, cannot be understood until this same process is analyzed in relation to the Native population. For actually, in any broad and over-all view of the situation in the Union today, the application of apartheid to the Coloreds is seen to be but a mere side show compared to the efforts of the Nationalists to apply apartheid to the Native population.

It is on the much grander scale, brought about by the more than nine million Natives, that one can better realize what it is that the Nationalists are seeking to accomplish by their policies. The application of apartheid to Cape Coloreds, however, does not lose its significance because of this, for, as has been shown, political tactics dictated that the more liberal concepts of race, in relation to the Coloreds, had to be attacked first by the Nationalists before apartheid on a much larger scale could be attempted. If the only outpost of liberal racial thought and practice (i.e., the Cape) could be stormed, and such a formidable obstacle to Nationalist designs for the Coloreds as the South Africa Act and its entrenched clauses could be circumvented, there would be much less chance of successful opposition to the Nationalist program of apartheid.

One faction of the Colored population, not living in the Cape Province, supports the prime minister's apartheid policy. As such it weakens the position of the vast majority of the Coloreds, who live in the Cape, by preventing them from presenting a united Colored opposition to the Nationalist government's program. In addition, it gives the Nationalists material for propaganda and is of no little comfort to them in their quest to reorganize the social structure of the Union. The Transvaal People's Vigilance Council has been formed in Johannesburg. The council's secretary, Mr. Albertus Pop, has stated:

> The Coloured people have been neglected because they have allowed themselves to become the tool of Communism, the Indian and other South African races. We see in the skeleton of Dr. Malan's policy the true beginning of a grand and glorious future for the Coloured people, especially in the northern provinces.[94]

Such Coloreds as Mr. Pop represents, living in the Transvaal, have, of course, never enjoyed the franchise; they have never known anything but segregation in municipal transportation, have always lived in strictly segregated residential areas, and their people have been traditionally considered to have their interests linked with the Natives rather than the Europeans. In short, they have never been exposed to a more uplifting and liberal racial policy. Coloreds, such as Mr. Pop himself, in the Transvaal do not have to go through the thoroughly demoralizing experience of having those rights stripped away which, by long practice and custom and even constitutional guaranty, have been granted to the Cape Coloreds.

Apartheid theory provides for the separation of the Coloreds from the other non-European groups; mixture of the non-European races is repugnant to Nationalist racial policy. As to be shown, the Indians will, under apartheid, become a negligible factor, for they are to be reduced to the "irreducible minimum" or repatriated. The Natives are to be separated territorially from the Europeans and the Coloreds. Although the Coloreds are to have their political interests more closely aligned to that of the Native, apartheid theory does not conceive of the Coloreds participating in the Native life of the Reserves and does not conceive of the Coloreds as being receptive to the Native culture.

The over-all effect, therefore, will be to reduce the area of intercourse between the non-European races as well as between them and the white race. The theory of "divide and rule" may be an underlying factor in this aspect of apartheid, although the Nationalists would no doubt counter to such an allegation with the assertion that the races will be happiest when each is left to develop within its own sphere.

It is now necessary to consider apartheid in relation to the Natives of the Union, for it is against them that the doctrine is principally directed. It is, in fact, only by reference to Nationalist Native policy under apartheid that the vast scope of the Nationalist effort becomes meaningful.

CHAPTER VI

Natives under Apartheid: The
Rural Population

THE ISSUES OF REVITALIZED TRIBALISM

WHEN A DEPUTATION OF TWELVE NATIVES PRESENTED AN ADDRESS of loyalty to him at the Cape Nationalist Party Congress on October 26, 1948, Prime Minister Malan stated:

> I regard the Bantu not as strangers and not as a menace to the white people, but as our children for whose welfare we are responsible, and as an asset to the country. My Government has no intention of depriving you of your rights or oppressing you. Nothing will be taken from you without giving you something better in its place.
> Your reserves will remain intact and where necessary will be enlarged. Your lands will be restored and your young men and women trained to improved methods of cultivation so that your reserves will be capable of supporting a larger population. What you want is a rehabilitation of your own national life, and not competition and intermixture and equality with the white man in his particular part of the country.[1]

This, in essence, is the heart of the apartheid program in relation to the Native population. As a theoretical and vague allusion to a better life for the Natives and the continued dominance of the white race, it has become a potent political weapon and an attractive panacea which would solve, once and for all time, the race problem between the whites and the blacks. To those Europeans who unreservedly support the doctrine, its logic and validity are obvious: merely keep the races separated into two distinct civilizations. Obviously, if there is little or no contact between the whites and the blacks, the probability of friction arising between them would be negligible.

Also forwarded by the advocates of such a theory is the assumption, referred to in chapter i, that the Native will be happiest when left "to develop along his own lines."[2] It includes the conviction that a very great deal of the best in Native life is bound up with the tribal system.

The disintegration of tribal life frequently has what can only be described as disastrous consequences, and the detribalized African of the towns and labour compounds very often compares unfavourably in character and behaviour with the "untouched" Native living in his ancestral surroundings.[3]

Such a concept, no doubt true in part, holds that the disintegration of tribal life results from contacts with European civilization. Detribalization does, to a considerable extent, undermine what has been the basis of good conduct and social order for the Native.[4] The tribal system is important to the stability of African society,[5] for the principal reason that African tribalism is conservative; it resists all change. Within it the younger men and women of the tribes are conditioned so as to keep their interests within the centuries-old organization of the tribal society. Other effects of the tribal system are that the movement of Natives into the European areas is discouraged by the tribal chiefs, since they realize that it will eventually lead to the breaking-up of the tribal organization. This has been relatively ineffective, however, in the face of economic pressure upon the Natives in the Reserves. In addition, the practices, superstitions, and tribal lore of the tribal organization keep the Natives separated from even a basic knowledge of modern scientific methods and processes by which they could benefit immeasurably. As such, African tribalism, though requisite, to a large degree, to good conduct on the part of many Natives, is not necessarily synonymous with the progress of the Native to a higher level of development.

As Broomfield points out,[6] there is a dilemma in that detribalization undermines what has been the basis of good conduct and social order, while, on the other hand, without the breakdown of the ancient tribal system, progress on the part of the Natives is impossible. The Nationalists contend, however, that such is not the case, for the Native can progress and realize his highest capabilities only while a member of tribal society.

Dr. E. G. Jansen, governor-general of the Union of South Africa and former Nationalist minister of Native affairs, while serving in his latter capacity, declared before Parliament in April, 1950:

Unfortunately, strong influences have been at work in the effort to destroy everything connected with the national character of the Natives. That steady background of his tribal consciousness and of his tribal links is gradually disappearing, and the Native is, as it were, suspended in mid-air; he has a feeling of instability which is nourished by people who are only too eager that he should be torn away from all his anchors, so that he can become an easy prey to their propaganda. The irresponsible teaching of equality and all kinds of ideas which are foreign to the Natives, and which many of them picked up when they were on military service abroad, are also factors which contribute to the present situation.[7]

It will definitely be worth one's while to consider whether this type of Native cannot again be part of a progressively oriented tribal relationship to the advantage of all concerned.[8]

Dr. Malan has attempted to show that the Native can never reach his highest level of development in competition with the European, for then the interests of the European must remain paramount, and the Native will always be relegated to an inferior status. It is therefore only by the movement of the Natives back to the Native Reserves that each will be able "to develop along his own lines."[9]

The picture which the phrase . . . ["to develop along his own lines"] . . . brings to the mind of those who use it is that of an amiable savage, the miraculous recipient of all the virtues, and none of the vices of European civilisation, sitting contentedly in a Transekei cottage weaving homespun while his family study the Old Testament in Xosa. Imbibing only the practical knowledge and none of the intellectual curiosity or philosophical ideals of western education, he will be content to leave his own destiny in the hands of his all-wise and benevolent masters. Contemptuous alike of economic and political ambition he will achieve in this blissful territorial isolation a degree of cultural integration and refinement that will rival the greatest achievements of Greece and Rome.

This is the philosophy and the intended practice of apartheid. . . .[10]

The opponents of Nationalist apartheid base their most effective criticism of the doctrine on the allegation not only that such a policy would in reality stifle Native progress but that in the final analysis the policy is impossible of accomplishment.

Tribalism cannot be preserved. The influences which lead inevitably to its disappearance are already too powerful and widespread. The African all over the continent is claiming liberty from the old tribal restrictions; he has seen or heard enough of a new world to make him frankly bored with village life on the customary model, and he is rapidly losing his respect for traditional lore. The tribes are breaking up from within, and it is too late for the process to be arrested.[11]

... African development and animistic tribalism are mutually incompatible.[12]

THE TRIBAL SYSTEM PAST AND PRESENT

One observer has written that the advantages and disadvantages of breaking up the tribal system are "so interwoven that it is difficult to differentiate and assess them accurately, and he is a clever accountant who can draw out a balance sheet."[13] Nevertheless, the controversy centering about apartheid requires, for intelligent participation, just such differentiation and assessment. It is requisite therefore to include a brief description of traditional tribal political institutions, their breakdown, and their present form.

The roots of the social policy of the Natives are to be found in their tribal system. According to this system, the Native races of South Africa are divided into a number of tribes, each of which is composed of a number of clans, which in turn consist of a group of families. The children are responsible to the father; he is responsible to the headman, who is responsible to the subchief or petty chief. The subchiefs are responsible to the paramount chief or king. Reversing this description, the paramount chief is concerned with the interests of the entire tribe, the subchiefs watch the interests of the various clans, the headmen watch the interests of their respective groups of families, and the father watches the interests of his family.

Each of these levels of tribal society are welded into a close union. Group association and responsibility are the essence of the system.[14] Schapera points out that the basic unit in Bantu political life is the tribe.[15] For all practical purposes, he defines the tribe as "the body of people organized under the rule of an independent chief."[16] Thus, he states, each tribe has its own name, occupies its own territory, manages its own affairs, and acts as a single united body in time of war. It is primarily through the chief that the consciousness of unity arises.[17] "The person of the individual belongs in theory to the chief; he is not his own, for he is the chief's man."[18]

In theory, the entire property of all members belongs to the chief of the tribe. The theory may break down in practice. While theoretically the individual has no right to part with the "property of the chief," when he covets the object offered in barter, he may part even with his weapons and thereby "conveniently forget all about the theoretical rights of his chief."[19] The individual, however, is allowed to hold private property and cattle only when this does not conflict with the good of the community. The system of the tribalized Native is based on obligations which are to be performed by the individual and not on any conception of man's rights.

It is the Kafir's primary obligation to sacrifice, if needs be, everything for the good of the clan, and his individual rights are wholly subservient, contingent, and secondary to the performance of his obligations. This . . . is undoubtedly one of the main causes of the stability of Kafir society.[20]

Although from time to time there have arisen in South Africa large Bantu states, in which many different tribes were amalgamated into a single political unit, most of these states have broken up and have reverted to the original system of small tribes.[21] The Bantu, although they have been referred to as a single nation, are actually composed of different tribes speaking different languages and practicing differing customs. There are, in fact, hundreds of such tribes in the Union. They have, however, been grouped from the point of view of similarity in language, customs, and history.[22]

THE CHIEFTAINSHIP

The chieftainship is hereditary, and the rules of succession may vary from group to group. In the families of tribal chiefs succession can pass by direct inheritance from father to son. Failing an heir, however, the succession is often disputed by rival claimants. This may occur even when the real heir is well known.

The chief is the executive head of the tribe and as such occupies a position of privilege and authority. Nothing can be done without his knowledge and permission. He is limited, however, in that he is obligated to consult with his councils, and one of his main duties is to summon the councils as occasion arises. Historically he has decided issues of peace and war. He sees that the local divisions of the tribe are effectively administered by his subchiefs and his headmen, he controls use of land and often regulates harvesting of crops, and he represents the tribe in external relations. He must maintain law and order throughout the tribe and punish wrongdoers. Traditionally he has been more concerned with maintaining existing laws than altering them. The chief is the religious head of the tribe, the representative of his ancestors, and plays an extremely important role in the ritual life of the tribe.

The chief's paternal relatives share to a varying degree the rights and privileges accruing to his position. As a rule, the more closely a man is related to the chief, the more powerful he is in tribal affairs generally.[23] "In honouring the chief, the tribe honours itself and its own past."[24]

THE CHIEF'S COUNCILS

The chief, in administering the affairs of the tribe, is assisted by his councilors. These councilors usually fall into two distinct groups. The first is composed of a small number of confidential advisers, usually his close relatives. The consultations are informal and secret. This small group helps the chief formulate policy and acts as an advisory body which deals with matters required to be placed before the second council, or *pitso*.

The second council is of a much broader base and is a more formally organized assemblage. Though its organization varies from group to group, it is traditionally made up of the chief's private advisers, more distant relatives, all subchiefs and headmen of local divisions, and commoners appointed because of ability.[25] It deals with all matters of tribal policy. Schapera writes: "The existence of these councils greatly limits the Chief's actual exercise of his power. Political life is so organized that effective government can result only from harmonious cooperation between him and his people."[26] Kidd has written, however: "The chief of such a tribe can do no wrong. His is the will of the people who do not complain about the abuses of power because it is the will of the people that the will of the chief should be supreme."[27]

Thus, as Kidd observes, "we have the strange phenomenon of self-government taking the form of Autocracy or Tyranny."[28] Even in those tribes in which the chief is less autocratic, the people only very indirectly and occasionally exert their power. "It is not true to say," he writes, "that the Kafirs are a 'pure democracy.' "[29] While therefore the chief of a tribe may be assisted by and responsible to a number of councilors, in another he may be a complete tyrant.[30] Schapera's observation that "a good deal, of course, depends upon the personal character of the chief"[31] probably most succinctly summarizes the situation. "His people will put up with much from him that would never be tolerated in one of lesser rank; and it is only under extreme provocation that drastic action will be taken against him."[32]

LOCAL ADMINISTRATION

Apart from the central government (i.e., the chief and his councils), there exists a system of local government in each tribe. The territory occupied by the tribe is divided into local units, each coming under jurisdiction of a recognized authority and each usually varying in size and importance.

The smallest effective political unit is identified by Schapera as the subdistrict or ward under control of a local headman. Being either a member of the chief's family or a commoner, he is responsible to the chief for the maintenance of peace, order, and government in his area. He acts as the chief's representative. By virtue of his office he, as a rule, is greatly respected by the tribe generally as well as by his own people. He may indeed play an important part in tribal politics.

The headman is assisted by a small council usually composed of his own eldest male relatives, some kraal heads, and any other elderly men of repute in his area. He confers with them upon matters generally relating to the public life of the group, and the council assists him in cases coming before the headman's court for adjudication. The council may even act as a check upon his behavior.

Larger districts are administered by subchiefs. These men may be related to the chief, commoners who have for some reason or another gained eminence, headmen of especially important clans or wards, or even hereditary rulers of vassal tribes residing in the district. The larger tribes may have several grades of subchiefs. Their functions are similar to those of the headmen, but they may take appeals from verdicts of the headmen and generally possesss superior authority over them.

The subchiefs are also assisted by councilors who comprise the headmen and their private advisers. The subchiefs, being directly responsible to the chief, must carry out his orders, and he may abrogate their authority in case of unsatisfactory service or conduct.

Thus, as Schapera points out, this system of local administration is one of ever increasing jurisdiction extending upward from the household or kraal. Each of these authorities have often identical functions; the difference lies, however, in the size of the group administered, its composition, and the consequent difference in range of power accruing to the person in charge.[33] Every official is usually dependent upon public support, and, as a result, Schapera concludes, "it is on the whole an equitable system of administration."[34]

BREAKUP OF THE TRIBAL SYSTEM

The tribal system has been broken up by undermining the authority of the chief. "In striking a blow at him we struck a deathblow at the very heart of the system, for it is in him that all the main girders of the structure are centred."[35]

The chief's powers have been reduced by removing his power to make war against rival clans. He was thus dishonored in the eyes of his people. Next, white magistrates took the law out of the chief's hands and refused to allow him to retain power of life and death. Third, a subsidy was given him, payable only on condition of good behavior. Fourth, chiefs were deposed and others put in their places by white authority, thus departing from Native conceptions of hereditary right. Finally, a white man was set up as the paramount chief.

The power of the chief having been effectively broken, the tribal or communal system of land tenure was attacked. In the Transkeian Territories, to be described more fully, administrative districts were set up which did not take into consideration tribal boundaries. In parts of the Transkei and the Ciskei, land which had been held communally by the tribes was broken up for individual tenure.

Missionaries directly aimed blows at the system. Finally, the dawn of economic individualism was brought about. The Natives became more reluctant to part with individual gains. They were taught the value of thrift and personal property. New wants were created, and they were urged to work for wages. They learned the use of money, and so a new economic era was introduced.[36]

THE REMAINING TRIBAL STRUCTURE

Diedrich Westermann has observed that "the chieftainships, though not altogether abolished, no longer have a decisive influence on the political life of the people."[37] He has also noted, however, that "chieftainship is one of those institutions which have preserved their vitality to the present day."[38] Such remarks, though seemingly in contradiction, are really descriptive of tribalism at the present time. In certain areas in Africa the chieftainships and councils have languished considerably, while in other, more primitive, areas the traditional tribal structure is found more or less *in toto.*

Portions of the existing tribal structure in the Union have been modified under present conditions so as to be metamorphosed into a system more amenable to ultimate authority for the European administrator. While such portions of the existing tribal structure may retain the outward traditional characteristics, the power epicenter is in European hands. Even in such a condition, however, the tribal system is popular, and loyalty to the chief, though not based on as much prestige as formerly, nevertheless is deep seated.

At the apex of the tribal system today is the governor-general of the Union of South Africa. The governor-general is the "supreme chief" of all Natives in the provinces of Natal, Transvaal, and the Orange Free State.[39] He is not the supreme chief in the Cape Province. The chief in charge of a tribe serves as the deputy of the supreme chief.

The governor-general is empowered to recognize or appoint any person as a chief or headman and to promulgate regulations setting forth their duties and responsibilities. The idea of councils dealing with matters on the various levels in the tribal structure has been retained, though the membership, as will be shown, may now be determined to a considerable extent by Europeans.

The chief in charge of a tribe now has his powers and duties as a judicial officer in petty matters defined by statute if jurisdiction criminal or civil has been conferred upon him. His present executive-administrative functions as a deputy of the supreme chief are based upon Native law and custom in so far as they are not defined by statute. Generally speaking, in matters concerning the internal affairs of a tribe the chief acts in accordance with Native law and custom.

There is no written tribal code of laws and customs, and consequently they are handed down to successive generations by word of mouth through chiefs and their traditional councils.[40] There is a system of special Native courts exercising civil and criminal jurisdiction in purely Native cases. These courts provide the Natives with not only a simpler and less expensive method of procedure than European courts but also a measure of recognition for purely Native institutions.[41]

The tribal chief is responsible not only for the general good conduct of his tribe but for discharging such duties as the supreme chief may assign to him. Thus, together with his headmen he must carrry out the provisions of proclamations in regard to local government and the directions of the Native commissioner (always European) of the district in which the tribe resides. In local matters these directions are in the nature of the advisory directions given to local councils, described below, by the Native commissioners who preside over them.

The council system upon which tribalism has traditionally been based has been, in some Native areas of the Union, supplanted under European auspices by a system of so-called local councils. These local councils are intended to be real local government bodies. The governor-general may establish local councils over purely Native areas. Though consisting entirely of Natives (usually six to nine members), one-third are generally nominated by the minister of Native affairs and the rest elected by the Natives. These councils, with the Native commissioner in his presiding and advisory capacity, are empowered to undertake a number of responsibilities and functions inherent in local government and which the governor-general may direct to be assigned to them. Twenty-eight local councils have been established thus far.

Whenever it appears that any powers conferred upon these local councils can more advantageously be exercised by a single body, the government may establish, under the Native Affairs Act of 1920 as amended, such a body to be known as the "general council" of the particular area it serves. The general council consists of a number of representatives from each of the local councils. The minister of Native affairs designates an officer of the Union's public service to act as chairman, and the European chairmen of the constituent local councils may be requested to act in an advisory capacity. The Ciskeian General Council, described later in this study, is as yet the only one to be established under these provisions,[42] the Transkei General Council being established before the turn of the century.

The Nationalist government has stressed the importance of local self-government in purely Native areas, and, because of this the council system will play an increasingly important role in the apartheid program.

The Nationalist leaders have based their Native apartheid program upon eight main points of policy:

1. Making the Reserves the national home of the Natives.
2. Giving the Native every opportunity and encouragement to retain his tribal affiliations.
3. Retaining only those tribalized Natives in urban areas necessary to industrial development.
4. Controlling the influx to the towns and establishing "labor bureaus" to insure that the Native is employed to the best advantage of the country.
5. Separating the Cape Colored and Native peoples, so that each may develop independently.
6. Making employers responsible to some extent for housing their Native employees in towns.[43]

These six major points were laid down in 1948 by the Nationalists shortly after they had assumed the role of the government party. Since that time, two additional major points have become discernible:

7. Industrialization of the Reserves.[44]
8. Extension of the council system and increased Native responsibility in local matters.[45]

The Nationalists having forwarded these cardinal points as most representative of their apartheid program for the Natives,

it is best to analyze each point and provide the detail necessary
to understand its scope and the obstacles to be surmounted if
the program is to be successful. These main points of Native
policy fall into three well-defined categories, that is, those affecting primarily the Native rural population, those affecting the
Native urban population, and those affecting the Native population as a whole, both rural and urban. With the preceding discussion of tribalism serving as an introduction to the problem of
the rural Natives, the effect of Nationalist apartheid upon them
may now be examined more fully.

Making the Reserves the National Home
of the Natives

In regard to this main point of Native policy the Nationalists
have announced:

Generally speaking, we propose that the Native areas shall be the
National Home of the Native, even of detribalized Natives who wish
to go back to the reserves. They should have all the rights and privileges that can be enjoyed by them in those territories. . . . The policy
for the Native areas should be that all services should be done by the
Natives themselves. . . .[46]

This phase of the Nationalist program is fundamental in any
consideration of Nationalist racial theory and practice; upon
its success lies the future of many other aspects of apartheid. As
will be shown, it will also be one of the most difficult to accomplish of the many formidable tasks already facing the
government.

A significant and disturbing feature of recent years has been the
rapidity with which the Native population in urban centres in the
Union has increased, a state of affairs which is to be attributed mainly to a steady and ever-growing influx as a consequence of the demand
for labour and the higher wages obtaining in industrial centres, combined with the meretricious attractions of town life, and in a sub-
sidiary measure, to the natural increase of what may be described as
the permanent Native population in urban areas.[47]

The movement of Natives from the Native Reserves to the
European urban areas has within the last decade assumed for-

midable proportions, leading some critics of Nationalist policies to point out that the movement cannot be retarded and that it is the natural consequence of the impact of European civilization upon a vast population which just now is awakening to the inadequacies of its own civilization. The extent of this movement, and its consequent impact upon the tribal organization of the Native population, can be appreciated by considering that more than 50 per cent of the Union Natives are established in the European areas, exclusive of migratory labor from territories outside the Union.[48] The government claims that many of these Natives are in excess of the labor requirements of such urban areas and serve only to congest even more the admittedly poor Native housing situation, increase the non-European crime rate, and contribute greatly to the vast increase in sanitation and health problems of the urban areas.

This Native movement from the Reserves has beeen carried out in spite of the Natives (Urban Areas) Act of 1923, which provides, among other things, that the governor-general has power to proclaim areas in which every male Native, with certain specified exceptions, must carry either a permit to seek work or a duly registered service contract and has the power to compel the Natives to leave such area if employment is not found within a certain time. The governor-general may also prohibit altogether the entry of Natives, for the purpose of residence or employment, into any specified urban area, save under conditions specially proclaimed.[49] This last provision has seldom been put into effect.[50]

The Nationalist government in December, 1948, announced, however, that Pretoria would be proclaimed under the Natives (Urban Areas) Act. This was to go into effect about April, 1949. The purpose was to place the peri-urban areas around Pretoria under strict administrative control to insure that only Natives required to supply the industrial and other legitimate needs of the city be allowed to enter. "Adequate steps will be taken gradually to 'freeze out' Natives who are leading useless or criminal lives in squatter camps in the peri-urban areas."[51] The government alleged that early in 1948 it was found that 28 per cent of Native men in the peri-urban areas could not give a satisfactory account of where they worked or how they made a livelihood and that at the end of the year the figure had probably increased to about 40 per cent.[52]

Such figures are presented to show the tremendous movement, increasing steadily, which has characterized the Native population in that last twenty-five years. It is only in the realization of the magnitude of this migration from rural to urban areas that one of the greatest problems in the Nationalist program can be fully understood. Indeed, those Natives, in excess of half the total Native population, who live outside the Native Reserves are already integrated into the Union's economic society.[53] The Malan government conceives, nevertheless, the establishment of a separate and economically self-sufficient Native nation. Opponents characterize it as an unattainable goal. "There is a good deal to say for it. Many of those most sincerely anxious for African welfare would regard it as ideal. The chief thing to be said against it is that in practice it is impossible."[54]

Another and not less significant factor enters into the establishment of the Reserves as the "homeland" or "fatherland" of the Natives. This is the reality of the land situation in respect to the Native population. "That the amount of land available for African use is grossly inadequate has long been recognized, not least, by a not inconsiderable body of South African opinion."[55]

A total of 10 per cent of the country is allotted to the Natives. In 1936 there were almost eight times as many rural Africans as rural Europeans, but they occupied only 7 per cent of the land.[56] Lloyd contends that in the Transvaal area alone, if apatheid were to be carried out as advocated, the area of Native Reserves would have to be quadrupled.[57] As a result, any effort to return the Natives already outside the Reserves back into the Reserves could only increase the present "deplorable beyond words" conditions in them.

The Fagan Report (the report based on the studies of the Commission on Native Laws under the chairmanship of Mr. Justice Fagan, K.C.) shows that 20 per cent of the cultivable land in the Ciskei area alone should be withdrawn from cultivation completely if the territory is to be saved from the most serious erosion.[58] In addition, Broomfield points out that, as it is, local production within the Reserves does not approach that necessary to maintain the population at a subsistence level and that, in part because of this, the adult males are compelled to spend a considerable part of the year away from the Reserves earning wages by working for Europeans.[59] "Their extreme poverty and their wretchedness are due primarily to the limitations of the area in which they live."[60]

In addition to being overcrowded already, the Reserves are neglected, and, though some are worse than others, even the best are deteriorating.[61] As a result of these considerations, General Smuts has declared:

The policy of separating and congregating our Native population as a whole in our Native Reserves is a policy which is impossible to carry out in this country. If that is the policy which is meant by apartheid then I have no hesitation in saying it is an impossible policy and it is a dishonest policy because it is impossible to carry out.[62]

From the standpoint of many economists the dependence of the European population upon the cheap Native labor supply makes the separation of races on the Nationalist pattern equally difficult. Professor Hoernlé effectively states this position:

The dream of prosperous, i.e., economically self-sufficient Reserves is in the spirit of true trusteeship. But it is a dream realizable only at the price of a heavy diminution if not stoppage, in the flow of Native workers into the white labour market. Reserves economically insufficient, i.e., Reserves in which the inhabitants do not and cannot prosper, but from which they are forced out to earn money, are alone in harmony with the requirements of the economic system of South Africa.[63]

Dr. Malan, as will be shown later in this study, has evolved a method of preserving this necessary source of cheap labor and at the same time of sending the Natives of the Union back to the Reserves. In addition, the Nationalist government, being fully cognizant of the facts and irrefutable statistics relating to the amount of land available to Natives, has announced a program of purchasing more land for the use of the Natives.

Lloyd gives a figure of 17 million morgen[64] as the intended goal of the Nationalists.[65] This figure represents the total amount of land which is to comprise the Reserve areas. He also provides figures showing that $13\frac{1}{2}$ million morgen, comprising 10 per cent of all land in the Union, is now available for Native use.[66] The intended increase will therefore be approximately $3\frac{1}{2}$ million morgen. This would still leave only 13 per cent of the total land area in the Union for a rural African population conceived under apartheid to be nearly twice the present African rural population. Considering the proposed apartheid program therefore only in the light of land distribution poses some of the enormous obstacles to the success of Nationalist endeavors.

Only one conclusion can be drawn from the figures presented. Since over 50 per cent of the Natives are situated outside the Reserves and since, at best, an increase of only $3\frac{1}{2}$ million morgen over the present $13\frac{1}{2}$ million morgen is contemplated, the movement of the Native population back to the Native Reserves would produce a situation infinitely worse than the present Native land shortage. The only other course would be a vast rehabilitation program seeking to improve the land already available to the Natives. Indications are that the Nationalist finance minister is having difficult times raising the million pounds necessary just to rehabilitate the present Reserves.[67]

The proposed Nationalist agricultural program has been outlined to some extent, however. The task facing the government in the rehabilitation of the Reserves is both difficult and of vast proportions. The Nationalists have vigorously applied themselves to the undertaking in spite of almost insurmountable obstacles. "In the interest of the country, it is indefensible to grant further areas to the Natives unless they are prepared and capable of making beneficial use of the land."[68]

This statement by the secretary of Native affairs is the basic premise upon which the agricultural program depends. This program rests upon two great principles—need for intensification of agriculture and need for conservation (i.e., protection and improvement of the soil).[69]

The secretary has pointed out that the traditional agricultural methods of the Native have permitted only enough food for each household and did not allow any surplus, from which the expenses of their growing needs such as better housing, better furniture, clothing, and other requirements could be defrayed. In his opinion the most important characteristics of traditional Bantu agriculture still practiced to a large extent today are: (1) use of land until the natural fertility is exhausted and a transfer is made to new fields and grazing areas; (2) every person is a farmer, quite apart from natural aptitude, and produces for himself only; and (3) status and riches are determined, not by the quality of meat and milk of one's herd, but by the strength of the herd.[70]

It follows that this type of agriculture is utterly wasteful and can have serious economic results not only for the Natives but for the country as a whole. While human and stock populations have generally increased, food production in the Native areas during the last 20 years has decreased by one-third. Great quantities of mealies have to be imported and the quality of the cattle has so degenerated that the "amasi" (soured milk) as a supplementary diet has become a thing of the past.

The question to which an immediate answer should be found is how, in spite of the shrinking food production and the increasing needs of the growing population, sufficient food is to be provided. The answer which the Natives give to this question in practice is that they endeavour to supplement this need by offering themselves for long periods as migratory workers, something which contributes further to the retrogression of their agriculture.[71]

The Nationalists refuse to accept this answer because they feel that it would mean the economic write-off of the Reserves. It also serves to strengthen the opinion that any expansion of the Reserves, in view of past practices, runs counter to the interests of the country as a whole.[72] The government realizes not only that the Reserves under apartheid must be expanded but also that European public opinion is loath to give us land for Native occupancy. The Nationalists' most fruitful approach to the problem is therefore to rehabilitate the present areas and show the Europeans that the Natives have altered their traditional soil-eroding and unproductive practices. The conservatism of the rural African, however, is something to be reckoned with.

There are too many instances where reclamation work is being done for them without any assistance or participation on their part. In some instances their attitude has been merely one of expectancy and passivity, while in others they have unfortunately gone over to sabotage of reclamation measures.[73]

Native opposition has assumed serious proportions. The crux of the problem lies in the government's stressing the need for culling stock. In the past cattle improvement in Native areas has been severely handicapped by the presence of many breeds, including vast numbers of scrub stock. The presence of inferior or scrub stock has come about in modern times due to the curtailment of grazing land and erosion of pastures from overcrowding of cattle in Native areas. This is the result of the importance of cattle in Bantu folklore, custom, and ritual.

[Cattle serve as] the means of keeping on good terms with the ancestral spirits and so of securing health and prosperity. . . . In folk tales the hero is often saved by a miraculous ox. . . . Cattle are also the means of obtaining sexual satisfaction, since a legal marriage cannot take place without the passage of cattle, the right to limited sexual relations is legalized by the passage of a beast, and the fines for illegal relations are levied in cattle. The possession of cattle gives social importance, for they are the means of securing wives and adherents, and of dispensing hospitality and showing generosity, on which virtues status largely depends. Also the possession of cattle in itself gives weight and dignity to the owner. . . . The pride of a small urchin when he is promoted from goat to cattle herd is great, and always he is conscious that cattle are a most important concern of men.[74]

Practically no important change has come about in this traditional attitude toward cattle. While the economic and dietetic value of African cattle has declined, owing to the fact that only the toughest and most resistant of scrub animals can survive under conditions in the Reserves today, they have lost little of their significance from the social and ritual point of view. Overstocking by sheep, donkeys, and goats as well as cattle has worsened the situation. Attempts by the Department of Native Affairs to encourage Africans to sell their stock and thus prevent the most serious cause of soil erosion have met with little success.[75]

In August, 1950, a large number of police were rushed to Witzieshoek Native Reserve (Orange Free State), where trouble was caused by Natives trying to combat the government's scheme for the culling of cattle. The authorities were attempting to reduce the number of cattle, with the object of improvement in the quality of the herds. The Natives destroyed sorting and branding pens, assaulted a Native official, and burned plantations.

> Cattle is such an obsession with them that despite continued representations by agricultural experts against overstocking, some Natives are actually bringing more beasts into the Reserve from outside its boundaries. Meanwhile, the spread of erosion outpaces all the efforts of the officials to check it.[76]

After the 1949 drought in the Ciskei, when the rains had appeared, the smallholders were already bringing in as many sheep and cattle as they could buy to replace their drought losses and the danger of overstocking was once more a reality. The drought killed nearly fifty thousand cattle and sheep in the Ciskei area. One senior official of the Department of Native Affairs at Kingwilliamstown commented:

> From our point of view this had its compensations because it eliminated thousands of very poor and old scrub cattle which were doing the land irreparable harm. Our agricultural officers have almost gone on their knees to the Natives to impress upon them that when conditions returned to normal they should buy one good cow in preference to five poor ones; but their pleas have obviously fallen on deaf ears. The Natives are interested in quantity, not quality.[77]

In order to carry out the proposed rehabilitation of the Reserves, the agricultural branch of the Department of Native

Affairs was reorganized in 1950.[78] The rehabilitation of existing Native areas depends upon the successful culling of stock, which in turn seems to depend to a large extent upon a change in Native public opinion. The proposed program of the Nationalist government therefore will admittedly require a considerable period before encouraging results become apparent. The Nationalists realize the necessity of carrying such a program over a long period of time. As one government officer stated: "On the basis of a productive agriculture, a many-sided and progressive community life for the population of our Native Reserves will undoubtedly develop, not with revolutionary suddenness but as a reward for initiative and the will to work."[79]

GIVING THE NATIVE EVERY OPPORTUNITY AND ENCOURAGEMENT TO RETAIN HIS TRIBAL AFFILIATIONS

Since the Native movement for the last twenty-five years has been toward the urban areas and detribalization, to the extent of over 50 per cent of the Native population, it is difficult in the extreme to see what factors can be changed so as to stem this flow and reverse its direction. Force could no doubt be used. But this would merely produce a dangerous social instability. If the Natives are to go back to the Reserves in the large numbers desired, the Nationalists will have to make the Reserves more attractive to them than ever before.

The government has announced that in addition to the segregation, to be rigidly adhered to, among European, Colored, Native, and Asiatic, the government also has in mind the tribal separation of Natives.[80] In this plan the Zulus, Basutos, etc., would be separated and housed in different areas.[81] It is not easy to see how this phase of their Native policy fits into their long-range objectives; there may be a basic contradiction in this aspect of the apartheid program. If the basic assumption is accepted that the unity of any people, especially when there are many different racial strains within such a people, is developed only by closer contact and common experiences with one an-

other, then the efforts of the Nationalists to develop the Natives
into a nation apart from the European sphere is doomed to failure. If the various Native tribes are to be, for all intents and
purposes, isolated from one another, from whence would grow a
unifying spirit?

Coupled to this factor is the obvious criticism that on a geographical thesis the plan is subject to substantial argument. Referring to the map of Native areas (Fig. 1), one fact is readily
apparent: the Native Reserves are not contiguous to one another.
They are scattered in many separate areas, some large and others
very small. Thus there would be a geographical isolation among
the various sections of the Native population as well as merely
tribal separation. The amount of control over the movement of
Natives, to prevent them from leaving the Reserves, will have to
be drastically increased under apartheid.[82] This is necessary in
order to keep the unwanted Natives out of the urban areas. As
such there will probably be little Native movement outside their
own Reserves or among the Reserves.

Again critics raise the question: From what source would rise
a common kinship and spirit of self-development among the
Natives as a group? Their Reserves consist of widely scattered
areas, and they are to be separated tribally. Nationalist apartheid,
in spite of allegations of the Malanites to the contrary, seems to
be a plan for dividing the Native people and keeping them divided. Nationalist allusions to the glories of the Natives' "national
life"[83] thus falls short of any meaning.

Controlling the Influx to the Towns and Establishing "Labor Bureaus" To Insure That the Native Is Employed to the Best Advantage of the Country

As part of their avowed apartheid program the Nationalists
propose to control the ingress and egress of migratory labor and
the flow of Union Natives into the urban areas by a system of so-
called labor bureaus. The government has outlined in very broad
form the largest features of the system, but as yet it is vague in

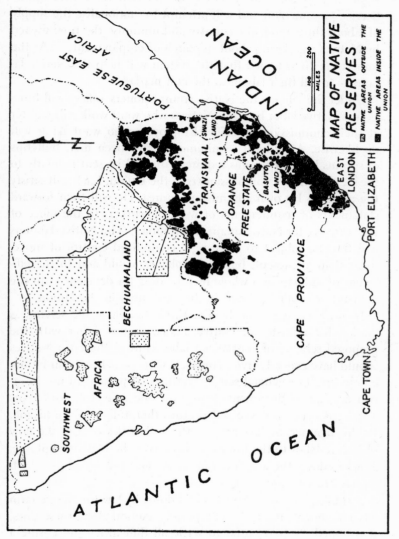

Fig. 1.—Map of Native Reserves

regard to details. The system is to function under the Public
Service Commission and will attempt to "rationalise the supply
of labour throughout the country and minimise the time wasted
by Natives wandering about in search of employment."[84] At the
same time "it is hoped that the system will help the Native la-
bourers to sell their labour in the best market."[85]

Under the scheme the Native commissioners' offices will function as Native labor bureaus. Natives who want work will register
at their commissioner's office. Employers who want labor will
do likewise. After local requirements have been met, bulletins
of surplus labor or surplus requirements will be sent regularly to
the six chief native commissioners in the Union. Each will satisfy
the needs in his own administrative area. He will then forward
statements of requirements of work or workers to the office of
the secretary for Native affairs in Pretoria.[86] The Native laborers
will thus be subject to more rigid centralized control of movement than at present, but this probably would add to the efficiency of industry as a whole by providing for deficiencies in the
demand or supply of labor in different areas in the Union.

It has been suggested by Dr. E. G. Jansen, while serving as
Nationalist minister of Native affairs, that together with the
proposed scheme of centralized labor control the farm Natives
should have general service contracts with their European farmer
employers. The general service contract, at present in use in urban areas, is a document giving, on one side, full particulars
about a Native employee and, on the other, full details of his job.
In this manner, besides helping the authorities control the flow
of Native labor to the towns, it also serves the Native employee,
as it lays down the wage he is to receive and the period for which
he has been engaged.

A similar form of contract is laid down by law for Native farm
laborers, but its use is not compulsory, Action along these lines,
it is hoped, "would go far to settle all difficulties and ensure a
better and more equitable distribution of Native labour."[87]

Any law aimed to make general service contracts mandatory

for Native farm labor would be aimed at halting the increasing exodus from farm employment by younger Natives. In addition to lower money wages, the conditions and terms of service on farms have deteriorated. In order to prevent young Africans from seeking urban employment, attempts have been made to restrict their movement and to increase the penal sanctions for any resultant breach of contract. Under the Nationalist apartheid program the general service contract will no doubt become compulsory for Native farm laborers, as it will provide another weapon to the Nationalists in their efforts to control tightly movements of Natives within the Union and in addition will stabilize the agricultural labor supply.[88]

CHAPTER VII

Natives under Apartheid: The Urban Population

INDUSTRIALIZATION OF THE RESERVES

INCESSANTLY THE NATIONALISTS HAVE STRESSED THE POINT THAT the Native would be allowed to develop to his highest capability in his own sphere. At the same time, however, if history can be used as a valid criterion, returning the vast numbers of urbanized Natives to the tribal organization will set a low limit on their development. The history of Native tribal life is certainly not representative of a highly developed people according to modern European standards.

Recently the Nationalist government has vigorously attacked such views as largely irrelevant to the apartheid program. The contentions of the Nationalists on this point reveal the dynamic character of apartheid theory itself. At the time the Nationalists were brought to power in 1948 little more than broad general statements concerning Native life on the Reserves under apartheid were forwarded. Such phrases as "rehabilitation of your national life," "the national home of the Native," "the opportunity of developing their national character," and "national development" to describe the future status of the Natives were aimed at both the European and the Native populations. They were aimed at the European to obtain their votes and at the Natives to gain their co-operation. Little in the way of detail was provided at the time.

What was not provided in detail, however, was furnished by the imaginations of both Europeans and Natives alike. The apartheid program had as yet barely emerged from the committee meeting rooms of the Nationalist party. It would have been

politically unwise and impractical to forward details about which
the party hierarchy itself was not sure and which would have
given the opposition additional Nationalist proposals to attack.

By late 1950, however, information provided by the Nationalist government showed that the criticisms concerning the role
the Natives were to play on the Reserves struck the Nationalist
program at a very weak point. As a result, carefully worded statements have been released providing, to a degree, some detail of
the envisaged life on the Reserves under apartheid. Taken as a
group, these statements reveal such a significant development in
apartheid theory that they constitute one of the main points
in Nationalist Native policy. As a refutation of criticisms aimed
at revitalized tribalism, they might well be described at this point
rather than at a later stage in the discussion of Native policy
where, chronologically speaking, they would belong.

This phase of the Nationalists' concepts of the future idealized state seem to have been substantially based upon views held
by some of South Africa's leading intellectuals.

On July 1, 1948, a few months after the Nationalist victory at
the polls, Professor A. C. Cilliers of Stellenbosch University,
in an address to the Cape Town Institute of Citizenship, urged
the gradual separation of the white and Native races and the
industrialization of the Reserves. The significant point of his
address was not only that the Reserves would have to be extended and improved but that "their present agricultural economy
would have to be changed, for work would have to be provided
for the Natives. Industries would have to be started to draw the
Natives to those places."[1]

Several days later W. W. M. Eiselen, professor of social anthropology at Pretoria University and a proponent of apartheid,[2]
in a speech before the South African Academy of Language,
Literature, and Art suggested the possibility of setting up factories
which would be dependent mainly on Native labor in the Reserves. Against the argument that if apartheid was carried out
there would not be sufficient land for the Natives, Professor

Eiselen said that the idea that every Native should be a land-
owner was old-fashioned. He envisaged instead self-supporting
Native communities with their own towns in addition to their
rural areas.[3] It is noteworthy that Professor Eiselen in October
of the next year was appointed secretary for Native affairs.[4]

That the Native Affairs Department has adopted this plan for
the rehabilitation of Native Reserves in the Union was revealed
in October, 1949, by Major M. L. C. Liefeldt, the chief Native
commissioner for Natal, before the Association of Chambers of
Commerce of South Africa in Pietermaritzburg. The plan, he
said, envisaged in broad outline the division of the Native population into peasant families and industrial workers. The peasants
would occupy the Native Reserves, and the industrial workers
would live in settlements.[5]

This same line of reasoning was given official credence in the
address of Dr. H. F. Verwoerd, Nationalist minister of Native
affairs, on November 21, 1950, before the Johannesburg Rotary
Club. He stated that the buying of land could not be continued
on the supposition that every Native would become an agricul-
turist. There would be industrial development in the Reserves,
including Native towns and villages with industrial populations.[6]

It is also significant that the Dutch Reformed church in the
1950 Bloemfontein congress passed a resolution, in support of
total territorial separation, which stated that the Natives should
be moved to an industrial system, yet to be established, in their
own areas and that apartheid did not mean returning the Natives
to a primitive existence.

By the beginning of the year 1951 these plans had been carried
so far that announcement was made that the Nationalist government was considering the formation of a Native Industrial Development Corporation to promote the establishment of industries in the Native Reserves. Mr. M. D. C. de Wet Nel, M.P.,
deputy chairman of the Native Affairs Commission,[7] in making
this announcement, stated that "raw Natives from the kraal
could be trained to a satisfactory level of industrial efficiency

within a reasonable time"[8] and that this was "opening up a new era for the Native in South Africa."[9]

Mr. de Wet Nel also revealed that the proposed corporation would be similar to the existing Industrial Development Corporation, which followed a policy of helping the establishment of industry by providing medium- and long-term finance on sound economic lines. The new corporation, however, would only promote industries in Native areas. At first, like the Industrial Development Corporation, it would be financed with government or European capital, but the Natives would be encouraged to invest capital in it also.[10]

Apartheid theory therefore has evolved into a program looking to an urban development in the Native Reserves based upon the growth of industry parallel with agricultural development and in harmony with "revitalized tribalism." As Dr. Verwoerd has said, "The future Bantu towns and cities in the Reserves could exist partly in conjunction with their own Bantu industries in those Reserves."[11]

The minister has also commented on the fact that the Europeans must be willing to help in the establishment of these industries with money and brains, "knowing that such industries must pass wholly into Bantu hands as soon as possible."[12] The European would thus withdraw altogether from the Native areas when the Bantu had no further need of him.[13]

Dr. D. L. Smit, vice-chairman of the Native Affairs Commission (which, together with the minister of Native affairs, is responsible for acquiring land for Native occupation under the Native Trust and Land Act of 1936), said that the commission was faced with a difficult situation because 5,000,000 morgen of land had been promised to the Natives by Parliament. Wherever the commission had sat, however, "there was a great deal of opposition to the buying of new land for the Natives."[14]

It is hardly conceivable that Europeans who are adamantly unwilling to give up land for Native occupancy in order to fulfil a parliamentary promise to the Natives would devote money and labor to developing industry in the Reserves and then turn the industries over to the Natives and withdraw from Native areas.

The issue, however, is even more fundamental. G. P. Lestrade, of the Department of Bantu Studies at Pretoria University, in his paper entitled "Some Aspects of the Economic Life of the South African Bantu" has written of the tribal Bantu:

> The Bantu are a pastoral and agricultural people, with, in the case of the South African Bantu at least, a strong pastoral bias, while the industrial side of their life is very little developed in comparison to the other two sides . . . industry . . . is exiguous in its role compared to pastoralism and agriculture, and is rather a cultural survival from an earlier stage of development than an integral part of economic life.[15]

In short, industry plays a small part in the Bantu economy. One might counter with the assertion that this refers only to the tribalized Bantu and not to the Europeanized Bantu, who have been industrialized to some extent. It must be borne in mind, however, that according to its own proponents apartheid looks to a cessation of the disintegration of tribal life and would put in its place a greatly revitalized tribalism. The Nationalists look to giving the non-Europeans an opportunity of developing their own "national character" and their own "national life." Whatever such terms may comprise, it will raise more than a few eyebrows to find it includes a black proletariat merged with the traditional tribal life. Tribal society has not, thus far, divided itself into the Nationalist-sponsored bifurcation of peasant families and industrial workers, each occupying its own areas.

The Nationalist plan is based upon the assumption that an intensive industrial development of the Reserves will not be competitive with European industry but, on the contrary, in harmony with and ancillary to industry in European areas. Such an assumption raises a vital question which is, perhaps, fatal to success of the plan. It is the question as to whether European industrialists in the Union will allow most of the Bantu people to be taken away as a market. Industrialized Reserves would mean that the needs of the Natives are to be met largely by their own factories. European industry at the present time would thus be confined to producing merely for its two and three-quarter million population. Such considerations have caused one commentator to write:

> If we are to look forward to industries in the Reserves, we must postulate at least a change of heart among Europeans, if not a radical change in the whole economic structure . . . to assume that the Reserves will be capable of creating industries ". . . in harmony with those established in European areas" must be considered the height of naïveté.[16]

Dr. Verwoerd has estimated that in fifty years there will be between five and six million Europeans and twenty-one million non-Europeans in South Africa. On these figures he bases his claim that not only agriculture but industries would have to be developed in the Reserves. The envisaged increase in the Union's population retains the same proportion of Europeans to non-Europeans as exists today. Similarly the same doubts as to willingness of European industrialists to allow the Bantu to produce industrial products to meet their own needs have lost neither their pertinence nor their validity.

It is thus a moot question whether this phase of Nationalist apartheid is compatible with the European capitalistic system. If industrialization of the Reserves is abandoned at a later date as impracticable or not capable of implementation, any attempts to send the urbanized Natives to these areas will bring forth the inescapable and valid criticisms earlier aimed at the concept of revitalized tribalism. Thus, exclusive of migratory labor forces, the Union's urbanized Natives would have their lives reoriented to a tribal existence and to a village level of development. The widespread skepticism directed toward the apartheid program is thus in many respects not unwarranted.

It must be realized that industrialization of the Reserves on a wide scale, which would be necessary to produce goods and provide employment for the great numbers of urbanized Natives to be returned to the Reserve areas, is only compatible with revitalized tribalism to a certain point. Native industry, like European industry, will require a plentiful supply of labor. How long the tribal system would remain revitalized or even intact to the degree present today alongside Native urban-industrialized areas in the Reserves is of course a crucial question.

It is still too early in the Nationalists' industrialization program to tell what aspects of their earlier apartheid policy may have to be abandoned if industry is to be carried out on any appreciable scale. These recently emergent aspects of apartheid theory leave the tribalism of apartheid a somewhat vaguer and less definable concept than in the first two years of the Nationalist administration. This theory of racial separation and development, however, being of the dynamic character it is, will in time reveal the details which are now lacking in its present stage of evolution.

Retaining Only Those Tribalized Natives in Urban Areas Necessary to Industrial Development

Dr. Malan is, of course, well aware of the dependence of the Union's economy upon the available labor supply. South Africa's wealth lies not only in the natural riches beneath the ground but also in the cheap Native labor employed in agriculture, mines, and industry. His concept of apartheid does not, in actual practice, mean that urban areas are to be without the benefit of cheap Native labor. If such were attempted for even a short while, the Union would be reduced to a pauper nation. Theoretically, apartheid calls for the life of the Native to be completely tied up with the civilization of the Reserves and for the life of the European to be tied to the civilization outside the Reserves.

European industry, mining, and agriculture, however, present the common ground upon which, under necessity, the Native and European must work together, the Native in an inferior capacity, as in the past, to be sure, but, nevertheless, working in the same area. It is at this point that apartheid appears to become most susceptible to criticism. It is at this point that critics of the program maintain that practice must deviate widely from theory. But it is also at this point that the Nationalists present a solution to this dilemma, that is, how to maintain the available cheap Native labor supply in urban areas while at the same time returning the Natives to the Reserves. The solution presented is, in view of the long-range Nationalist objectives, logical and possible of accomplishment.

The Nationalist solution to the problem is that the labor required for industry, mines, and, in the rural areas, agriculture is to be provided in large part by non-Union Natives. The system of migratory labor has been used in the Union for some time. The extent of "foreign" labor in the Union is provided in part by the report of the Commission on Native Laws:

> The Fagan report (Commission on Native Laws) gives the figure of 111,000 for Native labour employed in mines and industry from territories beyond the Union, including the British protectorates of Basutoland and Swaziland. It also estimates that there are 45,000 illegal immigrants from Mozambique employed elsewhere in South Africa.[17]

If such migratory labor forces were increased, under careful control of movements of these forces within the Union, a large number of Union Natives could be sent back to the Reserves by the government with little or no loss in the productivity of the total Native labor force. This essentially is what the Nationalists propose to do. The scale of migratory labor already in use is not done full justice in the excerpt above from the Fagan Report. As will be shown, the mining industry reaches into far-distant and remote portions of the continent to obtain its needed labor force.

As in the past,[18] the Union government will obtain the migratory labor by mutual agreements between the outside governments and the Union. The amounts of such labor will be increased considerably. The Rand mining interests, both British South African and Dutch South African, are agreed upon the essential need for cheap, readily available, and readily replenishable Native labor. Indeed, the unique factor of the possibility of mining such cheap low-grade ore as is mined in the Union can be "attempted nowhere else in the world."[19] This is due to the five main factors in the Union: (a) big-scale working, (b) technical efficiency, (c) group control, (d) the enormous areas of payable ore available, and (e) an abundance of cheap labor.[20]

For better or for worse, the gold mines have been able to exist only by the use of cheap, semicivilised labour. Almost the entire unskilled labour force is obtained from the Native Reserves in the Union, from South-West Africa, Nyasaland, Portuguese East Africa and the Rhodesias. To recruit this labour the mines have established a huge organisation consisting of over 120 recruiting centres, dotted all over Southern Africa, some of them in the remote tropical jungle where regular communication is had only by radio and from which Natives can be brought only along difficult tracks or by river barges. Natives are engaged to work on the mines under a contract system for a period of about a year. . . .[21]

As a consequence, the Nationalists, the United party, and the industrial and mining interests are agreed with Smuts's emphatic statement, "He [the African] is carrying this country on his back."[22] The Nationalists hold, however, that increased migratory labor would provide the required labor force and thus allow large parts of the Union's Native population to return to the Reserves. The United party asserts that the Union's Natives are already absorbed into the mining-industrial-urban economy to a large degree and should not be displaced. The mining interests of the Rand seem to be divided, like the political parties, upon this basic question.

In order to maintain economic stability the Malan Government has approved the policy of relying upon migratory labour where necessary. In this way, the Nationalists will be "ensuring the economic without in any way endangering the political and social hegemony of the European."[23]

This is the Nationalists' answer to one of the most widespread and effective criticisms leveled at apartheid: that it would reduce the Union's cheap labor supply. The Nationalist solution is relatively simple, being based on a system already in operation and which need be only expanded. This is a proposal which at one and the same time preserves the theory of apartheid as applied to the Union Native and also preserves the Union's productivity by use of cheap migratory Native labor.

It is doubtful if the Nationalist government envisages the entire Union urban Native labor force to be replaced by this migratory labor, though a large portion of the Union Native laborers would be replaced and sent back to the Reserves. This would uphold Dr. Malan's contention that the Union Natives could, to a very large degree, be removed from the industrialized urban areas without impairing the economy of the nation. It is a solution which is ingenious, and its effectiveness should not be underestimated. It has its own inherent problems of course, but they would not be insurmountable.

The yearly contract basis of such migratory labor, as now in use, would provide the Nationalists with the means of preventing a permanent Native population on the present scale in the industrial-mining-urban areas. The migratory labor population would be, in effect, a mobile labor force, transient in character, which could more easily be diminished or expanded in such areas according to the demands of the labor market at the time. With the approach of periods of slack employment the yearly contracts would soon lapse, and the migrants would be sent back to their own lands. This would prevent a large unemployed Native population of a permanent character being established and residing in the urban areas at a time when their presence was least desired.

The merits of expanding the migratory labor system, over the present system, have been supported by one faction of the mining industry which opposes the establishment of a permanent labor force, since it would "(1) destroy the tribal system in the Reserves which they consider should be preserved as long as possible; (2) in so doing destroy a system of 'social security' which the Reserves provided gratis as it were; (3) involve the provision of medical services on a scale which they could not contemplate financing; and (4) probably increase the Native silicosis rate which is at present kept very low by long periods of absence."[24] On the other hand, vehement criticism has been leveled at the concept of migratory labor in the Union:

> Its foundation [apartheid] is a system of migratory labour which is uneconomic and socially destructive and which has been condemned by the Permanent Mandates Commission of the League of Nations, by a Nyasaland Government Committee . . . the Transvaal Chamber of Mines, and by every responsible body which has had cause to examine the system impartially.[25]

Making Employers Responsible to Some Extent for Housing Their Native Employees in Towns

The Nationalist government is not assuming responsibility for Native urban housing on anything approaching the scale of the former government. The Nationalist government is attempting to shift a portion of the responsibility to the employers themselves. The employers of Native labor are reluctant to be made even partially responsible for so vast a task and, owing to the already desperate housing conditions in regard to urban housing for the Natives, have declared themselves opposed to this government policy.

The law places responsibility for Native housing in the urban areas on the local authorities. In the larger cities, however, the local authorities have arrived at a stage where they say that they can no longer afford the losses incurred on Native housing. Some years ago an agreement was entered into between the previous government and the local authorities whereby the losses on subeconomic houses were shared by the government on the basis of a fixed formula. The Nationalists allege that, owing to a tendency to build houses on too large a scale and because plans were executed for services to the Natives which were superfluous, large losses were incurred by both the local authorities and the government.

Commerce and industry have objected to the proposal that

they contribute toward the losses on subeconomic housing for urban Natives in their employ on the grounds that they have no say in the plans which are carried out but that any resultant losses will fall heavily upon them. The government has thus decided to form a board or committee on Native housing on which both industry and commerce will be represented. In addition, instead of employing the relatively expensive skilled European labor in the building of these houses, the Natives will be encouraged to construct the dwellings themselves.[26]

The Nationalist government also proposes to amend the law relating to the profits from the sale of kaffir beer to Natives in municipal beer halls, so as to allow two-thirds of the profits to be made available for general purposes, such as losses on Native housing, reduction of rentals to Natives, and capital and maintenance costs in connection with Native locations, villages, and hostels. This would be in addition to the limited purposes, such as social welfare and recreation among the Natives, for which such profits may at present be used. This plan for the extended use of kaffir-beer profits has been criticized on the ground that subsidies from municipalities for Native housing schemes will diminish and that the Natives will only have subsidies from the central government to rely upon. With the Nationalists' reluctance, however, to assume responsibilities for Native urban housing which former governments had undertaken, the subsidies of the central government would be grossly insufficient. Thus the losses which the local authority now undertakes to bear would in reality be ultimately borne by the Natives themselves. The municipal authorities are in favor of such a plan, and employers of urban Native labor can be expected to support the amendment, since it will similarly reduce their own financial responsibility.

CHAPTER VIII

Natives under Apartheid: Political and Economic Rights

EXTENSION OF THE COUNCIL SYSTEM AND INCREASED NATIVE RESPONSIBILITY IN LOCAL MATTERS

ANALYSIS OF THIS MAIN POINT OF NATIONALIST NATIVE POLICY provides the opportunity to examine in detail the political status of the Natives, rural and urban, under apartheid. It is essential to note that, as the Natives are headed back to the Reserves under the Nationalist program, they also lose their representation in the House of Assembly. As in the case of the Coloreds, the reasoning behind this removal of existing representation is: "It is our intention to take away their representation in this House. Then we can give them something else and we believe it will be something better."[1]

The Cape Natives at the present time are represented in the House of Assembly by communal representation.[2] In lieu of their present communal representation in the Assembly, however, the Cape Natives are to be allowed to retain representation in the Senate now allotted to all Union Natives. These senators, elected indirectly by the Natives, will not be allowed, as hitherto they had been, to vote on matters of confidence or no confidence in the government or on a declaration of war or on matters affecting a change of the political rights of the non-Europeans whose interests they are to represent.[3] Since the Union Senate plays only a secondary role in legislation and, when in controversy with the House, must ultimately bow to it, this "something better" of which Dr. Malan speaks is rather "something less." Thus, under Nationalist apartheid the Cape Coloreds and Cape Natives alike are to have their political status reduced.

Each of these Cape races will, so to speak, have its status in the political sphere reduced one step; that is, the Colored is to occupy the political status produced by communal representation in the House of Assembly which the Native now enjoys and the Native is to have his representation in the Assembly reduced to the communal representation now accorded to all Union Natives in the Senate.

As in other aspects of apartheid theory the principle of compensatory institutions underlies the proposed expansion of councils in Native areas. This program, to be carried out as quickly and efficiently as possible, is, according to the Nationalist government, to serve as a compensation for the proposed abolition of Native representation in the House of Assembly.[4]

As pointed out earlier, the powers conferred on the separate local councils may, if deemed advisable by the government, be exercised by a "general council" representative of the various local councils. The only two examples of such a general council system are those of the Ciskei and the Transkeian territories. The Nationalist government in the implementation of apartheid is looking to the Ciskeian and Transkeian councils as examples which might well be followed in the other Native areas of the Union.[5] The Nationalists will probably find over a period of time that expansion of the unattached local councils will serve their interests to a far higher degree than expansion of the general council system. It is requisite, however, prior to any consideration of the role of either type under apartheid to describe the Ciskei and the Transkeian general councils.

The earliest and prime example of the general council system is that of the Transkeian Territories, viz., Transkei, Pondoland, Tembuland, and East Griqualand. This area comprises 16,500 square miles in the eastern Cape Province between the Kei River and Natal. Within this area is a Native population approaching a million and a half. European ownership of land being excluded from much the greater of this area, no other province approaches the Cape in the proportion of Natives living apart from European society in reserved land.

After annexation of the area between the Kei and Natal the Cape authorities instituted a policy which was unique in South Africa, First, there was the administrative separation of the Transkeian Territories from the rest of the Cape Colony. Legislation by the Cape Parliament was not applicable beyond the Kei unless such was expressly stated. Legislation was provided by edictal law, that is, by proclamation. The second significant innovation was the recognition, as far as the Cape was concerned, of Native law and custom. Transkeian magistrates, from this time onward, were obligated to become acquainted with the laws of the tribe they administered. Although the penal code of the Territory enacted by the Cape Parliament was primarily based upon colonial criminal law, in the sphere of civil law the old tribal system prevailed. No attempt was made to codify Native laws, the magistrates thus having the opportunity of adapting the laws they administered to the variable needs of a Native society in contact with Western civilization.[6]

The present council system of the Transkeian Territories is based upon "the most famous law regarding Native policy in South African history"[7]—the Glen Gray Act of 1894. This law was enacted by the Cape Parliament for the administration of local affairs in the Glen Gray District of the Ciskei. The Cape administration, however, adopted by proclamation the broad lines of policy in respect of Glen Gray for application in the Transkeian Territories. These principles were applied in the four western districts of the Transkei before the act came into force in Glen Gray. The importance of the act itself therefore is not so much its operation in Glen Gray as in the extension of the council system to the Transkeian Territories and to other areas of the Union.

For the Glen Gray District the act aimed, in part, to give the Natives a share in local government. In each location the landholders were to elect a location board. For the district as a whole, a body known as the Glen Gray District Council was set up. This council was composed of six members nominated by the constituent location boards and six by the governor of the Cape Colony, with the district magistrate as chairman. The council was empowered to fix a local rate to be expended on such projects as cattle dips, roads, and agricultural improvements.

The Transkeian Proclamation, however, abolished the location boards and established instead district councils. Each district council, as first established, comprised six members, two being govenment nominees and four nominated, from among their own number, by a meeting of all the headmen of the district. The most original feature of the Transkeian scheme was the creation of a combined body representative of the various district councils and originally known as the Transkei General Council. Thus the district councils and the General Council in the Transkei stood to each other in a relationship akin to the location boards and district council in Glen Gray.

Today there are twenty-six district councils, and the Transkei General Council has evolved into the body known as the United Transkeian Territories General Council, on which each district is represented. Each district council consists of a European magistrate and six councilors. Two of these councilors are nominated and appointed by the government and four by the inhabitants of the district, except in Pondoland, where the chiefs nominate two councilors.

The United Transkeian Territories General Council is presided over by the chief magistrate of the Transkeian Territories, the twenty-six district magistrates are members, and, in addition, each district sends three councilors, one nominated and appointed by the government of the Union and two nominated by the district council. In addition, the chiefs of Tembuland, eastern and western Pondoland, and Gcaleka are members. It is thus composed of European administrators and Native members.

The seat of the United Transkeian Territories General Council is at Umtata. The annual meeting of the council at Umtata is called the *Bunga*, and the council system in the Transkeian Territories is often referred to as the Transkeian *Bunga* system. This general council or *Bunga* is the central feature of the system. It may deal with any matter affecting the welfare of the Bantu. The most-discussed topics are of a local nature dealing with matters of concern to the territories. Thus, agriculture, Native laws and custom, roads, Native education, revenue and expenditure, and general local improvements are topics to be found undergoing discussion and often lively debate in the annual sessions.

In local administration the district councils stand to the General Council as the individual parts of a single body.[8] There is also an executive committee composed of the chief magistrate, three other magistrates appointed by him, and four Bantu elected by the General Council itself. This executive committee is responsible for the implementation of resolutions passed by the *Bunga* and for administration of the council's affairs in such matters as appointment of officials, public works, education, and agriculture.[9]

The General Council is vested with those powers previously enjoyed by the district councils. The district councils send their representatives to the General Council, submit their work programs for official sanction, and, under direction of the executive, carry out the programs approved by the General Council. The district councils have no funds of their own, and money for work projects must be voted by the central body. The district councils are reponsible, however, for initiation of expenditure proposals. After being laid before the General Council in the form of annual estimates, and following the vote on such estimates by the council, the proposals are submitted for the approval of the governor-general. It should be noted that the functions of the General Council with respect to funds are purely advisory. "The Native Councillors talk, criticize and sometimes influence policy, but the European officials do the work."[10]

It can thus be readily seen that the General Council and the district councils constitute an auxiliary system to the Union's administrative structure, their primary and most important function being to associate Natives with control of public funds, to give them voice in the conduct of affairs ultimately affecting their own interests, to train them to constitutional methods of expression, and to keep the government informed of Native feeling.[11] There have been criticisms of the system, such as, for example, the charge that the Bantu are not really learning to control their own affairs and that the government asks advice but does not take or accept it.[12]

Although the Transkeian system has served to preserve Native society from expropriation of land and from commercial exploitation by Europeans, the tendency has been to weaken the integrity of tribal groupings. The territories are divided into districts quite irrespective of the traditional boundaries of the tribal lands of the Pondos, Tembus, Fingos, and other tribes. The Transkei governmental system, like the French system in Africa, ignores tribal units, adopts territorial divisions, and bypasses to a great extent traditional tribal chiefs.[13]

The Ciskei General Council since 1934 has linked together the Glen Gray District Council and eight local councils. Unlike the Transkeian *Bunga*, it is constituted on a federal basis. Local feeling is still too strong in some districts to recognize the administrative advantages of a unified rather than a federal system of local government.[14] The Ciskei General Council serves the same purposes and carries out the same functions as the Transkeian Council. Both may, generally speaking, be considered as representative of the general council scheme as opposed to the unattached or autonomous local scheme. These unattached local councils are not linked to any central or general council, and in this respect they differ from the linked or attached local councils of the Ciskei and the district councils of the Transkei.

It is essential to note that the general councils, district councils, and local councils are designed to operate in the more advanced Native areas. Some unattached local councils have been set up, however, in areas where the Natives are not so advanced as those in the eastern Cape, and as a result the extension of the council form of local government has not met with anything like the same success it enjoys in the Transkeian Territories.

Other types of local government organs are widely used. For the more primitive areas the tribal system itself is utilized, the chiefs and headmen thus acting as local government organs in certain respects though to a lesser degree than the councils. Native Reserve boards, in use in the Orange Free State, consist of variously numbered elected Natives and a government-appointed European chairman. Native advisory boards established under the Natives (Urban Areas) Consolidation Act of 1945 serve to represent every location or Native village under control of an urban local authority or for any portion of an urban area in which Natives reside. These boards consist of not less than three Natives resident in the area, with a European chairman, who is usually superintendent of the location or village. Each of these local bodies for Natives serves to express to the government the views of Natives on matters of immediate local concern.[15]

The Nationalist government is considering the linkage of presently unattached local councils in certain areas of the Transvaal. Thus, the unattached local councils of Natives in the Pietersburg area were convened in 1949 to discuss the proposal.[16] If such a third Native general council materializes, it, together with the Transkeian *Bunga* at Umtata and the Ciskeian General Council or *Bunga* at Kingwilliamstown, would serve, the Nationalists assert, as a step toward a more uniform administrative and local government system for the Reserves. Thus the "chaos" which the Nationalists claim they inherited from the former government, dating "from the days when each of the present four provinces was a separate entity with its own approach to the Native problem,"[17] would, they contend, be eliminated.

In opposition to this view, however, it must be pointed out that these unattached local councils in the Transvaal, actually on a tribal basis, have been slow in developing.

Most of the Natives have been in contact with Western civilization for a shorter period than the Cape Bantu.

In addition, the Glen Gray Act looked to "a thoroughgoing experiment in detribalization based upon a complete change in land tenure."[18] Thus all arable land in the Ciskei was divided into individual holdings, although Bantu land tenure was traditionally tribal or communal.[19] In the Transkei, although individual tenure was applied to only a few of the twenty-six districts, nevertheless, the districts themselves, as shown, were drawn without any regard whatsoever of customary tribal boundaries. This land policy, together with the circumvention of authority of the chief, served to break up the tribal system to a considerable degree. By these means, it was hoped, the Natives in great numbers would be more prone to go out of the Reserves and labor for Europeans. One has only to read Buell's account of the administration of the Transkei to realize the extent to which "persuasion" was used in these areas as an accepted part of European policy to get the Natives to work in the mines.[20]

Apartheid, however, looks in the opposite direction. The main task is to get the Natives outside the Reserves back into them and keep them there. The only manner in which an extended general council system could be made compatible with the apartheid program is by retaining or instituting, as the case may be, the tribal basis of those local councils which are to be linked and not inaugurate representation on councils based upon arbitrarily surveyed districts. In this manner the revitalized tribalism of apartheid would not be undercut by a system originally designed to do just that.

Considering the expansion of the *Bunga* and local council system as compensation for the Natives' loss of representation, it must be remembered that only the Cape Natives have representation in the Union's lower house. Since the majority of Cape Natives are already being served by the councils of the Ciskei and Transkeian territories, this supposed compensation is incognizable. These councils never have exerted an influence comparable to the Cape Natives' communal representation in the

House. Extension of the council system in any form to the other provinces cannot be considered to be in lieu of any existing parliamentary arrangement enjoyed by the Cape Natives.

As Barnes so succinctly stated in 1931 when agitation was rampant for removal of the Cape Native franchise: "It is already abundantly plain that for the loss of the Cape vote the Native is to receive no *quid pro quo* which could by any stretch of fancy be called reasonable."[21] This statement is remarkably apropos to the proposed removal of the Native communal representation in the Assembly today.

The Nationalist government in its propaganda concerning the extension of both the general and the local council schemes has placed great stress on the increased responsibility which Natives are to enjoy in their own areas. In the past most of the work has been done under European guardianship. The Nationalists have announced, however, that they now hope steadily to loosen the administrative ties between whites and Natives. The future of the Transkei and other Reserve areas therefore is to lie largely in the hands of the Native.[22]

The government has vehemently denied, however, that it has any intention "of creating a sovereign independent Native state."[23] Thus references to "Bantustan," a term coined by the Natives in South Africa to refer to such a visualized independent Native state within the borders of the Union, have for the Nationalists no concrete foundation. The establishment of more councils cannot be tied up with any concept of ultimately independent Native areas.

Although there are repeated Nationalist references to increased responsibility of the Natives in local matters, these must be examined in the light of other Nationalist announcements. Dr. E. G. Jansen, governor-general of the Union and former Nationalist minister for Native affairs, while serving in the Malan cabinet declared in the Senate on May 9, 1949: "While we would like to see more powers given to the Natives, they must realise that full control in their own areas cannot be granted while a large part of the finances is provided by the Government."[24]

If the Nationalist government is waiting for the Natives to begin paying a "large part of the finances" toward maintaining the Reserves and keeping themselves at a subsistence level in their own areas, the future is exceedingly dismal for the Native cause. Under apartheid most of the Natives will be cut off from employment outside the Reserves and thus lose the benefit of the higher wage scale in the European areas. In addition, as pointed out, the land in the Reserves is not adequate in quantity or quality to support the vast numbers of Natives intended to be within them. The proposed industrialization of the Reserves, while theoretically it might provide such financing, can be realized only in the far-distant future. As long as European industry demands continuing markets, the success of industrialization of Native areas becomes problematical in proportion as the visualized scale of such a development increases.

One is led to question the meaning of the term "full control in their own areas" in view of later pronouncements by Dr. Jansen. "The idea is that local and general councils should gradually be given the power eventually to control their own affairs as *far as possible with the retention of white trusteeship*. That is the intention as far as Native areas are concerned."[25] He has also revealed that the tribal chiefs' councils must be approved by the government as before[26] and, in speaking of Native urban life, stated that "in their own separate residential areas . . . the local authorities will naturally remain in control."[27]

Thus the biggest inducement to the Natives—responsibility in their own sphere without European restrictions—probably means, in the last analysis, little more control over their own affairs than they have at the present time. Nationalist pretensions to the loosening of administrative ties between whites and blacks must therefore remain suspect.

The new councils in Native areas are to serve, according to Nationalist pronouncements, not only as compensation for alteration of the present parliamentary representation of the Cape Natives but also as compensation for the government's abolition of the Natives' Representative Council.[28] The use of an expanded council system in this respect brings to light several vital issues not otherwise apparent. Unlike abolition of Native representation in the House of Assembly, this phase of the apartheid program affects all the Natives in the Union.

The Natives' Representative Council was established under the Representation of Natives Act of 1936, by which the Cape Natives were removed from the common roll and given communal representation.[29] This body, representative of all the Union's Natives, in practice meets several times a year (by law it is required to meet once a year), and before it must be laid the estimates of the South African Native Trust Fund[30] and all proposed legislation affecting Natives. "In addition it has very full powers of initiative and may and does discuss other matters affecting Africans and even general issues of national life."[31] It is, nevertheless, a purely advisory body. Although its resolutions have no force of law, "there is no doubt that it has exercised quite a considerable influence on the deliberations of Parliament and the decisions of government."[32]

The history of the council has been somewhat erratic, the members feeling frustrated not only because the council is purely advisory but because its advice on significant issues has been so often disregarded.[33] The council has been in a condition of "suspended activity" several times over disputes with the government, the most recent of which has been the issue of apartheid. Dr. W. J. G. Mears, secretary for Native affairs at the time, reported in 1948:

The greatest weakness has been the fact that the Council has little responsibility to carry. In other words, it has been an advisory body. As its requests, particularly in the political sphere, have not been acceded to, it not unnaturally became disgruntled and queried the reason for its existence.[34]

In December, 1949, the council adjourned indefinitely after a two-day session. In his opening statement of that session, as chairman of the council, Dr. Mears said that the government agreed with the opinion of the council that it was serving no useful purpose and that the government, as a result, was considering its abolition.[35] The essence of the dispute, however, was revealed when Dr. Mears declared:

The Government will at all times be prepared to consider any reasonable and practical suggestions as to the manner in which better co-operation between white and black can be made possible, but Councillors must know that no Government could abolish all discriminatory legislation and that such a course is quite impracticable. . . .

It is questionable whether the Council has ever presented the real needs of the Natives. Matters affecting the every day affairs of the bulk of the population . . . have received relatively little attention; on the other hand the Council turned its mind to politics and in a demand for political equality insisted on the removal of all distinctions between blacks and whites.[36]

In December, 1950, the council adjourned *sine die* to enable its Native members to apply to the courts to test a ruling of its chairman, Dr. W. W. M. Eiselen, who succeeded Dr. Mears as secretary for Native affairs. The dispute arose when the Nationalist minister of Native affairs, Dr. H. F. Verwoerd, complied with the council's request to explain the government's apartheid policy. The minister had then asked the council to proceed with the practical work on the agenda, but they resorted instead to debates on political issues. The chairman ruled according to the powers conferred on him by regulation under the Representation of Natives Act of 1936 that the council must proceed with the agenda placed before it before discussing matters arising from the minister's speech.

Mr. Quintin Whyte and Mr. J. D. Reinallt Jones, while both were serving as officers of the South African Institute of Race Relations, asked Dr. Eiselen to agree to a limited discussion, in an attempt to prevent the proceedings from breaking down, but he would not allow it. The council took the position, however, that since the minister's speech was placed on the agenda on the resolution of the council in January, 1949, the consideration thereof was not in the discretion of the chairman.[37] The Nationalist government has felt that by its adjournment in this manner the council had again shown that it "was not in earnest about its obligations towards the Bantu people, to whom housing, employment and training were much more important than the exposition of political theories."[38]

To this allegation several observations may be made. First, it must be borne in mind that the council was set up at the time and under the same act by which the Cape Natives were removed from the common roll and given communal representation in the House of Assembly; it was a compensatory device. Second, the broad terms of reference with which this body was vested with functions allowed it to discuss all proposed legislation affecting the Natives of the Union. This must, of course, include apartheid legislation. The changes to be effected upon the Natives by apartheid certainly demand expression representative of all Union Natives which this council provides to a limited extent. If the rules of procedure do not allow for adequate discussion or debate by the Native members of such a far-reaching program as apartheid, then the rules should be modified by the government.

The council was originally intended as a channel of communication between the government and the Native community. If opinion representative of the vast Native population is to be stifled at the council meetings, where will Native opinion on grave national issues such as apartheid be expressed? Certainly not in the present Ciskeian or Transkeian *Bunga,* where local matters are uppermost, or in any future councils set up by the government for local government purposes. The only other alternative, since under apartheid Native representation is to be abolished in the lower house, is the Natives' representation in the upper house, that is, the four European senators who represent the interests and welfare of the Natives.

These senators may give expression of Native sentiments, and indeed they have traditionally been exceptionally well qualified for their responsibilities and keenly aware of their duties. In many instances they have espoused the Native cause with energy and devotion. However, as shown earlier in this chapter, under Nationalist apartheid these four senators are to have their own parliamentary rights reduced. Native opinion, though only advisory, as in the council, must have an adequate outlet on matters of national as well as local concern.

On the other hand, the Native councilors must approach their problems with a realistic attitude—an attitude that reflects the fact they have important, though advisory, functions to perform. This would exclude the attitude of previous councils which had refused under the former government to carry out its statutory duties until all legislation discriminating against non-Europeans had been repealed.[39]

Dr. E. G. Jansen, while serving as Nationalist minister of Native affairs, stated that the trouble with the Natives' Representative Council was that it drew representatives from all over the Union and that it was accordingly out of touch with local needs and therefore turned to political issues. Thus it was that the government had in mind the establishment of more Native councils equivalent to the *Bunga* in the Cape Province.[40]

It is this same Union-wide representation which gives the council its present value, however. It is out of touch with local needs because it was never devised to concern itself with such. The general councils, district councils, local councils, location boards, Native Reserve boards, Native urban advisory boards, and even the use of the tribal system for certain local government functions have all been utilized by successive government administrations to keep in touch with local needs. Their widely variant forms serve to adapt them to the particular requirements of each Native area, whether it is rural or urban, primitive or more advanced. The Natives' Representative Council serves a needed national purpose and should not be abolished, because it carries out those functions for which it was originally established.

Although there are large sections of Native opinion which would abolish the Natives' Representative Council even if the government were to make significant concessions on major points, the Ciskeian General Council (Ciskei *Bunga*) has unanimously adopted a resolution asking the Nationalist government not to abolish it, "as the body is a good link between the Government and the Native people."[41]

A parallel development to the extension of the council form of local government in the rural Native areas is found in Nationalist announcements that a system of Native councils for urban Natives is to be created. This is the result of the criticism of the Nationalist government as to the Natives' Representative Council being created "without taking into account the differing interests of the Natives in the Reserves, in the towns and living on European farms."[42]

This scheme of urban Native councils envisages that over a period of time progressively more local authority could be intrusted to the urban councils than is proposed for the councils in the Reserves. If this scheme were carried out, each council would represent part of the Native population more or less of the same group or tribe.[43]

This seems to point up the fact that the Nationalists are seemingly, more and more, coming to realize and accept as a condition of their own well-being a considerable, fairly stable Native labor force in the carefully controlled locations bordering the European urban-industrialized areas. The theory of greatly expanded and highly mobile migratory labor forces for these areas, described earlier in this study, may thus at the time of writing be evolving under practical necessity into notions of a less mobile labor force. The Nationalists have not provided much detail on this new scheme, and the author reserves further judgment until more adequate information becomes available.

The Nationalists, like past governments, are aware that both the general and the unattached local council systems are not readily applicable to all Native areas in the Union. The greatest part of the rural Native areas are inhabited by Natives who, in the local government sphere, have not advanced very much further than to administer their own affairs in connection with the dipping of their cattle, the eradication of scab and weeds, improving the land for increased yields, managing their own locations, fencing, and the cutting of firewood. The Transkei seems to stand apart in this respect.[44]

Thus, in the more primitive areas where the tribal system is firmly entrenched, the authority of the Native chief will, no doubt, remain and will even be buttressed by the Nationalist government. Dr. E. G. Jansen, in the early months of the Nationalist administration, considered that it would be in the interests of the Natives if tribal discipline were restored and more use made of chiefs in Native administration. His successor, Dr. H. F. Verwoerd, has announced that the government favors revival of chiefs' councils and that the government recognized the rights and traditions of the chiefs, the fact that they had reigning houses, and the right to govern within their own areas.[45]

Although the expansion of the unattached local council system and general council system seems to undercut the earlier stress of apartheid upon a greatly revitalized tribal life, owing primarily to the circumvention of the authority of the chief and the circumvention of the traditional tribal councils, there is, nevertheless, up to a certain point, no basic contradiction. It fits, in fact, into the recently evolved program of industrialization of the Reserves and emerged as a main point of Nationalist Native policy at about the same time. It is merely recognition that the Natives returned to the Reserves from the European urban-industrialized areas will no longer be responsive to traditional tribal authority or even traditional tribal lore. They will be most responsive to an urban-industrial environment. This will be provided for by the proposed industrial development of the Reserves.

As a necessary concomitant of this type of society, however, a more advanced system of local self-government and administration is required. Thus the general council system of the Transkeian Territories, which has been eminently successful for more advanced rural Natives, and the unattached local councils, with their more independent and flexible administrative potentialities, have been stressed. This advanced type of local government body and the traditional tribal hierarchy of authority will attract and be amenable to different types of Natives according to the environment with which they are most compatible. The Nationalists hope thus to attract Natives from every stratum of Native society to support the apartheid program.

It is important to note that the expansion of the council systems in no way precludes or undermines the isolation, both geographical and social, between the tribes which, as the author has pointed out, is inherent in apartheid theory. Even in the councils envisaged for the Native labor force allowed in the European urban-industrialized areas the Natives are to be grouped with due regard for the characteristic Nationalist stress of ethnic and tribal affiliations. The unattached local council system rather than the general council system with its linked constituent bodies is more amenable to Nationalist designs. The unattached and administratively independent (independent of course of only a central body) local councils are particularly adaptable to tribal separation and isolation not only in the urban areas but in the rural areas where they can be based upon the small and scattered Native Reserves.

The general councils may also be adapted to ethnic division of the Native population, however, as long as the tribal basis of the constituent bodies is retained. Thus, as Dr. Jansen has revealed, the proposed general councils for the Transvaal are to be established for the Northern Sotho and the Tswana, respectively. The general council for Natal is to be predominantly Zulu.[46]

Tribal isolation of the Native population is intimately tied up with the issue of Native nationalism. Sir Charles Dundas, long familiar with the African scene and former governor and commander-in-chief of Uganda Protectorate, in his analysis of apartheid has emphasized that Nationalist administrative policy under apartheid "is designed to keep the tribes apart."[47] He points out that, although the Nationalist government has set up local councils, it has virtually suppressed any co-ordinating intertribal body.[48] Thus the mere setting-up of unattached local councils or of general councils throughout the Union in no way lessens the isolation between the ethnic sections of the Native population as long as there is no provision, as there is not, for co-ordination between the tribal groups.

These councils, unattached or general, ostensibly set up to train Natives in local government tend, under apartheid, to become ends in themselves rather than means to an end. Beyond the horizon of routine local matters concerning only their own tribe, there is little hope of the Natives applying the experience gained to higher levels of government. Dr. Jansen has stated that the Nationalist government proposes a central body of Natives representative of all the general councils which are to be set up.[49] However, the proposed abolition of the Natives' Representative Council is illustration enough that any such centralized focus of Native opinion cannot be successfully meshed into the sociopolitical structure of a society based upon apartheid theory. It is also contradictory to the Nationalist policy of tribal isolation, a pivotal and cardinal feature of their program.

Thus apartheid, which as first enunciated in Nationalist election pronouncements was mistakenly taken by many persons as the beginning of a sort of Native state, must prove to them a disappointment. The name "Bantustan" itself implies unification of the Bantu peoples—at least of southern Africa. The very word "apartheid," more significantly, however, denotes a separating of races and of tribes.

Sir Charles has observed that the Bantu extend all the way from the Cape to the Equator and that there is hardly more than tribal distinction separating them. With Native nationalism active and on the increase, it will respond to stimulation.

Nationalism of this sort is, of course, inimical to white dominion, and one must agree with his conclusion that "it would be the irony of fate were its strongest incentive to come from White Nationalists in Africa."[50]

An interesting sidelight of the political status of the Natives under apartheid is the Nationalist government's introduction of a bill to abolish the right of appeal to the Privy Council in England. Before the establishment of the Union there was an appeal as of right from the superior courts of the colonies in South Africa to the Privy Council. The South Africa Act repealed this right and left only the right of appeal to the king-in-council for special leave to appeal. Any law by a dominion parliament, in so far as it intended to prevent the king from granting leave to any of his subjects to appeal an order of a dominion court, was repugnant to the statutes of the United Kingdom regulating this right and void under the Colonial Laws Validity Act of 1865. Only the United Kingdom Parliament could negate this right.

With the passing of the Statute of Westminster in 1931 and the Status of the Union Act in 1934, the force of the Colonial Laws Validity Act was swept away. Though the Status of the Union Act left the right of applying for special leave to appeal intact, the Union Parliament now has the power, if it so chooses, to prevent any citizen of the Union from asking such leave, or it may pass legislation enacting that judgments of the Privy Council have no effect in South Africa.[51] The Nationalist government in its bill before Parliament is thus on indisputable constitutional grounds.

The proposal, however, has implications for the Native population. Thus Mr. W. H. Stuart, Natives representative (Transkei) in the House of Assembly, declared he was convinced that any Native who thought at all on this topic "would feel the psychological reprecussions of the repeal of the leave to appeal to a palladium of justice which had covered him for nearly 150 years."[52] He termed it as a "factual blow to the Coloured and

Native communities of South Africa."[53] Mr. Stuart has pointed out that, with rare exceptions, only matters of the greatest political or constitutional importance could get through to the Privy Council. Only those matters in which there was much public feeling would make an appeal wise and financially possible. Appeal on the abolition of the Native vote, he stated, was such a matter.

The Nationalist government, however, takes the position that the judicial committee of the Privy Council is not versed in Roman-Dutch law, which, together with the Roman and Germanic law and English law, forms an important constituent of the blend of these three great legal systems upon which the common law of South Africa is based. The government contends that South African interests are best served by adjudication of its own appellate division and judicial system.[54]

SEPARATING THE CAPE COLORED AND NATIVE PEOPLES SO THAT EACH MAY DEVELOP INDEPENDENTLY

The Nationalist government looks to a stricter segregation between the Colored and Native peoples in both rural and urban areas. In this manner, conditions will be provided, the Nationalists contend, conducive to the races developing independently of each other.[55] Long-bred antagonisms and the traditional lack of common interests between the two races will no doubt help this aspect of the apartheid program along its path.

Dr. Malan has stressed the economic implications of such a development and has forwarded the thesis that as a result each race will be in an improved economic position. Thus the prime minister has announced that in their own areas the Colored people would be given preference in the issue of trade licenses and would occupy a privileged position compared with the Native.[56] In Native areas suitable Native applicants would have preference in the granting of trade-store sites, and it has been revealed by the government that Natives had been granted such sites in preference not only to Coloreds but also to Europeans.[57] In addition, the minister of Native affairs is seeking power to order licensing authorities to issue licenses to Native traders in urban areas in those cases where refusals to issue had not been based on reasonable grounds.[58] It is also declared Nationalist policy that the mixed living of Coloreds and Natives must be stopped.[59]

The Group Areas Bill, passed by the Union Parliament in 1950, is described by Dr. T. E. Donges, minister of the interior, as "positive apartheid," and Dr. Malan has called it the "kernel" of apartheid. Its overriding principle is to provide for the establishment of separate areas for the different racial groups in the Union by compulsion if necessary. The provisions do not make the demarcations necessary for the various areas; they merely create the necessary machinery for doing so over a period of years.

The groups for which areas may be assigned are the Europeans, Coloreds, and the Natives. The latter two groups may be subdivided, as in the case of the population register, into further groups. In a controlled area there would be no change of ownership, that is, no transfer of ownership to a member of another group than that of the existing owner without a permit.[60] A disqualified member of a group area for ownership is one who does not belong to the group for which the area has been set aside. If he holds property there on the date of proclamation of such a group area, he can retain ownership during his lifetime, but he cannot sell it except to a qualified member.

A disqualified company is to be treated differently, because legally it does not die; it is to be allowed ten years in which to dispose of its property to a qualified person or company, unless it has a permit to retain the property for a longer period.[61]

To permit people of a different group to live in a group area, it must be clearly in the interests of the persons belonging to the group for which the area had been declared. With regard to trading licenses the issuing authority would have to be satisfied that the applicant had a right of occupation in the group. The Land Tenure Advisory Board is the agency to carry out the provisions of the act, and representations might be made to the board by interested parties.[62] The act did not come into operation immediately, so that time was provided in the year following the passage of the act for wills affecting people in proclaimed areas to be changed.[63]

During parliamentary debate on the Group Areas Bill, opposition forces censured the government for rushing through this legislation without ample time being given for a thorough inquiry. While the Opposition emphasized that there was no difference between any of the parties in the House on the question of the principle of social and residential segregation or separation, there was nevertheless a vast difference between them on how such a policy should be carried out.

The bill, it was alleged, did not provide for the placing of legal responsibility for providing alternative accommodations for those evicted, and it failed also to provide for some form of compensation. Thus vested rights were abolished without due recompense. This applied to Europeans as well as non-Europeans affected by the bill.

Notwithstanding the objections raised by the Opposition, that the bill was based on "fear" and "hate" of the non-European races,[64] Dr. Donges declared:

> The desire to live among one's own people is not a desire limited only to white persons in South Africa. It is shared by other sections of the community, by other groups. There is a natural, if slow, gravitation towards this end by all members of the same group. That is the experience of all of us in South Africa. It is the natural feeling of oneness and of group awareness which makes the members of the same group desire to live in the same area.[65]

The Group Areas Act will be applied first to the Cape Province because of Nationalist allegations that there is no protection there against Asiatic penetration as there is in Natal and the Transvaal.[66] The Nationalist government is also becoming increasingly apprehensive of Colored hostility to the Natives, especially in the Cape Town area; this is another factor which has probably influenced the Nationalists to apply the act to the Cape Province as soon as practicable.

As part of the program which the Nationalists claim will raise the economic status of the Natives, the government has placed before Parliament a Native Workers Bill. This is an example of what is termed "practical apartheid." It seeks to raise the Native builder's economic level in his own area. The bill is also aimed at safeguarding the interests of European artisans in European areas against infiltrating Natives employed in such areas at lower rates of pay.

This bill, it is alleged, provides a *quid pro quo* for the removal of such Natives from European areas under apartheid in that these Natives will be the nucleus of a Native builders' force which would come into being in the Native areas. The bill not only provides for training of these Natives to the stage required for erection of simple Native dwellings but sets a higher rate of pay than they previously enjoyed, though it is lower than wages determined from Europeans. The bill also provides for excision of these Native builders from regional wage determination agreements.[67]

As a result of the amendments made by Parliament in 1949 to the Unemployment Insurance Act, all Natives have been excluded from its benefits as of January, 1950.[68] The withdrawal of the Natives from unemployment benefit insurance illustrates another point at which the United party and the Nationalist party policies conflict. The United party has broken with the theory that welfare services for Natives should be financed from their own taxation. Although the Nationalists realize that this cannot be done, they nevertheless continually repeat the theory, which has the effect of retarding increases in such commitments and endangering the existence of some which have already been made.[69]

The material presented has shown the extent of the social reorganization which Nationalist apartheid envisages for the Union's Natives. The program is bold, ambitious, and born of a long history in Nationalist political theory. This is true without even considering the apartheid program in relation to the Union's Indian population, the subject of the next chapter.

It would be an underestimation of the theory itself, however, to merely attribute it to the Dutch South Africans alone. In this theory, which has such a broad base and involves significant moral, social, and economic problems, it is inevitable that support will come, and has come, from outside the strictly Afrikaner-Nationalist fold. Some British South Africans, many of them of established reputation in politics and other fields, have indorsed such a Native policy. A hard-and-fast line, never violated, cannot be drawn on either racial lines or political lines.

The late General Smuts, one of the most outspoken critics of the Native policy herein presented and until 1950 leader of the United party in Opposition, for a long time supported this same theory. Broomfield points out that Smuts took the same view of segregation in 1929 as Prime Minister Huggins of Southern Rhodesia, who has been one of the most consistent advocates of apartheid on the Nationalist pattern. In fact, Broomfield shows that only experience with efforts to institute this policy caused Smuts to regard it as a failure to solve the Union's foremost racial problems.[70] Smuts has stated:

The high expectation that we entertained of that policy has been sadly disappointed. . . . The whole movement of development here on this continent has been for closer contacts to be established between the various races and the various sections of the community. Isolation has gone in South Africa and it has gone for good.[71]

Regardless of the impossibility of establishing an infallible party-race division on the apartheid issue, the concept has nevertheless, and rightly so, been associated with the Dutch Nationalist element of the population. The historical tradition of conservative Native policy on their part and the emergence of apartheid as a party platform in 1948 have reinforced this association.[72] The absence of an infallible racial division on apartheid extends also to the non-European races. There are Natives, like the Coloreds, who are opposed to the apartheid program, and there are others who support it.

A few months after the Nationalists were brought into power the African National Congress (Transvaal), at its annual provincial conference in Pretoria, pledged itself, and called on other non-European organizations, to resist and oppose the apartheid policy of the government.[73] A "Protest Day" was called by the African National Congress and other bodies on June 26, 1950. All Natives were urged to stay away from work as a protest against Nationalist bills before Parliament dealing with the suppression of communism.[74]

On the other hand, the government claims considerable backing among the Natives for its apartheid policy, and it has published several letters received by Dr. Verwoerd from Natives pledging their support. One writer from the Transkei addressed the minister of Native affairs as follows:

> We look up to you as our father who cares for the welfare of his children. The Natives in this area have much hope and trust in you. The policy of Apartheid sponsored by our present Government is that for which we Natives have been praying for all these years. . . . We, the people of the Reserves, are very happy, because through the Government's policy we will be in a position to trade among our own people and practice as doctors and practitioners among our own people under the trusteeship of the Minister of Native Affairs.[75]

There is one school of Native opinion which withholds judgment until apartheid is developed further. Representative of this group is Mr. C. A. R. Motsepe, who stated in his presidential address before the Pietersburg District Transvaal African Teachers Association: "Let us not be in a senseless hurry to condemn. Let us not conclude that the reptile whose tail we see is a snake, for it may turn out to be a lizard."[76]

CHAPTER IX

The Indian Population under Apartheid

THE ROLE TO BE PLAYED BY THE INDIAN POPULATION OF THE Union under the Nationalists' apartheid program is unique in many respects. It is in relation to the Indians in the Union that the apartheid program differs least from the objectives of the other political parties. It is difficult to separate the Nationalist conception of the status of the Indians from that of a large segment of the European population which does not align itself with the Nationalist party on other issues.

The "Indian problem," nevertheless, is an integral part of Nationalist apartheid, and, though the Nationalist solution parallels in many respects that posed by other groups of the European population, it is still a basic tenet of the party's program; and it is the Nationalist party today, as the government in power, which is meeting a steadily rising opposition to its Indian program from other nations of the world.

Nationalist apartheid in respect of the Asiatics in the Union, mostly Indian, though there are some Malays and Chinese, has to be considered in two separate aspects. The first is the ultimate objective of the Nationalist government of seeking to reduce the Indian population in the Union to the lowest possible minimum. The second aspect to be considered is the role of the Indians until such time as they are reduced to the irreducible minimum.

The government's policy toward the Indian community in South Africa was outlined by the Nationalist minister of the interior, Dr. T. E. Donges, when he declared that it was

the ultimate target of the Government to reduce the Indian population in South Africa to the irreducible minimum.

Referring to the tension between Indians and Europeans in the Union, the Minister said the hardening of the attitude of the Europeans was due to the attitude taken by India in placing South

157

Africa in the dock at the United Nations for three successive years, to the exaggerated and irresponsible statements made by Indian leaders in South Africa and to the entry of illegal immigrants from India. It would have eased the tension considerably had the South African Indian Organization in the past repudiated irresponsible utterances by Indian leaders.

Another fundamental fact was the feeling that the Indians, no matter what the legal position might be, were not considered an indigenous portion of South Africa.[1]

The Indian problem revolves in large part upon economic issues. "Land looms large in any attempt to review the situation of the South African Indians."[2] Webb attempts to explain the present European-Indian tension in the Union in terms of successive land restrictions placed upon the Indians since 1891, when a Natal law was passed which provided that the previous granting of crown lands to former indentured Indians was to be discontinued.[3] He places emphasis upon the Europeans' fear of Asiatic "penetration" into the areas set aside by legislation as European residential areas, particularly in Natal and the Transvaal.

Appasamy, on the other hand, places stress on this land legislation as the outgrowth of European fear of the economic conflict between European and Indian, since both are competing for the labor and patronage of the Native, who is the mainstay of the South African economy.[4] He points out that, although the purchasing power of the Natives is low, their large number creates a lucrative demand for products and presents the problem: Who is to satisfy their wants, the white trader or the Indian?

The problem has a historical emergence, and an examination of the legislation directed against the Indians reveals a constant attempt on the part of the Europeans in the Union to keep them politically and economically on a level considerably below that of the European population. Investigations and legislation adverse to the Indian population seem to become more widespread and numerous in periods of Indian prosperity, when there is a natural tendency to invest in land, and also in periods when the

Indians fear for the future, since they seem to find security in property ownership. From whatever cause, however, as Indian bidding for land increases, European agitation against the Indian grows.[5]

The status of the Union's Indian population today is governed, in part, by the Asiatic Land Tenure and Indian Representation Act of 1946. This bill was introduced by the United party and represents the party's attitude toward the Indian population. The act provides for a limited measure of franchise[6] and sets aside certain areas in Natal and the Transvaal as "unexempted" areas in which no Asiatics are permitted to buy or occupy fixed property without a permit from the minister of the interior.[7] In the "exempted" areas the Indians are free to buy, occupy, and obtain loans on property from any person irrespective of race or color, There are also other provisions relating to inspectors and certain changes in the Transvaal laws which previously, according to the government, on account of legal technicalities, made "illegal occupation" possible by Indians.[8] A Land Tenure Advisory Board to advise the minister upon applications for permits by Indians, upon the declaration of new exempted areas, and upon the excision of such areas and a number of other matters is also provided for in the act.

The passing of this act was deeply resented by the Indians in the Union, and they have refused to submit their nominations to the government for minority membership on the Land Tenure Advisory Board. The government of India, upon the passage of this act, withdrew its high commissioner from the Union, broke off trade relations, and took the treatment of Union Indians by the government to the United Nations.

In the Cape the Indians are placed on the common voters' roll, along with Europeans, if they meet the voting qualifications. In Natal, no Indian is allowed upon the common voting roll unless registered before the Disenfranchisement Act of 1896. Under the Act of 1946, however, Indians are allowed to vote on a separate roll, provided they possess the qualifications as required for an Indian electing a senator.[9] In the Transvaal the Indians are granted a franchise similar to that of Natal. The Orange Free State has an absolute exclusion of all non-Europeans from the voters' rolls.

The Nationalist party, as part of its apartheid program, repealed those provisions of the Asiatic Land Tenure and Indian Representation Act of 1946 relating to the Indian franchise. This was the first step in the government's anti-Asiatic policies. During the discussion of this act in Parliament the Nationalists had urged the introduction of more clearly defined segregatory clauses and took their stand on placing a complete embargo on the purchase of land by Indians in European areas. They opposed the franchise provisions *in toto* and finally voted against the bill, since in their view it did not go far enough in its restrictive land provisions and too far in the direction of giving political rights to the Indian community.[10] The party has stated that it will strive "to repatriate or remove elsewhere, as many Indians as possible, with the cooperation of India and other countries."[11]

Repatriation of the Union's Indian population is the means by which the Nationalists are to achieve the reduction of Indians to the so-called "irreducible minimum."[12] In the meantime, while the repatriation process is taking place, the Indians are to be placed under an apartheid program which is much more restrictive than the status afforded under the former government.

The Nationalist goal of reducing the Indian population in the Union to the irreducible minimum is vague and nebulous in its connotations; just what constitutes this minimum is a matter of conjecture, as the government does not specifically state when that number is to be reached. Since, however, the government regards the Indian as not an indigenous portion of the population and seeks to repatriate as many Indians as possible, the goal which it would desire to achieve is no doubt the complete exclusion by repatriation of the Union's entire Indian community. (Over 80 per cent of the Indians in South Africa were born in that country and have not even seen India.)

The policy of Indian repatriation is not a characteristic of Nationalist doctrine alone. The Union government under Smuts in the mid-twenties also attempted repatriation of the Indian population but was forced to relent due to the overwhelming pressure of world opinion. The Nationalists are determined that such will not be the fate of their own Indian repatriation program. Dr. Donges, in elaborating upon the repatriation of Indians, declared that "there was nothing unjust nor anything that might be called a stigma."[13] Full compensation was to be paid, and meanwhile the policy of apartheid would be applied.

The Nationalists are, at the present time, using two approaches to implement the repatriation of Indians. The first is to encourage as many Indians as possible to leave the Union by means of inducements offered by the government. The second approach is to reduce the status of the Indian population to the point at which Indians will literally be forced to accept repatriation or remain under apartheid on a level somewhat between that of the Colored and Native population. Politically, under the Nationalist apartheid program, since the Indians are to have no franchise in any form, they would be inferior to the Natives. However, the Indians would be able to own land in their own areas and thus would be on a higher economic level than the Native, as is now the case.

In order to make repatriation as attractive as possible, Dr. Donges has announced:

The Government is prepared, as a temporary measure and for a limited period, to increase the bonus payable to Indians who wish to return to India. . . . The scheme provides for financial assistance and a free passage from any place in the Union to any place outside the Union for any adult Indian and his family under certain conditions. Emigrants are also provided with food during the journey.

The financial assistance consists of a bonus of £20 an adult and £10 a child under the age of 16. The Government is prepared, as a temporary measure and for a limited period, to increase the bonus from £20 to £40 an adult and from £10 to £20 a child under the age of 16 in the hope that the increased bonus will assist Indians to establish themselves in their homeland.[14]

M. K. Gandhi, who became the spokesman of the South African Indian population in pre-Union and post-Union years, stated on the occasion of the Smuts-Gandhi Agreement of 1914:[15]

Compulsory repatriation is a physical and political impossibility; voluntary repatriation by way of granting free passages and similar inducements will not, as my experience teaches me, be availed of to any appreciable extent. The only real effective remedy for a great State to adopt is to face responsibility fairly and squarely, to do away with the remains of the system of indenture and to level up this part of the population and make use of it for the general welfare of the Union.[16]

If the inducement method fails to reduce the Indian population to the extent desired, the Nationalists will use the other method which has as its objectives not only pressure to increase repatriation but the lowering of the Indian in social, political, and economic status to a point at which, even if considerable portions of the Indian population remain in the Union, they will offer no threat to white supremacy in the economy of the Union. In addition to the lack of representation in Parliament and the tightening of land laws in respect of Indians, "the Nationalist Government has decided to abolish family allowances for Indians, introduced . . . by the United Party Government as part of its social security scheme."[17]

The Nationalists contend that the payment of family allowances to Indians encourages polygamy and have published figures purporting to show that for the Cape Coloreds, who outnumber the Indians by more than three to one, the family allowances amounted to less than one-third those of the Indians.[18] It is interesting to note also that, although the government has canceled provisions in the Asiatic Land Tenure and Indian Representation Act in respect to the Indian representation, the Indians themselves had never accepted these provisions but have steadfastly maintained their right to be placed on the common voting roll with Europeans as in the Cape.

Dr. Malan revealed during debate on the Act of 1946 in the

House of Assembly, that he wholeheartedly agreed with the leader of the Opposition, General Smuts, that the Indians themselves were responsible for the feelings that had been aroused against them. Dr. Malan has also stated in reiterating the government's policies:

> The Government would do its best to bring about the repatriation of as many Indians as possible. Those satisfied to remain in South Africa will have to do so under restrictions because, by systematically going abroad with their grievances instead of submitting them to the South African Government through the proper channels, they had proved themselves to be a foreign element which did not belong in South Africa.[19]

The prime minister neglected to state, however, that previously Dr. Donges had told the Natal and Transvaal Indian congresses, the traditional groups representing the Indians in those provinces, that he was *not* prepared to accord the two executive committees an interview on difficulties that have arisen over the Asiatic Land Tenure and Indian Representation Act. In a letter to the president of the Transvaal Indian Congress, Dr. Donges wrote:

> I am not prepared to extend this facility to any organization of Indians which sponsors or associates itself with any organized flouting of the laws of the country. I also exclude organizations which are Communistic in their orientation of leadership, of which, while claiming to be composed of Union citizens, invoke the political aid of another country. . . .[20]

If these groups had broken any laws in the Union, there was no formal charge brought against them by the government. On the other hand, the government seems prone to listen to the grievances of only those Indian groups, assuming that such exist, which agree already with the government's anti-Indian policies and which repudiate India's action in bringing the treatment of Indians in the Union before the United Nations. By excluding all groups which "are Communistic in their orientation of leadership," the Nationalist government, by such broad phrasing, could conceivably exclude all Indian groups which are liberal in racial policy but not connected with the Communist movement in any manner.

This could exclude all Indian groups guilty of no more than wishing to revise the Indians' status under Nationalist apartheid. It is similar to the Dutch Reformed church's accusations that other churches in the Union which are critical of Malanite racial policies are Communist dupes. "The Union Government has decided to appoint a commission to investigate and report on the desirability of introducing legislation in connection with acquisition and occupation of property by Asiatics in the Cape."[21] This announcement was made in the House of Assembly at Cape Town on September 16, 1948, by Dr. Donges, the Nationalist minister of the interior.

He made this statement as a warning to individuals who might claim protection for vested rights acquired between that date and the date of any legislation that may become necessary, should such rights become affected. If the Government decides after receipt of the report of the commission, to institute legislation dealing with acquisition and occupation of land and buildings by Asiatics, such legislation will be of retrospective effect from today, September 16, 1948.[22]

This is, in effect, the application of an *ex post facto* law. The Cape Colony under British colonial administration imposed no restricting legislation on the Indians. After union, however, the Immigrants Regulation Act of 1913, under which no prohibited immigrant can own or lease land, became the only restrictive legislation that applied to the area of the former Cape Colony.[23]

The Dominion party has been very closely aligned with the Nationalists on the Indian problem. The Dominion party bitterly opposes the political clauses of the Indian Act of 1946 and in this respect identifies itself with the Nationalist party. It thought that the land restriction clauses did not go far enough to restrain Indians in the purchase and occupation of property and are implacably opposed to the granting of any political rights to Asiatics.[24]

The Labor party literally split asunder during the parliamentary debate on the Asiatic Land Tenure and Indian Representation Bill. Wide divegencies of opinion between members of the Labor party became evident. The result was the resignation of both the leader and the deputy leader of the party, the late W. B. Modeley and M. J. van den Berg. Both opposed the political provisions of the measure and thought the land-tenure provisions did not go far enough in their restrictive effect, a stand which the Nationalists supported.[25]

It is evident therefore that on the Indian issue the Nationalists have considerable support from outside their own party. On this basis the Nationalists can reasonably expect the success of their Indian policy at home, and a continued determined defense of Nationalist apartheid, directed against the Indian, in the United Nations will no doubt result.

The Indian population, as a consequence of renewed Nationalist vigor in applying the apartheid policy, is faced with a dilemma. Should they regard themselves as apart from the other non-European segments of the population and thus demand equality and rights for Indians alone, or should they consider themselves as just one part of the non-European population, gain the advantages of overwhelming numerical support, and thus regard the Indian issue as the issue involving all non-Europeans in the Union? Appasamy holds that this is the most important question facing the Indians today, and the choice must eventually be made:

Danger ... in the failure to recognise that the difficulties of the Indian settlers are part of the base position assigned to all non-Europeans in South Africa. To demand special consideration for Indians as a group is to isolate the Indian settlers from the majority of Africans who form eighty per cent of the population of the Union.[26]

... When Africans and Coloreds are equally the victims of the racial arrogance of the whites, it is suicidal for the small Indian group to isolate itself because it happens to be today slightly better treated than the mass of the people, who are the Natives of the country.[27]

The harsh duty of breaking the system falls upon the African who is in a majority. The Indian has the power of choice: he may continue to live at the mercy of the European, thanking his stars every day that he is still slightly better off than the African, or he may decide to throw his experience and ability into the common pool and carry on the long struggle for equality side by side with the people of the country which is now the land of his birth.[28]

Dr. E. G. Jansen, former Nationalist minister of Native affairs, in outlining alleged Indian designs on the African continent, declared in a speech at Durban that through the United Nations the Asiatics were endeavoring to become established in South Africa and throughout all Africa.

That is the reason for a great deal of the adverse, and very often untrue propaganda that is being made against us in India, in America, in Britain, on the continent of Europe and especially at the meetings of the United Nations. I sometimes wonder how it is possible that the white races do not realise what is going on on this southern part of the continent of Africa. Here there is a struggle going on of vital importance to them.

It was not the Indian workers in South Africa who were causing all the agitation, said the Minister, it is the man who is flourishing under the white man's laws. He has been allowed to compete with him, to oust the white man and to grow fat and prosperous.

They are the people who are crying about oppression overseas. They give examples of shacks where Indians are living but you can go to parts of Durban where Europeans are living under worse conditions in the back yards of Indian-owned property, and you could not call that oppression.

That is the result of economic conditions which we should not allow to continue.[29]

The treatment of people of Indian origin in the Union of South Africa has, since 1946, been an issue before the regular sessions of the Assembly of the United Nations. On May 14, 1949, the Assembly of the United Nations took action again. Forty-seven member states voted "inviting" the governments of India, Pakistan, and South Africa to hold a round-table conference to discuss the matter. The resolution added that at such conference the purposes and principles of the Charter and the Universal Declaration of Human Rights should be taken into consideration.[30]

Earlier India had proposed a Commission of Inquiry to delve

into the situation in the Union. However, in the interests of a more rapid solution to the problem, this proposal was withdrawn in favor of the French-Mexican proposal for a round-table conference. The one vote against this French-Mexican proposal adopted by the Assembly was that of the Union of South Africa.[31] This was cast by her representative, Eric Louw. His argument was based upon Article 2(7) of the United Nations Charter, and the Union's position was that the treatment of Indian, Asian, and other non-white citizens was essentially within the jurisdiction of the Union government. He stated that the issue was outside the competence of the General Assembly and that Article 2(7) of the Charter was "the cornerstone of the foundation upon which the United Nations rests."[32]

Mr. Louw contended that it was generally recognized from the records of the San Francisco Conference that such matters should not be regarded as warranting United Nations interference. In this matter the United Nations was moving away from the intentions of the founders, and the General Assembly has assumed for itself a competence which it did not in fact possess. He also took the position that India's complaint in the past had related only to Indians in the Union but that it now dealt with "Asians" and "other non-whites" as well. This showed the extent to which interference in the domestic affairs of sovereign states could go.[33]

Mr. Louw forwarded the fact that the Union of South Africa is not the only country in the world with racial minorities and separate religious and racial groups.

If the United Nations followed up complaints about their treatment, "there is no saying . . . to what extent in the future there is going to be interference in the domestic affairs of a state in relation to the subjects of a state, by the United Nations and its organs."[34]
We in South Africa do not wish to be told by people outside how to solve our problems.[35]

Dr. Malan has stated, "We, as the Nationalist Government, refuse to allow UNO or any foreign country to interfere in our domestic affairs."[36]

An interesting development akin to this problem is the role of India as a member of the Commonwealth of Nations. Dr. Malan is aware of the strategic importance of India in the present world situation and declared of the London Conference:

The problem which had to be solved in London was whether or not India was to remain a member of the Commonwealth after becoming a republic. . . . India is at present anti-Communist, and in the present dangerous world situation, that fact is important to us. If we lose India we lose a foothold in Asia which is extremely important.[37]

To accept India as a member of the Commonwealth and at the same time to apply Nationalist apartheid to South African nationals of Indian descent presents one aspect of apartheid which is uneasily reconciled with the long-range strategy of Commonwealth defense.

Correspondence between the governments of the Union, India, and Pakistan released on June 8, 1950, by the Union Department of External Affairs disclosed that India had decided not to participate in the round-table conference on the Indian question in South Africa because the Union government had declined to postpone the Group Areas Bill in Parliament.[38] Some of the provisions of the Group Areas Bill were based on recommendations of two committees that investigated the whole question of land tenure by Asiatics in the Union. Evidence on the question had been taken over a period in Natal and the Transvaal.[39]

The Durban riots of January, 1949, present another facet in the Union's racial tension. Bands of Natives stormed and burned Indian property, and many Indians were murdered and their shops destroyed. The carnage followed an uneasy day in which hundreds of Indians were attacked in the center of the city by Natives. The final tabulation listed casualties as 142 killed and 1,087 injured.[40]

The U.S.S.R. representative in the First Committee considering the Indian complaints against the Union of South Africa, Mr. Alexander Panyushkin, declared that there were attempts in

South Africa by ruling circles to sow interracial dissension, recalling the Nazi pogroms in Germany. This policy, he declared, had such consequences as the Durban riots.[41] Regardless of the validity of these charges, there can be little doubt that the riot had a significant impact upon the members of the Assembly and helped to frame the completely overwhelming vote against the Union government's position on the interpretation of the charter.

A large part of the Native population is as one with the Nationalist government's apartheid policy, that is, as it affects the Indians. "All we desire is that the Government provide ships and we will see the Indians on their way to India. We will help them back." These are sentiments expressed by the Union's Natives.[42] An investigating commission blamed the riots on Zulus, who had three major complaints against the Indians. The first was the alleged immoral assaults by Indians on Zulu women; second, the assertion that Indian traders were exploiting the Natives in Native areas by high prices and inferior goods; and, third, that Indians receive privileged treatment from the government.

The position of the Indians vis-à-vis the Natives, despite various alleged relationships, is determined more by the "objective" relationship arising from the economic competition between the two races. Thus Mr. Paul Sauer, Nationalist minister of transport, stated that if certain bus services in Durban had been operated by Natives instead of Indians, a great deal of trouble might have been avoided.[43] Native hostility to the Indians in this instance was due to the virtual Indian monopoly of licenses for the operation of bus service along certain routes heavily traversed by Natives and in predominantly Native areas. The government, following the Durban riots, issued licenses to operate bus service to a number of Natives.[44] Preparations were also made to alter the Road Transportation Act if necessary.

Another significant aspect of this same problem is the growing realization by the Natives that they are capable of conducting commercial transactions in their own areas. A bitter resentment has therefore arisen over a period of years concerning the licensing of Indians as traders in certain of the Native Reserves. The Natives feel that the profits from such trade should accrue to their own people.

The Coloreds, more on a par with Indian astuteness in trade and commerce than the Natives, also view the Indian as an economic competitor. A Colored deputation presented a memorandum to the government in 1948 stating that Indian conduct was "presumptuous" and, more significantly, that Indian penetration into Colored areas had assumed serious dimensions and that in the business world Coloreds were being exploited by Indians. If the Indians could be removed from their midst, the memorandum added, the Coloreds could build up their trade. The memorandum concluded that the government's first duty was to the Colored rather than to the Indian community and that the Indians should not be allowed to strengthen their economic hold on the Colored people.[45]

The significance of the Durban riots was to serve notice that the Indians are caught between the apartheid policies of the government, on the one hand, and millions of uneasy Natives, on the other. The *Sunday Express*, an Opposition newspaper, stated:

> The Durban riots have nothing to do with Representative Councils, Entrenched Clauses or any other constitutional issue. During the wild few hours of the fighting, the Zulus felt the spirit of Chaka, or what many of them still regard as the "glorious past. . . ."[46]

This may be a sign that the Native struggle for self-expression which is being frustrated in its direction against the government's apartheid policies is being redirected, by the Natives, against the Indian community. The Natives' frustration is a tremendous force which could conceivably be unleashed against the small Indian minority; all other avenues of expression being closed, the Durban riot may be a forerunner of things to come.

This would cause extreme uneasiness not only throughout Africa but in all nations which have racial problems.

It would also negate any efforts on the part of the Indians to unite with the Natives and Coloreds for a common non-European front against the apartheid policies of the Nationalists.

Pictures of the riots should be posted on the wall of the United Nations committee room to show the world that South Africa is struggling with problems more terrible and realistic than those which can be settled by political theorising. . . .[47]

The Government's policy has been stated as "not isolationist, but it was not prepared to commit race suicide in order to satisfy world opinion on the colour question as expressed in the United Nations Assembly."[48]

On the basis of such contentions, which it believes to be irrefutable, the Nationalist government, with its apartheid program, is attempting to reorganize the social structure of the Union—a structure in which the Indian population, under ideal conditions, has no place.

CHAPTER X

Apartheid and Africa South of the Sahara

Nationalist racial policy is of extreme importance not only to peoples within the Union itself but also to those within territories adjacent to the Union and even farther north. British Native policy in the high commission territories (commonly referred to as the South African protectorates) of Basutoland, Bechuanaland, and Swaziland is acutely sensitive to changes in racial policy in the Union of South Africa. This sensitivity is largely due to their economic dependence upon the Union, which in turn arises from their geographical position. These territories depend upon the Union as a market for their products. In addition, because of the very restricted number of openings for employment in the territories, large numbers of Natives are forced to migrate to other areas.

This labor migration is extremely large. In Basutoland the number of able-bodied males away at any one time is between 50 and 60 per cent, with a similar proportion in Bechuanaland and Swaziland. The greater number of Natives stay away for at least a year. About two-thirds find their way via labor contracts to the Union's mines. Others may serve as unskilled factory laborers.[1] The protectorates are thus dependent upon the Union for the employment of their Native populations.

While the Union has no great part in their administration, since they are under direct British control, neverthelesss there is a tendency to follow Union rather than colonial legislation and practice. This includes not only economic matters but racial discrimination, though to a lesser degree. General administrative policy is modeled, however, on that of the colonial territories.[2]

The high commissioner has his main offices not within the territories he administers but within the Union of South Africa.

172

When the Union Parliament is in session, his offices are in Cape Town, the legislative capital of the Union; at other times in Pretoria, the administrative capital.

This unique situation is merely a manifestation of the long-recognized principle that the interests of the protectorates are intimately tied with the interests of the Union. As late as 1930 the governor-general of the Union of South Africa also served as the high commissioner. Today the high commissioner serves in a dual capacity: as a diplomatic representative of His Majesty's government to the Union government and also as a colonial governor.

The channel of communication between the protectorates and the British government, unlike other British colonial areas, is not through the Colonial Office but through the Commonwealth Relations Office (known formerly as the Dominions Office). It has been pointed out that "there is a danger that the interests of the territories may sometimes be subordinated with the more weighty interests of Dominion affairs and harmony"[3]

At the time of the union of the South African colonies, the British government agreed that the protectorates should be transferred to the Union at some future date to be determined by the British authorities.[4] The transfer was to be subject to conditions specified in a schedule attached to the South African constitution. Since 1909 the question of their transfer has been thoroughly discussed in articles, speeches, and debates in both Great Britain and the Union of South Africa.[5]

Successive Union Parliaments have been subjected to an unrelenting pressure of public opinion formally to request the carrying-out of the transfer within the "meaning and intent" of the provisions. The Nationalist government, owing especially to its nationalistic outlook and avowed ideal of a South African republic,[6] has been queried on this issue. Dr. Malan, in reply, stated in the Union Senate:

I have not yet approached the British Government formally. We do not know what may happen tomorrow or the day after. There may be a change of Government, and I do not want this question of the transfer of the Protectorates to the Union to be a matter of dispute in any coming election between the various parties in England ... for that reason I am adopting an attitude of wait and see, waiting for more stability in the British Government.[7]

This "wait and see" attitude of Dr. Malan does not diminish the pressure the Union is capable of exerting upon the British government. The still smoldering controversy centering around Seretse Khama of Bechuanaland, the Oxford-bred chief of the Bamangwato tribe, is a case in point. While studying law in England, Khama had married a white woman. According to most reports, the Bamangwato, except for a small dissident group, did not object to a white queen. The case, however, raised issues which the Union government felt it could not ignore. Though admittedly difficult to assess, it is nevertheless generally conceded that the Nationalist government brought great pressure to bear upon the British government. Britain, occupied elsewhere in the postwar tension of international politics, did not take issue with the Union. Khama was exiled from his land and wife.

Time was led to remark:

With South Africa's rabid racist Prime Minister Daniel Malan ready to seize on any excuse to step into Bechuanaland ... British Ministers seemed more willing to heed his wishes than those of the Bamangwato. ... In its timid efforts to propitiate Malan, His Majesty's Government seemed to be sacrificing both the Bamangwato and its own principles.[8]

In addition, the recent "taking over" of the former mandated territory of South-West Africa by the Union government in the face of United Nations opposition[9] has added over 300,000 more Natives to the Union's population who would be directly affected by Union Native policy. The Malan government, with the support of the United party, has integrated South-West Africa into the Union's Parliament. As pointed out earlier, the Nationalist government considerably strengthened its parliamentary position by this move.

In August, 1950, an important election was held in South-West Africa to fill the six seats allotted to that territory in the Union's House of Assembly. This was the first election to give South-West Africa representation in the Union Parliament. After the election the state of the parties in the House of Assembly was announced as follows (in comparison with the results of the Union's 1948 general election):[10]

		After South-West Africa Election	After 1948 General Election
Government parties	Nationalist party ...	77	70
	Afrikaner party	9	9
		86	79
Opposition parties	United party	64	65
	Labor party	6	6
	Natives' representatives	3	3
		73	74

The results are not surprising in view of the fact that, of a total European population of 30,677 in South-West Africa in 1937, there were 18,128 who were Afrikaans-speaking.[11] The election confirmed very clearly that the postwar United party has no message which can entice the Afrikaner. The Nationalist party, however, received a go-ahead signal for the realization of Nationalist concepts and ideals. The election enabled the Malan government to overcome its "minority complex," and its dependence upon the Afrikaner party disappeared. The balance of power went from Mr. Havenga to the six representatives of South-West Africa. It is a sobering thought that the Union's destiny may be determined by the Afrikaner-German voters of South-West Africa. Not only has the geographical frontier of the Union been pushed northward but likewise the frontier of apartheid.

Regardless of the arguments pro and con which have been

raised in this controversy between the United Nations and the Union government, the complete integration of South-West Africa with the Union is now an accomplished fact. The area concerned is three-quarters that of the Union, and its geographical position is of great strategic value. South-West Africa not only guards the Atlantic approaches to the southern portion of the continent but provides the Union with another common frontier with Bechuanaland Protectorate. Bechuanaland is, therefore, surrounded on three sides by Union territory. Thus, the position of the Union in regard to the protectorates is considerably strengthened.

The relationship of Union Native policy and European public opinion in the British territories north of the Limpopo, particularly the "White Settler" colonies of East and South Central Africa, is one of the significant characteristics of the postwar African scene. The broader considerations of British colonial policy in Africa have a direct bearing upon this relationship. Examination of recent developments in British West Africa will aid in illustrating the dilemma facing the British government in Africa and the consequent role the Union of South Africa is to play in the affairs of colonial areas beyond its own borders.

A new concept of partnership between Great Britain and its colonial empire emerged during the last war. Besides the subsidizing of a large-scale program of colonial economic development and the introduction of needed social reforms, the new philosophy was based upon providing experience in self-government for the Native peoples. The enlightened colonial partnership is to consist of a number of self-governing units tied to Britain only by mutual bonds of economic and political self-interest.[12]

The Gold Coast in West Africa is the British African colony in which the social and constitutional reforms have been most conspicuous and spectacular. In 1948 the Gold Coast was rudely disturbed by country-wide disorders, many of them very serious. Under the pressure of these outbreaks a Commission of Enquiry recommended constitutional changes on all levels of government. In particular, a greatly enlarged legislature with a very large proportion of members popularly elected was recommended. The recommendations received the general approval of His Majesty's government.

Later in the same year the Coussey Committee, a local committee under the chairmanship of Sir Henley Coussey, was set up to "examine the proposals for constitutional and political reform" as set out in the previous report. Significantly the Coussey Committee consisted entirely of Africans representing the main sections and interests of the community.

In place of the existing constitution the committee proposed a system designed to provide responsible government under an administration composed mainly of elected Natives and responsible, with certain qualifications, to the elected Legislative Assembly. A second chamber, the Senate, was also to be formed. The membership of the Assembly was to be composed of Natives, subject only to the usual disqualifications for age, allegiance to a foreign power, penal servitude, a party with a government contract, etc. The franchise for election to both houses was to be granted to all males and females (Natives and resident non-Natives) of twenty-five years or older who are registered and have paid their taxes or rates.

In 1949 a select committee was appointed to consider the organization necessary to hold elections based upon the Coussey Report[13] and to divide the country into suitable constituencies. The Gold Coast was subsequently divided into electoral divisions, registration of eligible voters was effected, and the general elections were held in 1951.

Hand in hand with these developments, the higher reaches of the civil service were opened to Natives. In addition, a reform of local government took place. The new theory of local government, though allegedly a transitional phase and not a violent break with the past, involved a drastic reorganization of the Native local government structure. Native local government bodies (usually chieftain's councils of various sorts) were based on more democratic representation, and the reforms also looked toward the adaptation of English local government principles to colonial territories.[14]

The new approach has been explained in the following terms:

> There has been a definition and authoritative confirmation of the idea that the evolution of traditional institutions must be directed more decisively and rapidly towards democratic self-governing bodies of the English type. . . . The aim is now laid down as representative local government bodies on the English model . . . it symbolizes the adoption for Africa of the democratic ideal of English local government to an extent hitherto unknown.[15]

The British government is now dedicated to the declared aim of leading her colonies toward self-government. It is essential to note, however, that British colonial policy is founded upon the assumption that self-government is not construed as vesting power in the white minorities.

In the Gold Coast this cardinal assumption raises no serious problems due to circumstances peculiar to that part of the continent. The extremely small resident European population is the underlying factor in this situation. For example, in 1945 the population of the united territories of the Gold Coast was estimated at 3,963,000; of this number, only 3,443 were resident Europeans. The ratio of blacks to whites was thus more than 1,000:1. Nearly one-quarter of the European population, moreover, consists of civil servants. There are few whites therefore engaged in "non-official" occupations. There is no settled agricultural European community. Missionary work, trading, and mining are carried on by the small number of whites who are not colonial officials.[16]

Under such conditions the whites do not conceive of the Natives as primarily a threat to white labor. There is little white labor in this sense in Britain's West African territories. The colonial civil servants thus find it easy to consider themselves as the guardians and instructors of the Native population, and the other sections of the European community are also amenable to contemporary Colonial Office policy. The interests of the

Natives which are to be paramount are not regarded as inimicable to white interests.

On the contrary, among the white civil servants the rise in status of the Natives is regarded as an indication of European skill in long-range planning and the culmination of efforts to prepare the Natives for increased responsibilities. When the Gold Coast general elections were conducted with decorum as well as widespread enthusiasm, the colonial officers regarded this as a signification that they themselves were instrumental in the success of this bold yet inevitable political evolution.

In addition, the absence in the Gold Coast of a large Indian trading community, which would compete with the white traders, spares this area from many of the social and political problems which have characterized other parts of Africa. A large Arab community is also absent. The movement toward self-government for the Natives is not retarded by disputes centering around the sociopolitical status of varied indigenous and immigrant communities.[17]

On the other hand, those conditions which are conducive to the interests of the Native being regarded as paramount in West Africa do not exist in East and South Central Africa. Of the British territories in this portion of the continent the most important are the "white settler" colonies of Kenya, Northern Rhodesia, and Southern Rhodesia. During the last several years the British Colonial Office has been bitterly critcized by the white settlers for its inauguration of a more liberal Native policy in the West African colonies. Preparations made by the Colonial Office for similar, though perhaps less extensive, political devolopments in Uganda, Tanganyika, Kenya, and Northern Rhodesia have caused the white settlers to consider this as interference with the spread of white Christian civilization and as contrary to the ideal of permanent white political and economic dominance in their portion of the continent.

The racial issues facing the white settlers are similar to those facing their brethren in the Union of South Africa, and, generally speaking, their racial theory and outlook on life are similar, though the Union is admittedly the country where the color bar finds its most rigid application. There is a considerable Afrikaner population among the white settlers, owing to successive treks of Boers from South Africa.[18]

In Kenya, Northern Rhodesia, and Southern Rhodesia the proportion of whites in the population far exceeds that of the Gold Coast.[19] Although still overwhelmed numerically, the white settlers nevertheless regard themselves as a permanent resident community of sufficient strength to maintain the interests of the whites as paramount rather than those of the Native. The European population of the white settler territories is far more dependent upon occupations outside of government service than in the Gold Coast. There is a settled European agricultural community, and the white farmers form one of the most conservative groups in these territories. Large capital investments have been made by the white settlers in mining and industrial enterprises. White trade-unions are engaged in a never ending struggle to keep the Natives from undermining the white monopoly of the skilled and higher-paying occupations. In short, unlike the Gold Coast, there is white labor to be protected.

The whites in Kenya and the Rhodesias, like those in the Union, are troubled by the breakdown of tribal society and are also afflicted by a similar Indian problem. The Indians not only outnumber the whites but are characterized by their aggressiveness and have amassed considerable wealth. In 1947 an Indo-Native front was formed in Kenya. The Indians are in close touch with political movements in India and are well fitted to serve as the leaders of Native opposition to white-race dominance.[20] Most of Kenya's commerce has already been monopolized by the Indians.[21] There is also a considerable Arab community in East Africa, and, while the Arabs pose no threat at the moment to the Europeans' economic position, they nevertheless make the uneasy racial situation more complex. It is hardly to be wondered at therefore that the white settlers conceive of self-government in a vastly different frame of reference than the whites in the Gold Coast.

The fact that Mr. Arthur Creech Jones, while serving as secretary for colonial affairs in the Attlee cabinet, had introduced an experiment in Northern Rhodesia by appointing two Natives to the executive struck the whites at a particularly sensitive spot. It stirred white opinion in Southern Rhodesia to a considerable degree, and that territory immediately rose to challenge this affront upon her neighbor to the north. The Legislative Assembly was the scene of heated and spirited speeches directed against the "Leftists and Fabians" of the Colonial Office. It was reiterated time and again that the white settlers do not believe in a black state and that to give an undeveloped race or people the vote is dangerous.

It was pointed out that unless white civilization was strong and determined enough to retract that sort of intervention, they would never see a federated white southern and central Africa. Instead, they might see "stagnation, Communism and misery."[22] One member of the Assembly stated: "For our own salvation we who have come to maturity must do all in our power to rescue our Northern neighbours from being submerged. I feel confident the Rhodesian Government can do a lot to persuade the British Government to revise their Colonial Policy."[23]

Sir Godfrey Huggins, prime minister of Southern Rhodesia, made a suggestion to the people of England upon a visit there that it would be more profitable and desirable if they sank some of their capital in the colonies to assist in the advancement of the Natives rather than to supply them "with political dogma of which they understood practically nothing"[24] He also proclaimed that the English did not understand the white settlers.

The growing uneasiness of the white settlers regarding their own future has led to proposals to draft a joint statement representative of the whites in East and South Central Africa stating their policy of the permanency and supremacy of white settlement. The British government will be subjected to unrelenting pressure by the white settlers, and the issues involved have driven them to renewed efforts to obtain more devolution of responsibility from Whitehall and eventual self-government for themselves.

Southern Rhodesia's recurring pleas for self-government in the form of Dominion status have been consistently rejected by the British government since full racial equality and political representation are repudiated *in toto* by the white minority.

> In such circumstances it is clearly necessary that the ultimate control of Native policy should be in the hands of the colonial administration, and this excludes Dominion Status. One can now observe the political significance of the difference between these two types of colonial society, the one tending towards independence and the other necessarily remaining under the authority of the home country.
>
> And, in fact, we should harbour no illusions: to turn a colony into a Dominion means to hand over the Native to the mercy of the settler, that is to say, to withdraw the protecting hand of a metropolitan colonial administration, more liberal because it is further away and less directly interested. . . . Logically therefore we are bound to conclude that if Great Britain really regards herself as the protector of the Native she cannot desire the formation of any new Dominions in Central Africa.[25]

The Union of South Africa is in the foreground of any broad discussion of Native policy south of the Sahara. Events in one African territory affect conditions in other parts of Africa. Political and constitutional reforms in the Gold Coast and Nigeria have an impact upon the Union as well as the white settler territories. Mr. M. D. C. de Wet Nel, a guiding light of the Nationalist party, stated that apartheid is the only policy which could bring about peace and healthy development for all sections of the population in the territories north of the Union and in Central Africa. "The large measure of similarity between their problems and ours results in numbers of the people looking to the Union for leadership in these territories."[26]

Mr. de Wet Nel has urged in Parliament the convening as soon as possible of a conference of European states and communities in the whole of South Africa, with the special object of defining afresh and very explicitly the place and task of the Europeans in Africa, and a common course of conduct in regard to relations between Europeans and non-Europeans, to impart lucidity and clearness to important matters of policy. The topics such a conference would consider would include a common attitude toward communism and toward the rearming of non-Europeans and a common attitude throughout the whole of Africa as to the place that non-Europeans would take in the machinery of government and in the legislative bodies of the European states of Africa. Such a conference, Mr. de Wet Nel declared, would also offer South Africa the opportunity to explain the policy of apartheid that would be followed in the future in the Union.[27] Dr. Malan concurred in the feasibility of such a conference and expressed his desire to extend an invitation to the United States, because of its direct interest in Liberia, and to the nations of Europe having possessions in Africa.[28]

Both Crocker and Siegfried in their postwar studies of Africa point to the existence of a "Mason-Dixon line" south of the Sahara.[29] British Africa is rapidly dividing itself into two hostile blocs of white opinion, one representing the prevalence of the Colonial Office point of view, and the other the white settler–South African attitude toward the non-European races. Although there is not complete agreement as to the exact geographical demarcation such a line will follow, it may be generally assumed that it extends from the Kenya Highlands through the Highlands of East and South Central Africa thence westward over South-West Africa to the Atlantic.

The pole of the northern bloc would be the Gold Coast (ultimately the Colonial Office), and the pole of the southern bloc would be the Union of South Africa. As the white settlers feel their interests are not being served by the "Leftists and Fabians" of the British Parliament and the Colonial Office, they will become all the more closely linked with the Union of South Africa, the most vocal and effective champion of white supremacy in Africa. The Nationalists' own proposals for a Pan-African control movement and joint Native policy throughout the continent may thus be thwarted.

Alexander Campbell in his work *Empire in Africa* warns: "Clearly this sharp division of Africa into two spheres, where two opposing doctrines are preached and practised, cannot long endure. . . . One or the other doctrine must go down."[30] Only then will there be uniformity in Native policy, and such uniformity will be gained only as the culmination of strife and violence. The white settler territories are relatively small, economically weak, and together they represent only a handful of whites. The Union of South Africa is the most powerful and influential white state in Africa. It is well qualified to provide the leadership which the white settlers, not unnaturally, feel to be compatible with their own good, and such leadership will not be found wanting.

Although white settler and South African opinion cannot hope to force a retraction of developments in West Africa, it can nevertheless impede the advance of similar policies from Kenya to the Cape. With South Africa now in exclusively Afrikaner hands, the significance of apartheid in the emergent cleavage south of the Sahara becomes increasingly apparent.

CHAPTER XI

The Issue Today

THE PROBLEM OF NATIVE POLICY IS NO LONGER ONE WHICH CAN be sidestepped and its solution postponed until such vague or convenient time as the European may desire. The moral issues have been more sharply delineated since the nations of the world have found themselves divided into two hostile power blocs. This uneasy bifurcation has taken place as a post–World War II phenomenon, and ideological battle lines have been drawn. The prewar balance of power has been unbalanced, and the resultant shift in power is hastening decisions on many problems which had until now been capable of postponement. In the Far East and Asia, colonial peoples have emerged from their prewar status in new guise and have raised vital questions which can no longer be met with an attitude of complacency and misty phraseology. Can such an attitude still be used in Africa?

The fact that the Nationalists were voted into power in 1948 at a time when non-Europeans in India and the French and Dutch colonial possessions in the Far East were experiencing a great upsurge of determined and widespread independence movements leads one to ask if Nationalist apartheid might not be, in part, a reaction to this. A not inconsiderable segment of South African public opinion believes in "uplifting" the Natives by granting to them the benefits of European culture. With this, however, is the tacit assumption that the non-Europeans by inherent biological inferiority will not, regardless of the uplifting process, present a threat to permanent white-race dominance. In other portions of the world the allegedly inferior non-Europeans are, however, steadily rising in political status,

185

and the accuracy of such an assumption of permanent white-race dominance increasingly requires more critical analysis of events elsewhere.

Africa remains, since World War II, the only colonial area of large extent remaining in the world. No longer should the European feel secure behind allegations of non-European biological inferiority. The Nationalist apartheid program became a potent political weapon therefore at a very strategic moment in postwar Union politics—a moment when a reappraisal of this attitude toward the non-Europeans seemed imperative and more restrictive measures seemed attractive to the European.

Although it is difficult to gauge, the effect of some Negroes in the United States rising to positions of influence and prestige on both national and international levels may be another factor in making the South African non-Europeans increasingly aware of their own restrictions. This is but another manifestation of the total picture of world-wide events and trends by which the South African non-Europeans appraise their own situation. Thus world affairs have a primary significance to South Africa, and apartheid as perhaps a reaction to these events has, conversely, a significance for the world.

Granted that moral issues may be postponed as man has postponed them so well throughout his history, but strategic shifts in the international balance of power cannot be postponed and must be reckoned with. Any significant change in the public policy of a government today must therefore take on increased importance, especially when that nation occupies a strategic geographical position. The apartheid program represents an attempt on the part of the Nationalist government to alter the existing social structure of the Union. There are few who would deny the strategic geographical position of the Union, controlling, as it does, the approaches by sea or land to the southern portion of the continent and dominating the maritime shipping lanes at the confluence of the Atlantic and Indian oceans.

The forces with which the South African Government is tampering, under the misguided impression that it controls them are of cataclysmic strength, and every civilised European, both within and outside the continent, is not only entitled by a concern for human rights, but obliged by pure self-interest to observe the actions of the admittedly sovereign South African administration.[1]

It is primarily in terms of such self-interest, apart from the moral questions involved, that the Nationalist apartheid program affects millions of people, whites and nonwhites alike, who have never heard of "apartheid" or conceived the scope of what is being attempted at the present time in the Union.

CHAPTER XII

Conclusion

THE NATIONALIST PARTY CAME INTO POWER AFTER THE 1948 general election, having won the election on the apartheid platform. Though 1948 marks a new era in South African politics, the historical foundation for the philosophy underlying apartheid should not be underestimated.

Though born of a past rich in racial conservatism, there are nevertheless aspects of the doctrine which are meaningful only when considered in relation to contemporary South Africa. Herein lies a great deal of the strength and vigor of the doctrine and also a significant factor in its attraction for the European population. For that which has a historical emergence becomes deeply rooted in the lives of a people, and tradition often becomes precious of its own accord. When the traditional views are made to appear to be the effective solution to current problems, they may become virtually unassailable as a political platform.

The same outlook on life as the early Boer trekkers possessed is in part the basis for the doctrine of apartheid today. The label is new, but the assumptions are old. Originating in a deep-rooted psychological fear of miscegenation and intermarriage, it has been reinforced by a harsh environment consisting of overwhelmingly numerically superior Natives whose grandparents were hostile and ferocious enemies of the whites, and the peculiar physical, economic, and social realities of South Africa which combined to isolate the nineteenth-century Boers from the gradual emergence of English and Continental liberalism, though they felt its impact and found it distasteful. But more than distasteful—they found it immoral. Their church preached

188

the inequality of white and black and carried this inequality into both church and state.

This accounts for the Dutch Reformed church's support of the Nationalist program. The leadership of church and party are closely intertwined. They share a common moral consciousness, which, while it is founded on "unique" Christian theology (unique from the standpoint of the other Christian churches in the Union and from some of their own theologians), is nevertheless based upon Scripture and teachings they feel to be the true "morality" and ethical justification for avowed supremacy of the white race. It is precisely at this point that one is apt to fall into gross error on the apartheid program. To contend, as does Lloyd, that the Malan government's theories "have no moral content"[1] shows a lack of insight into the philosophic implications of apartheid itself.

To the Dutch-Nationalist of today, as to the Boers of the last century, racial inequality as an avowed doctrine expressed in public policy is Christian, moral, and ethically justified. To brand Nationalist racial theory as lacking in morality is merely to reassert one's own views and impose a standard upon the Dutch-Nationalists which their own church rejects—a rejection which is carrying the political battle on apartheid into the church groups of the Union.

The Dutch South Africans are deeply religious as a group and highly conscious of the role of the church in the social and political life of their people. Though the Nationalist campaign was, considering the close link between party and church, devoid of religious fervor or appeals to moral or ethical justification for apartheid, there is in the background of the doctrine the ultimate defense that can be made: to follow any other policy than complete inequality in both church and state would be immoral. This is not an example of Nationalist "misty phraseology." It is clear-cut, easily defined, and deeply rooted church doctrine.

Apartheid does not lack so-called "morality." This is an aspect which is seldom brought to light. Apartheid must be approached from the Nationalists' traditional frames of reference as well as those of one's self if any examination of the theory is to be meaningful.

Lloyd also makes the assertion that the government's apartheid theories have no logical structure.[2] This must be qualified. If the doctrine were based upon non-Nationalist assumptions, which Lloyd's are, the entire program would no doubt be highly illogical. But these are not the assumptions upon which the doctrine has been developed, and they are not the assumptions which the Nationalists forward. To consider apartheid therefore from the point of view of its being illogical on the basis of one's own assumptions rather than the Nationalists' assumptions is not a valid test for determination of logical content.

On the assumptions that the non-Europeans can develop only at the expense of the European community and that the nonwhite races present a threat to the continued survival of the white race, the Nationalist program is logical. Its conclusion, the avowed confirmation and reinforcement of white-race dominance, is the logical outcome of such assumptions.

It is, in fact, the "paternalism" of the Opposition which is not logical in content. It should be pointed out here that paternalism is the traditional South African attitude and is confined neither to the Nationalist party nor to the United party. It is based upon the broad allegation that the charges are not conceived of as adults and that authority over them should not be abrogated. Both the Nationalists and the United party want residential and social segregation. Both want to maintain white supremacy—Smuts said that "it will last forever."[3] But can it under the United party's program?

The paternalism of the former government was based, in addition to the common Nationalist-United party goals of white supremacy forever and segregation both residential and social, upon several points. First of all, the segregation of the former government was much less restrictive and on not so broad a scale as that of the Nationalist government. Second, it did not attack existing rights of the non-Europeans; it stands for the "status quo" in racial policy. Third, it did not look to territorial segregation as does Nationalist apartheid. It looked rather to a close co-operation of the various races. Fourth, it considered the interests of the Coloreds as nearly synonymous with the interests of the white race.

Under the former government, for instance, the influx of Natives to the urban centers was not regarded with apprehension but with the conviction that the Reserve life was neither adequate nor particularly desirable. The growing signs of the Natives becoming more "Europeanized" and the resultant detribalization, with the consequent increased integration of the Native into the Union's economic srtucture, was felt to be the natural consequence of, and requirement for, both European and non-European development in the Union.

Though dedicated to the proposition that all men are not created equal and that white supremacy must be permanent, the actual policies followed would have led in time to other conclusions. In many respects the paternalism of the former government was of a nature to "uplift" the Natives and Coloreds. The increase in facilities for Native education and health, the linking of Colored and white interests though still maintaining social segregation, the educational facilities for non-Europeans at some white institutions, the integration of Natives into the economy and their increased urban employment, the proposed social security schemes for non-Europeans and unemployment benefits, and the acceptance of detribalization with little effort to stem its rate of acceleration would have tended to produce a leveling-up process. Though the United party is not a liberal party, and it would be a grave injustice to regard it as such, the tactics of the party were not compatible, in many respects, to a *permanent* European supremacy.

The point would have eventually been reached wherein the gradual uplifting policies of the government, though veneered over with reiterations of racial inequality, would have produced and developed in the non-European a "spirit" of equality with the European and the quest for the realization of the rights inherent in such an assumption. Had the Smuts government fostered a policy of eventual, be it ever so far in the future, recognition of the equality of all races in the Union, its paternalism would have been logical. But, as it was, it pointed up a glaring contradiction between public policy and the ultimate avowed goal.

It is the United party's paternalism and not Nationalist apartheid which is illogical on the basic assumption of the inequality of races and the final goal of permanent white dominance. They both profess unending white supremacy in all spheres of endeavor, but only the oppressive and restrictive Nationalist policies have never deviated from this goal.

This may account in part for the Nationalist success at the polls. The election victory was a surprise even to themselves. Why were they brought to power? In part perhaps because of a reaction against the status quo of the former government which stemmed from its basic contradictions. The European South Africans had been seeing the gradual betterment and uplifting of the non-European races. They saw it as incompatible with an economy based upon cheap semicivilized labor and considered the consequences of a rising non-European standard of living and rising price scales for Native labor. They saw such a program as incompatible also with the professed ideal of a South Africa forever white. A point would be reached where the uplifting process could not be curbed—at any price. The proverbial fork in the road had been reached.

The reaction for many was to support apartheid and the Nationalist leaders, whose policies, though repugnant, were nonetheless logical in relation to the goal envisaged. Apartheid is therefore, in part, a reaction against the relatively liberal-uplifting policies of the United party's paternalism. This paternalism is incompatible with its own professed goal, and the valid conclusion may therefore be inferred that it is, to its own chagrin, conducive instead to eventual racial equality rather than the opposite.

Thus, in a sense, the Nationalists have been much more realistic than their political foes. Though less paternal, they have the foresight to see that the "wards" are growing up. They realize the inherent implications of such a situation and are doing everything they can to prevent its unpleasant consequences for the white population.

On the other hand, the policies of the United party may be approached from another point of view. It has been stated that an effective defense of the logical structure of United party policy can be made on the assumption that the uplifting of the non-European will not displace or threaten European dominance due to the inherent biological inferiority of the non-Europeans. In such case the paternalism of the United party would be logical in theory, although the practical application may admittedly lead to the opposite result. On such an assumption the difference between Nationalist theory and United party theory lies largely in the social consequences which each party holds will result from the uplifting policies such as United party paternalism has revealed.

Both parties share therefore a common "value-judgment" as to the inequality between the white and black races; the white race is the biologically superior race. Both share the same avowed goal of a permanent white supremacy in South Africa. The consequences which are held to result from the application of more benefits to the non-European races will therefore become the standard of determining the logical content of the political-racial theories of both parties.

Recent events in Asia and the Far East seem to indicate that the European assumption that the mere biological inferiority of the non-Europeans is sufficient to prevent them from displacing the Europeans, particularly in a predominantly non-European country, is an assumption that is found wanting. Though it preserves the logical structure of United party policy, it never-theless is forcing on the part of many South Africans a re-appraisal of their views on non-European issues. The United party is no doubt composed of both schools of thought, one of which has been found illogical in view of basic assumptions or value-judgment and the professed goal. The other has been found to be logical in theory but highly questionable as to its being a correct interpretation of world-wide events. Those who hold to either school of thought therefore have reached a dilem-ma within the United party.

To explain, as some commentators have done, the apartheid program as merely the temporary manifestation of a political party suddenly come into power is an underestimation of the significance of the doctrine. Whether the Nationalists win or lose the next election, the philosophy of social relationships underlying the doctrine will live on. It is not liberalism which has characterized South Africa but on the contrary it has been a conservative outlook in racial affairs. It has not been the early liberalism of the Cape which permeated South African public opinion but rather the conservatism of the other provinces led by the Orange Free State.

It must be noted that the United party, the parliamentary Opposition, itself offers nothing more than the status quo in racial policy. The initiative has been taken by the Nationalists. The United party may at the most hope to gain a delaying ac-tion; it cannot hope for a letup of the constant pressure for more restrictions on the non-European population. The United party, far from supporting the Cape Colored vote for the sake of the Coloreds alone, is at the same time protecting the inter-ests of the English-speaking white community. The equality of the English and Afrikaans languages rests upon a constitutional provision, likewise entrenched, and equally susceptible to Na-tionalist machinations.

It has not been conservatism but rather liberalism which has been on trial in South Africa; and liberalism in even its most elemental form, that is, United party liberalism, has been found wanting. When the most liberal of the provinces had the direct Native franchise reduced to communal representation in the Disfranchisement Act of 1936, this served notice that liberalism not only was waging a losing battle in the Union but for all intents and purposes was dying at a rapid rate. It was but the portent of things to come which have now been fairly well crystallized in Nationalist apartheid.

The other provinces have been little affected by the liberal tradition of the Cape, but the Cape lost a major battle on the Native issue and faces prolonged pressure and a bleak future on the Colored issue. The conservative outlook on racial policy has typified South African statesmen and writers, and those who do not have this attitude are the exceptions, not the rule.

To lay the inception of apartheid or its repressive policies to the prime minister and party leader, Dr. Malan, is therefore wholly unrealistic. He is merely leading the movement whose principles and policies, while adapted of course to contemporary South Africa, emerged in the South African past when the first white settlers came into contact with the Natives. When Dr. Malan is no longer in the political struggles, others with equal vigor and determination and belief in the righteousness of the cause will be found to take his place. They will be but carrying on the traditional South African attitude.

It is in this respect also therefore that apartheid must be considered as something more than the mere brain child of a Nationalist committee meeting to determine pre-election strategy. It is this in part, it is true; but it is a program which seems to meet the needs of a large segment of the European population which looks to the future with apprehension and to the past for the solution.

In addition to the unique morality which the Dutch-Nationalists contend justifies, on moral and ethical grounds, the apartheid program, there is the theoretical balance between the in-

creased restrictions imposed on the non-European races and
vague allusions to a higher level of self-development for them—
a development which, the Nationalists hold, is higher than is
now possible under the present social structure of the Union.
For that which is to be taken away something better is to be
substituted.

That "something better" becomes more in the character of
something less, however, since the fulfilment of the promised
higher self-development lies in the future—a future which the
Nationalists regard as ideal but which critics regard as illusory
and highly problematical. The positive rights and privileges, already established in many cases by custom and tradition, which
are to be replaced by something better, are being removed at the
present time in the name of this nebulous future life.

Apartheid theoretically consists of positive and negative aspects; so far only the negative, the taking-away, aspects of the
doctrine have characterized the Nationalists' apartheid program.
Herein lies a fundamental danger. The positive aspects of the
program will be the most difficult to achieve, for example, the
allocation of sufficient land for Native occupation and use and
the establishment of industries in Native areas. The negative aspects are relatively easy to carry out, such as further restrictions
upon the non-European population by government decree. This
brings to light a characteristic of the Nationalist approach to the
implementation of their theories. They are using the regulatory
power to alter policy, not merely to implement it. For example,
the government regulation introducing segregation on the Cape
transportation system was invoked by an administrative order,
even though it represented a significant change in public policy
which shoud have emerged as the result of parliamentary action.

In addition to the vertical segregation of races, the caste system type of organization which has traditionally been practiced
by both British and Dutch South Africans, the Nationalists conceive a "separation" of races on a geographical basis. The Colored population of the Cape Province are to have their interests

more closely linked with those of the non-European races. In this respect the apartheid program looks to increased segregatory practices where already in existence and the instituting of segregation between Coloreds and Europeans in many instances where it had not existed previously. Separate Colored villages are to be established within the urban areas. For the Cape Coloreds this will be a reorientation of social status unlike anything practiced by previous governments, and communal representation has already replaced Colored voting on the common roll in the Cape.

With the former intermediate status of the Coloreds reduced to a status more closely aligned to that of the Native, the apartheid program could more easily be administered with fewer exceptions to the rules. With the Cape Province more in line with the conservative racial policies of the other provinces, a uniform racial policy could be applied throughout the Union. In fact, when such had been achieved, the whole liberal concept of race would have been undercut in the Union, and the only social laboratory where liberal racial theories could be put into practice would be, to all intents and purposes, destroyed.

The Indian population is to be reduced to the "irreducible minimum" and will be controlled by a strict application of apartheid. This includes denial of representation in any form and such reprehensible devices as *ex post facto* laws which have already been put into practice by the government. The ideal of complete repatriation of the Indian community will always remain the ultimate goal of the party.

It is interesting and also significant to note that the Nationalists attack the existing rights of all three non-European races at once rather than concentrating on one race at a time. One would ordinarily expect the Indian issue, the most unpopular cause in the Union, to be the first target of Nationalist strategy because of the wide non-Nationalist support. The pressure on the existing rights of all non-Europeans has remained constant, however, and the apartheid program as regards Indians seems to be co-ordinate with, rather than dominant over, the policies toward the other non-European races.

The United party, while united as regards support of the Nationalist anti-Asiatic policies, is deeply split into factions over the Native and Colored issues. The Nationalists therefore are taking advantage of this internal dissension by attacking the political enemy at these weak points.

The Nationalist party is blessed with vigorous and capable leadership, with leaders who sincerely believe their program to be in the best interests of the white community in Africa and who, in fervently extolling the righteousness of the cause, attack all opposition as Communist inspired. This factor is a potent one in preventing the effective rise of a sincerely liberal, not Communistic, spirit. It places liberalism on the defensive, and the liberal spirit, already weak, must divert its strength to denying the Communistic association, thereby lessening the magnitude of its own attack on conservative racial policy.

The Dutch Reformed church has also resorted to this stratagem in its attack against the non-Afrikaner churches. As a result it becomes imperative that the non-Afrikaner churches abandon a laissez faire attitude as far as everyday politics are concerned. Their attention must increasingly be devoted to their own existence as an effective social force in South Africa. They must not only morally but politically oppose those who are detrimental to their best interests. The Dutch Reformed church has, in effect, its own political party to mirror its doctrine. The non-Afrikaner church groups must likewise become fully politically conscious. They must present a politically cohesive and politically vigorous bloc if their own position is not to become untenable.

Theological irreconcilability does not remain merely as such but manifests itself via the Nationalist party into political irreconcilability. Thus the non-Afrikaner church and missionary groups are, for better or worse, whether they like it or not, drawn irresistibly into the political vortex.

The Nationalists are, of course, merely in the first stages of their apartheid program, which must, they admit, be accomplished by gradual processes. They have certain tools with which to work, namely, the parliamentary system of government and the Union's civil servants. The gauging of the strength and disposition of both European and non-European opposition in the Union is a delicate and difficult task which the Nationalist leadership must carry out with a very high degree of skill. To push the program at too rapid a pace or to emphasize certain aspects of the program at an unpropitious time could easily result in widespread non-European demonstrations. Lack of political acumen in the administration of the program, therefore, could retard Nationalist aspirations indefinitely.

The fate of the apartheid program lies just as surely in the ability of the civil administrators as on the floors of Parliament. The proposed movement of Natives back to the Reserves, the centralized control of expanded migratory labor forces, and the necessity of enforcing the restrictive legislation and increased administrative regulations which such a program envisages place the public servants in a position of primary importance.

The land problem is, at the present time, the most formidable obstacle to the eventual success of the apartheid doctrine. Whether the full implementation of the theory of apartheid could ever be achieved depends upon the solving of this problem. Thus far, it is of such scope that it is seemingly not capable of solution. Besides the financial aspect of the problem, the setting-aside of vast tracts of good quality land sufficient for the proposed Native population would require a literal reversal of the European frame of mind, a phenomenon which has so far been conspicuous by its absence. Even the rehabilitation of present Native lands will require a change of the Native frame of mind. Agricultural demonstrators of the agricultural branch of the Department of Native Affairs have met with little success in convincing the Natives to desist from erosion-producing practices; they have even been met with violence. Although the

government can point to a few "betterment areas" where the
Natives are co-operating in model agricultural projects, the outer
shell of Native resistance has yet to be pierced.

The Nationalists' concept of industrialized Reserves has an
attraction for those acquainted with the perplexing land problem. As an answer to criticisms that urban Natives cannot be
returned to a tribal society and that the quality and quantity
of land is insufficient for an increased agrarian population, the
concept of industrialized Native areas is an effective political
weapon against the opponents of apartheid.

This whole new concept of the Natives' role under apartheid
is such a recent development that any attempted analysis of this
phase of the program is apt to be premature and for that reason
particularly susceptible to erroneous conclusions. It cannot be
denied, however, that there is much in such a concept which is
desirable. Light or secondary industries in the Reserve areas are
advisable to take up the slack of some of those Natives not able
to eke out a living in agriculture. In addition, the Reserves
would be made more self-sustaining, though financing of the rehabilitation and improvement programs of these areas by Native
means alone could hardly be expected. The Natives in the Reserves need not necessarily therefore be oriented to an agricul-
tural-pastoral economy and need not be fettered by traditional
tribal lore. There is little doubt that previous criticisms directed
against apartheid in these respects are considerably undermined.

As the envisaged scale of industrial development increases,
however, its ultimate success becomes more problematical. It
can hardly be expected, despite Nationalist hopes, that Europeans will invest and build up such industry in the Reserves and
then withdraw to enable the Natives to produce for themselves.
The European capitalistic system is paralyzed by a great and
prolonged diminution of markets for its products. The South
African capitalistic economy cannot afford to have the present
Native population or the envisaged Native population of fifty
years hence removed as a profitable and permanent market. The

Europeans in South Africa will not turn the cheek in losing their markets any more than they have been prone to do in giving up their land for Native occupation.

There are of course other barriers to Nationalist designs. The attempted reversal of the movement of Natives from rural to urban areas is itself one of the most ambitious phases of the apartheid program. It is a moot question whether it can ever be effected. Failing in this, apartheid must remain in the theoretical stage.

It is interesting to note that the republican propaganda of the Nationalist party has been toned down considerably since the apartheid program became the political platform of the party. Care has been taken not to accelerate republican propaganda due to its frightening off overseas investors, of which South Africa has great need. There is little doubt, however, that the traditional republican theme will be reverted to whenever the apartheid program is lagging and the Nationalist hierarchy feels that attention should consequently be drawn to other issues.

The Dutch South African is no longer characterized by his long rifle and his ox wagon. While the Scriptures still play a large part in his life, they no longer monopolize his thoughts as in the past. He is now partaking of broader experiences. Where once his people trekked into the virtually unknown wilderness, they are now returning to the urban areas to take part in the social intercourse and commerce of modern society. The Boers have ceased to regard themselves as impervious to the influences and repercussions of international events. Proof of this is found in the Nationalist government's dispatch of a South African fighter squadron to Korea in support of United Nations policy immediately following the outbreak of hostilities in that theater.

The body of Afrikaans literature is steadily expanding as Afrikaner authors are gaining acclaim and prestige in many fields. The Afrikaans-speaking universities of South Africa are making great strides in developing an academic consciousness among the

Afrikaner people, and prominent scholars from these universities have imparted an intellectual flavor to the apartheid program. Further substantiation of the fact that there is a thread of intellectualism woven into the pattern of apartheid is provided by the presence of a Nationalist cabinet which can boast that nearly one-third of its members hold Doctors' degrees from leading universities in South Africa and abroad.

While one may appreciate those imperious forces which have molded the Afrikaners' sociopolitical philosophy, the basic assumptions upon which the theory of apartheid rests are not acceptable to many persons who regard the uplifting of the non-European races as not necessarily incompatible with the interests of the Europeans. For them the doctrine is one of oppression and only increases the dangers already facing the European minority. They believe the philosophy of apartheid to be the *coup de grâce* to liberal thought in the Union and stress the difficulties inherent in the Nationalists' reactionary concepts of social organization and its resultant "apartness." To the consternation of the Nationalist government forty-seven sovereign states, through the United Nations, have taken a keen interest in the issues involved.

To those persons who have viewed with apprehension the "pigmentocracy" already existing in the Union, the rise of the Nationalist party to power in 1948 has heralded with renewed vigor the forces of bigotry and fear which carry on their nefarious activities in the name of the *Afrikanervolk*. To them the development of apartheid from the realm of Nationalist political theory to the attempted actual implementation of the doctrine is the most significant and disheartening movement in contemporary South African politics.

Notes

CHAPTER I

1. Following the coalition of the Nationalists and the South African party under the name of the United party in 1933 due to pressure of the economic crisis of world depression, Dr. D. F. Malan, the present prime minister, condemned fusion and seceded with some followers to form a Purified Nationalist party. Nationalist forces reunited in 1939 under the name Herenigde Nasionale party (Reunited Nationalist party), which is the government of the Union today. The literature dealing with contemporary Union politics sometimes refers to this party as the HNP, but most often it is merely labeled the Nationalist party.

2. "The Doctrine of Apartheid," *Round Table*, XXXIX (December, 1948), 32.

3. Sarah Gertrude Millin, "Fear in Africa," *Foreign Affairs*, XXVIII (October, 1949), 102–3.

4. I. S. Lloyd, " 'Apartheid'—South Africa's New Native Policy," *Political Quarterly*, XX (April–June, 1949), 127.

5. W. K. Hancock, *Survey of British Commonwealth Affairs* (London, New York, Toronto: Oxford University Press, 1942), II, Part 2, 101.

6. The term "Afrikaner" or "Afrikander" denotes those South Africans of Dutch descent who are also commonly referred to as Boers or the *Boervolk* (Boer people). The Afrikaner party represents only a very small minority of the Afrikaner people. The Afrikaners have traditionally been represented by the Nationalist party, which was formed in 1912, the Purified Nationalist party, and the HNP of today.

7. Alexander Brady, *Democracy in the Dominions* (Toronto: University of Toronto Press, 1947), p. 352.

8. James Bryce et al., *Briton and Boer: Both Sides of the African Question* (New York and London: Harper & Bros., 1900), pp. 30–31. This in spite of the fact that Brady regards Nationalist anti-Semitism in Afrikander politics as an "innovation" and that "in republican times wealthy Jews at least were among Paul Kruger's closest friends" (*op. cit.*). Cf. C. W. Van der Hoogt, *The Story of the Boers* (n.p., 1900), p. 66.

9. See Lewis Sowden, *The Union of South Africa* (Garden City, N.Y.: Doubleday, Doran & Co., 1943), pp. 211, 214–16, for an account of the relationship between Nationalist anti-Semitism and the immigration laws of 1930 and 1937–38.

10. Brady, *op. cit.* (Italics mine.)

11. The terms "Native," "Bantu," and "African" are hereafter used as synonymous.

12. Brady, *op. cit.*, p. 364.

13. *Ibid.*

14. "The Doctrine of Apartheid," *op. cit.*, p. 33.

15. *Ibid.*

16. South African Supplement, *Continental Daily Mail* (March, 1949), as quoted in *Weekly Newsletter* (State Information Office, Pretoria), No. 486 (March 26, 1949), p. 2.

17. Figures provided by Brady, *op. cit.*, p. 362.

18. W. Douglas Mackenzie, *South Africa, Its History, Heroes and Wars* (San Francisco: J. Dewing Co., 1899), p. 154.

19. LeRoy Hooker, *The Africanders* (Chicago and New York: Rand McNally & Co., 1900), p. 125.

20. M. J. Farrelly, *The Settlement after the War in South Africa* (London: Macmillan Co., 1900), p. 20.

21. "The Doctrine of Apartheid," *op. cit.*, pp. 33–34.

22. *Ibid.*

23. Gerald Broomfield, *Colour Conflict: Race Relations in Africa* (Cambridge: University Press, 1934), p. 9.

24. "The Doctrine of Apartheid," *op. cit.* p. 33.

CHAPTER II

1. Le Roy Hooker, *The Africanders* (Chicago and New York: Rand McNally & Co., 1900), p. 12.

2. *Ibid.*, p. 13.

3. James Bryce et al., *Briton and Boer: Both Sides of the African Question* (New York and London: Harper & Bros., 1900), p. 3.

4. Hooker, *op. cit.*, p. 15.

5. *Ibid.*, p. 16.

6. *Ibid.*

7. Bryce et al., *op. cit.*, p. 5.

8. *Ibid.*

9. William Miller Macmillan, *Bantu, Boer and Briton: The Making of the South African Native Problem* (London: Faber & Gwyer, 1929), p. 1.

10. *Ibid.* One of the points which the nationalist faction among the Dutch colonists demanded of the Dutch East India Company government in return for their resistance to British occupation of the Cape was "permission to hold in perpetual slavery all Bushmen captured by commandos or individuals" (Hooker, *op. cit.*, p. 49). One thus gains an insight into the tremendous impact the freeing of all slaves had upon the Dutch South Africans.

11. Macmillan, *op. cit.*

12. Bryce significantly observes: "Like all Europeans dwelling among inferior races, the mass of colonists, *English as well as Dutch*, looked upon the natives as existing for their benefit, and resented the efforts which the home government made to secure for the blacks equal civil rights and adequate protection" (James Bryce, *Impressions of South Africa* [New York: Century Co., 1900], pp. 139–40). (Italics mine.) Hooker seems to confirm this view in his implication that English as well as Dutch colonists "cordially disliked" the English missionaries (*op. cit.*, p. 75).

13. Alexander Brady, *Democracy in the Dominions* (Toronto: University of Toronto Press, 1947), p. 304.

14. Bryce, *op. cit.*, p. 116.

15. *Report of the Native Affairs Commission, 1852–53*, p. 8, as quoted in Edgar H. Brookes, *The History of Native Policy in South Africa from 1830 to the Present Day* (Pretoria: J. L. Van Schaik, 1927), p. 22.

16. Brookes, *op. cit.*

17. *Ibid.*, p. 119. For a detailed analysis of Natal Native policy from the period of Voortrekker rule to Union in 1910 see *ibid.*, pp. 22–87.

18. W. Douglas Mackenzie, *South Africa, Its History, Heroes and Wars* (San Francisco: J. Dewing Co., 1899), pp. 45–46.

19. Macmillan, *op. cit.*, p. 179.

20. Hooker, *op. cit.*, p. 84.

21. Mackenzie, *op. cit.*, p. 41.

22. Bryce, *op. cit.*, p. 85.

23. Macmillan, *op. cit.*, p. 179. Brookes (*op. cit.*, pp. 22–23) maintains that the Native population increase was due to an influx of Natives from Zululand following the downfall of the Zulu Military Empire at Bloody River and nowhere implies an underestimation of Natives on the part of the Boers.

24. Macmillan, *op. cit.*, p. 179.

25. I.e., a Council of the People in the form of a unicameral legislature.

26. Macmillan, *op. cit.*

27. *Ibid.*

28. *Ibid.*, p. 303. Macmillan also observed that in 1929 the Reserves constituted little more than one-eighth part of Natal proper. Roux, however, provides the figure of 27.9 per cent of the total area of Natal set aside for Native Reserves as adjusted by the Land Act of 1913 (Edward Roux, "Land and Agriculture in the Native Reserves," in *Handbook on Race Relations in South Africa*, ed. Ellen Hellmann [Cape Town, London, New York: Oxford University Press, 1949], chap. vii, p. 172).

29. *Ibid.*, p. 306.

30. Early in 1839.
31. See Brookes, *op. cit.*, p. 24; Macmillan, *op. cit.*, p. 178; and John H. Bovill, *Natives under the Transvaal Flag* (London: Simpkin, Marshall, Hamilton, Kent & Co., 1900), p. 18.
32. Macmillan, *op. cit.*, p. 178.
33. Brookes, *op. cit.*, pp. 23–24.
34. *Ibid.*, pp. 119–20.
35. Macmillan, *op. cit.*, p. 305.
36. *Ibid.*, pp. 305–6. (Italics mine.)
37. W. K. Hancock, *Survey of British Commonwealth Affairs* (London, New York, Toronto: Oxford University Press, 1942), II, Part 2, 6.
38. Mackenzie, *op. cit.*, p. 161.
39. *Ibid.*
40. As quoted in Macmillan, *op. cit.*, p. 308.
41. Par. 96 as quoted *ibid.*
42. Pars. 104 and 105 of the *Grondwet* as described *ibid.* (English translation mine.)
43. The following description of early Boer local organization under the rule of the Dutch East India Company at the Cape is helpful in that it represents essentially the same type of government which was carried over into the independent Boer republics:

"Magistrates and assessors were appointed in some of the distant stations, but they failed to control the wandering stockmen, who . . . 'trekked' from place to place. Being good marksmen and inured with wild beasts and wilder men, they formed among themselves companies of fighting men whose duty it was to disperse or destroy the savage Bushmen. The independent military organizations the government recognized and approved by appointing over them a field commander for each district and a subordinate called a field cornet for each subdivision of a district. These officers and their respective commands became permanent features of the system of local government, and the war bands—called commandos—have always been recognized in the records of military operations by the Boers" (Hooker, *op. cit.*, pp. 18–19.

For a more detailed description of the Boer commando system and its method of operation see Macmillan, *op. cit.*, pp. 54–57. For a brief description of the *Landdrost*, or magistrate system, of the Boer republics (described in the case of the Orange Free State) see John Ormand Neville, *Boer and Britisher in South Africa* (Chicago: Thompson & Thomas, 1900), Appendix B, IV.
44. Macmillan, *op. cit.*, p. 308.
45. *Ibid.*
46. Par. 104 of the *Grondwet* as quoted in part *ibid.*
47. *Ibid.*
48. *Ibid.*, pp. 308–9.

49. *Ibid.,* p. 309.
50. *Ibid.,* p. 308.
51. Mackenzie, *op. cit.,* p. 161.
52. *Ibid.*
53. *Ibid.*
54. As quoted in Bovill, *op. cit.,* p. 11.
55. *Ibid.,* p. 13.
56. For a detailed discussion of the Transvaal Boers' failure to uphold these four "elementary principles" see *ibid.,* pp. 11–31.
57. Macmillan, *op. cit.,* p. 309.
58. *Ibid.*
59. *Ibid.*
60. *Ibid.*
61. *Ibid.*
62. *Ibid.,* p. 310.
63. *Ibid.*
64. Hooker, *op. cit.,* p. 124.
65. See Mackenzie, *op. cit.,* pp. 163–69.
66. See Hooker, *op. cit.,* pp. 123–34.
67. Mackenzie, *op. cit.,* p. 163. This is difficult to reconcile with Macmillan's contention that actually the settlers in the Transvaal were faced with the problem of "surplus Natives" (Macmillan, *op cit.,* pp. 178–79, 300, and 310).
68. Mackenzie, *op. cit.,* p. 163. Nevertheless, such an eminent authority as Brookes (*op. cit.,* p. 123) states: "It is important to insist that the annexation [Transvaal] of 1877 *did not involve* the deliverance of multitudes of oppressed Natives from cruelty and semi-slavery. It is a legend which ought to be exploded today." (Italics mine.)
69. Hooker, *op. cit.,* p. 124.
70. *Ibid.,* pp. 124–25.
71. Mackenzie, *op. cit.,* p. 164.
72. Hooker, *op. cit.,* p. 125.
73. Mackenzie, *op. cit.,* p. 167. (Italics mine.)
74. "The Native Policy of the Union, 1910–1932," *Round Table,* XXII (June, 1932), 660.
75. *Ibid.*
76. *Ibid.,* p. 661.
77. Brookes, *op. cit.,* p. 139.
78. M. S. Geen, *The Making of the Union of South Africa* (London, New York, Toronto: Longmans, Green & Co., 1947), p. 157.
79. Brookes, *op. cit.,* p. 139.
80. Sec. 24.
81. Brookes, *op. cit.,* p. 140.
82. Roux, *op. cit.,* p. 172.
83. See A. M. Keppel-Jones, "Land and Agriculture Outside the Reserves," in *Handbook on Race Relations in South Africa,* ed.

Ellen Hellmann (Cape Town, London, New York: Oxford University Press, 1949), chap. viii, pp. 191–92, for a concise review of pre-Union land legislation.

84. Ellen Hellmann, "Urban Areas," in *Handbook on Race Relations in South Africa*, ed. Ellen Hellmann (Cape Town, London, New York: Oxford University Press, 1949), chap. xi, p. 232.

85. "The Native Policy of the Union, 1910–1932," *op. cit.*, p. 661.

86. *Ibid.*

87. Roux, *op. cit.*, p. 172.

88. "The Native Policy of the Union, 1910–1932," *op. cit.*, p. 661.

89. Brookes, *op. cit.*, p. 143.

90. Roux, *op. cit.*, p. 172.

91. Lord S. H. Olivier, "General Hertzog's Eirencion to the Native," *New Statesman*, XXVIII (October 16, 1926), 8.

92. Hancock, *op. cit.*, p. 74.

93. "The Native Policy of the Union, 1910–1932," *op. cit.*, pp. 662–63.

94. *Ibid.*

95. *Ibid.*, p. 664.

96. *Ibid.*

97. *Ibid.*

98. *Ibid.*

99. "The South African Race Problem in the Light of General Hertzog's Proposed Legislation," *International Review of Missions*, XVI (April, 1927), 183.

100. Brookes, *op. cit.*, p. 141.

101. "The South African Race Problem in the Light of General Hertzog's Proposed Legislation," *op. cit.*, p. 182.

102. *Ibid.*, p. 184.

103. *Ibid.*, p. 182.

104. *Ibid.*, p. 186.

105. *Ibid.*, p. 187.

106. *Ibid.*, p. 188.

107. "General Hertzog's Native Policy," *New Statesman*, XXXIII (June 8, 1929), 263.

108. "The South African Race Problem in the Light of General Hertzog's Proposed Legislation," *op. cit.*, p. 190.

109. *Ibid.*, pp. 190–91.

110. "General Hertzog's Native Policy," *op. cit.*, p. 263.

111. *Ibid.*

112. *Ibid.*, p. 264.

113. As quoted in Roux, *op. cit.*, p. 173.

114. *Ibid.*

115. One morgen is equal to 2.1 acres.

116. Basil Williams, *Botha, Smuts and South Africa* (London:

Hodder & Stoughton, 1948), p. 149. Since the death in 1946 of the single remaining Native voter in Natal, there are no Natives on the general or common voters' roll.

117. Geen, *op. cit.*, p. 183.

118. Williams, *op. cit.*, p. 150.

119. Geen, *op. cit.*, p. 183.

120. A location is an area of land set aside for the exclusive use of Natives. It may be a heavily populated suburb of a European city, a Native village, a collection of huts or houses, or a large area of land inhabited by Natives.

121. Hellmann, *op. cit.*, pp. 258–61.

CHAPTER III

1. I. S. Lloyd, " 'Apartheid'—South Africa's New Native Policy," *Political Quarterly*, XX (April–June, 1949), 126.

2. "The Doctrine of Apartheid," *Round Table*, XXXIX (December, 1948), 33.

3. Leonard Barnes, *Caliban in Africa* (Philadelphia: J. B. Lippincott, 1931), p. 43.

4. A memoir by I. D. MacCrone in R. F. A. Hoernlé's *Race and Reason* (Johannesburg: Witwatersrand University Press, 1945), p. xxviii.

5. *Ibid.* There are, however, easily discernible groups in the Union which are dedicated to the furtherance of more liberal principles in Native policy. The liberal influence of the English-speaking missionaries mark them as perhaps the most outspoken European group advocating a greatly liberalized segregation and the full franchise for all qualified non-Europeans. The African National Congress, the Bantu Union, the Industrial and Commercial Union, the Industrial and Commercial Workers Union, the Negro Mutual Improvement Society and African Communities League, the Coloured Peoples National Union, the Natal and Transvaal Indian Congress, and other non-European groups also strongly advocate a more liberal non-European policy. Many of these groups have been attacked, in varying degree, by political commentators and the Nationalist government as Communist-front organizations.

6. *Ibid.*

7. *Ibid.*, p. xxix.

8. *Ibid.*, p. xxx.

9. The Union lies roughly between 22° S. and 34° S. (with the latitude decreased northward to approximately 18° S. if South-West Africa is included).

10. Forty per cent of the total area is over 4,000 feet above sea level. The largest urban center (Johannesburg) is about 6,000 feet.

11. Alexander Brady, *Democracy in the Dominions* (Toronto: University of Toronto Press, 1947), p. 296.

12. J. M. Tinley, *The Native Labor Problem of South Africa* (Chapel Hill: University of North Carolina Press, 1942), p. 15.

13. Brady, *op. cit.*, p. 296.

14. W. Douglas Mackenzie, *South Africa, Its History, Heroes, and Wars* (San Francisco: J. Dewing Co., 1899), p. 23.

15. Brady, *op. cit.*, p. 296.

16. Mackenzie, *op. cit.*, p. 27.

17. Brady, *op. cit.*, p. 296.

18. H. D. Leppan, *Agricultural Policy in South Africa*, p. 64, as quoted in Brady, *op. cit.*, p. 297.

19. Brady, *op. cit.*, p. 297.

20. James Bryce et al., *Briton and Boer: Both Sides of the African Question* (New York and London: Harper & Bros., 1900), p. 29.

21. Brady, *op. cit.*, p. 297.

22. *Ibid.*

23. See P. A. Silburn, *South Africa White and Black—or Brown?* (London: G. Allen & Unwin, 1927), p. 146; cf. William Miller Macmillan, *Bantu, Boer and Briton: The Making of the South African Native Problem* (London: Faber & Gwyer, 1929), p. 8.

24. The date of the battle was December 16, 1838.

25. Tinley, *op. cit.*, p. 248.

26. *Ibid.*, pp. 248–49.

27. Lloyd, *op. cit.*, p. 126.

28. "The Doctrine of Apartheid," *op. cit.*, p. 33.

29. Barnes, *op. cit.*, p. 338.

30. Brady, *op. cit.*, p. 358.

31. *Ibid.*, p. 359.

32. *Ibid.*

33. Barnes, *op. cit.*, p. 31.

34. *Ibid.*

35. Howard Hillegas, *Oom Paul's People* (New York: D. Appleton & Co., 1900), p. 100.

36. There were no non-European representatives of the mission churches at the Bloemfontein congress because it was felt that clear policy was essential before mutual talks could profitably be held. A congress composed of both Europeans and non-Europeans, similar to that held in 1923, was proposed however.

37. "The Dutch Churches Call for Root and Branch Separation," *South African Outlook*, LXXX (May 1, 1950), 68–69. This article provides summaries of some of the more important resolutions passed by the congress. See also *Weekly Newsletter*, No. 541 (April 15, 1950), p. 7.

38. "The Dutch Churches Call for Root and Branch Separation," *op. cit.*, p. 69.

39. The congress maintained that the economic sacrifices caused by such complete separation should be accepted in the spirit that economic security meant nothing without racial security and that on the whole the elimination of Native labor from the European economy would increase European productivity.

40. "The Dutch Churches Call for Root and Branch Separation," *op. cit.*, p. 69.

41. The *Cape Times* as quoted in "Noted D.R. Church Scholar and Apartheid," *South African Outlook*, LXXX (January 1, 1950), 15.

42. *Ibid.*

43. *Ibid.*

44. Henry Gibbs, *Twilight in South Africa* (London: Jarrolds, 1949), p. 234, n. 1.

45. "Church Opposition to 'Apartheid' Growing," *Christian Century*, LXVI (November 16, 1949), 1348–49.

46. "Defiant South Africa," *Christian Century*, LXVI (September 28, 1949), 1127.

47. *Ibid.*

48. Africanus, *Transvaal Boers* (London: Horace Marshall & Son, 1899), p. 13.

49. *Ibid.*

50. *Ibid.*

51. Spenser Wilkinson, *British Policy in South Africa* (London: Sampson Low, Marston & Co., 1899), p. 24.

52. Africanus, *op. cit.*, p. 14.

53. Wilkinson, *op. cit.*, p. 25.

54. *Ibid.*, p. 27.

55. W. E. G. Fisher, *The Transvaal and the Boers* (London: Chapman & Hall, 1900), p. 99.

56. *The Cambridge History of the British Empire*, ed. A. P. Newton and E. A. Benians (New York: Macmillan Co.; Cambridge: Cambridge University Press, 1936), VIII, 78–79.

57. L. Marquard, *The Native in South Africa* (Johannesburg: Witwatersrand University Press, 1948), p. 70.

58. *Cambridge History of the British Empire*, VIII, 839.

59. Marquard, *op. cit.*, p. 70.

60. W. M. Eiselen, "Christianity and the Religious Life of the Bantu," in *Western Civilization and the Natives of South Africa*, ed. I. Schapera (London: George Routledge & Sons, 1934), chap. iii, p. 65. Chief among the societies that sent out volunteers were the Moravian Missionary Society, the London Missionary Society, the Baptist Missionary Society, the Wesleyan Missionary Society (British Methodists), the Church Missionary Society, the Glasgow Society, the South African Mission of the United Free Church of Scot-

land, the Berlin and Barman Missionary Societies from Germany, the Paris Society, and the Rhenish Society.

61. Eiselen, *op. cit.*, p. 65.

62. Edgar H. Brookes, *The Colour Problems of South Africa* (Lovedale, South Africa: Lovedale Press; London: K. Paul, Trench, Trubner & Co., 1934), p. 153.

63. *Ibid.*

64. Eiselen, *op. cit.*, p. 65.

65. Marquard, *op. cit.*, p. 71.

66. S. M. Mokitimi, "African Religion," in *Handbook on Race Relations in South Africa*, ed. Ellen Hellmann (Cape Town, London, New York: Oxford University Press, 1949), chap. xxiii, p. 563. See also Diedrich Westermann, *The African Today* (London: Oxford University Press, 1934), chap. ix: "The Supernatural World"; Newell S. Booth, "The Ministry in Bantu Religion," *International Review of Missions*, XXVI (July, 1937), 334–44.

67. Mokitimi, *op. cit.*, p. 556.

68. *Ibid.*

69. Eiselen, *op. cit.*, p. 70.

70. Ray E. Phillips, *The Bantu in the City* (Lovedale, South Africa: Lovedale Press, 1938), p. 249.

71. Mokitimi, *op. cit.*, p. 557.

72. *Ibid.*, p. 562.

73. *Ibid.*

74. Brookes, *op. cit.*, p. 154. (Italics mine.)

75. Mokitimi, *op. cit.*, p. 563.

76. Brookes, *op. cit.*, p. 155.

77. Eiselen, *op. cit.*, p. 70.

78. *Ibid.*, pp. 70–71.

79. Mokitimi, *op. cit.*, p. 563.

80. J. H. Oldham and B. D. Gibson, *The Remaking of Man in Africa* (London: Oxford University Press [H. Milford], 1931), p. 56.

81. *Ibid.*, p. 57.

82. Brookes, *op. cit.*, p. 157.

83. In 1658 a school for slave children was opened where instruction was given by the Dutch *Sieckentrooster*, or sick comforter. Although the attempt was made to teach the three R's, most of the emphasis was upon religious instruction. "The school lasted only three weeks, for in spite of being bribed with brandy and tobacco the slaves ran away" (M. E. McKerron, *A History of Education in South Africa [1652–1932]* [Pretoria: J. L. van Schaik, 1934], p. 156).

84. Oldham and Gibson, *op. cit.*, pp. 49–50.

85. Seth M. Mokitimi, "Apartheid and the Christian Spirit," *International Review of Missions*, XXXVIII (July, 1949), 277.

86. *Ibid.*

87. "Minister Indicates Native Education Policy," *Weekly Newsletter*, No. 534 (February 25, 1950), p. 7. (Italics mine.)

The state has manifested an ever increasing interest in education of the Native population. The control which the government exercises in return for its financial assistance is far-reaching. "The liberal support accorded to mission schools and the inclusion of religious teaching in the school curriculum do not alter the fact that the educational system in South Africa is in principle a system of state education" (Oldham and Gibson, op. cit., p. 123).

Previous to 1922 the provincial governments provided the necessary funds. Since 1945, funds for Native education have been drawn from the Consolidated Revenue Fund. The part played by missions and Natives in paying for Native education has never been set down in detail. A large number of schools have not been "registered" by the education departments of the provinces and must necessarily be supported therefore entirely by the missions and Natives. In 1935 missions contributed 12 per cent of the cost of educating each child in primary schools and 13.5 per cent in all schools.

The fundamental fact in the government-Native education relationship is the constitutional provision (85iii) that all higher education (defined in Sec. 17 of Act 38 of 1945 to include the university colleges, South African Native College, technical, mining, etc.) shall be under control of the Union Department of Education and all other education under control of the four provincial governments. The legislative authority in regard to Native education therefore lies in the provincial councils of the provinces and the administration in the hands of the head of the provincial education department. In each province there is an advisory board on which representatives of the missions controlling schools are strongly represented.

In the Cape many managers of Native schools are Native ministers, while in the other provinces the usual requirement is that the managers be Europeans nominated by the mission concerned (P. A. W. Cook, "Non-European Education," in *Handbook on Race Relations in South Africa*, ed. Ellen Hellmann [Cape Town, London, New York: Oxford University Press, 1949], chap. xv, pp. 362–65).

88. Ernest Gideon Malherbe, *Education in South Africa* (1652–1922) (Cape Town and Johannesburg: Juta, 1925), p. 109 and n. 19, p. 110. "Most of the spade-work in educating the Bantu has been done by the various English-speaking churches" (A. J. Friedgut, "The Non-European Press," in *Handbook on Race Relations in South Africa*, ed. Ellen Hellmann, chap. xx, p. 501).

89. A. W. Blaxall, "South Africa Belongs to Us," *International Review of Missions*, XXXVIII (July, 1949), 302. In the Union the church conducts its mission work largely among the Hottentots and Colored people.

90. *Ibid.*, p. 302.

91. In 1936 the Christian Council of South Africa was established as a co-ordinating agency of the Christian forces of the country. This council represents interchurch and interracial co-operation. Non-

Europeans take full part in its discussions and serve on its council and executive committee. For an excellent article dealing with the formation of the Christian Council of South Africa and its doctrinal differences with the Dutch Reformed churches see Robert H. W. Shepherd and Edward W. Grant, "The Christian Council of South Africa," *International Review of Missions,* XXXIII (July, 1944), 258–66.

92. The two churches withdrew in April, 1941.

93. Shepherd and Grant, *op. cit.,* p. 258.

94. *Ibid.,* p. 259.

95. *Ibid.,* pp. 259–60.

96. *Ibid.,* p. 260. Reverend Nicol has correctly pointed out that, had the other churches of the federated Dutch Reformed churches co-operated in joining the Christian Council of South Africa, they together with the sympathetic German societies (the Berlin, the Rhine, the Moravian, and the Hermannsburg societies) would have had sufficient representation to insure the Dutch Reformed church point of view with regard to Native questions.

97. *Ibid.*

98. William Nicol, "Why the Christian Council Failed," a translation of a report published in the *Transvaler* (October 23, 1941) and appearing in the *South African Outlook,* LXXI (December 1, 1941), 251.

CHAPTER IV

1. The official policy of the United party toward the Native and Colored races is presented in "Policy of the United Party towards Natives and Coloureds," *Weekly Newsletter,* No. 462 (October 11, 1948), p. 7. See also "United Party Summarizes Its Native Policy," *Weekly Newsletter,* No. 479 (February 12, 1949), p. 8.

2. Leonard Barnes, *Caliban in Africa* (Philadelphia: J. B. Lippincott, 1931), p. 45.

CHAPTER V

1. Alastair Matheson, *The Coloured People of the Cape* (London: Public Relations Office, South Africa House), p. 7.

2. *Ibid.*

3. Report, 1938, of the Commission of Inquiry regarding the Cape Coloured population, as quoted *ibid.,* p. 8.

4. R. F. A. Hoernlé, *Race and Reason* (Johannesburg: Witwatersrand University Press, 1945), p. 69.

5. Matheson, *op. cit.,* p. 7.

6. *Ibid.,* p. 8. Since the 1946 census figures were published, the Union government has issued supplementary figures placing the Colored population at one million.

7. "Apartheid on Cape Trains," *Weekly Newsletter,* No. 455 (August 23, 1948), p. 7.

8. Matheson, *op. cit.,* p. 11.

9. *Ibid.,* pp. 50–51. On September 11, 1950, the death of General Smuts was announced. On September 28, 1950, Mr. J. G. N. Strauss, M.P., was elected to succeed the late general as chairman of the United party.

10. "Prime Minister Pledges Racial Co-operation," *Weekly Newsletter,* No. 446 (June 21, 1948), p. 6.

11. South Africa Act (1909), Secs. 33, 34, 35, 36, 137, and 152.

12. *Ibid.,* Sec. 35, as amended by Sec. 44 of Act 12 of 1936.

13. W. P. M. Kennedy and H. J. Schlosberg, *The Law and Custom of the South African Constitution* (London: Oxford University Press, 1935), p. 197.

14. South Africa Act (1909), Sec. 36.

15. "Nationalist Non-European Policy," *Weekly Newsletter,* No. 478 (January 29, 1949), p. 3.

16. "Proposed Abolition of Native Representation," *Weekly Newsletter,* No. 445 (August 23, 1948), p. 7.

17. "Dr. Malan Reiterates His Colour Policy," *Weekly Newsletter,* No. 470 (December 4, 1948), p. 2b.

18. "Decision on 'Entrenched Clauses,' " *Weekly Newsletter,* No. 478 (January 29, 1949), p. 2.

19. *Ibid.* It should be noted that the Status of the Union Act (1934) requires that an imperial act, i.e., an act of the Parliament of Great Britain, such as the South Africa Act originally was, in order to be applicable to the Union, must be re-enacted by the Union government. The principle is thus maintained that, in matters concerning the Union, a British statute can no longer be repugnant to a Union statute. The English Parliament therefore has no role as regards Union legislation, i.e., statute law or the repeal or amendment of the South Africa Act (see Alexander Brady, *Democracy in the Dominions* [Toronto: University of Toronto Press], pp. 327–28). See also Sec. 59 of the South Africa Act and Sec. 2 of the Statute of Westminster, 1931.

As far as judicial review in constitutional enforcement is concerned, the most prevalent theory has been that the courts of South Africa cannot declare any portion of an act of Parliament unconstitutional and therefore void because it does not conform to the provisions of the South Africa Act. "If a later act of Parliament is inconsistent with the South Africa Act, the Court may hold that the later act impliedly varies such portion of the South Africa Act as is inconsistent with the later act. The court cannot say that acts of Parliament must be interpreted as to conform to the South Africa Act and that no other interpretation is admissible" (Kennedy and Schlosberg, *op. cit.,* p. 104). Such is no longer true, however, according to the recent Colored vote case decided by the Supreme

Court on March 20, 1952. The case is described later in this chapter.

20. "Dr. Malan Reiterates His Colour Policy," *op. cit.*, p. 2b.

21. Kennedy and Schlosberg, *op. cit.*, p. 103.

22. *Ibid.* Kennedy and Schlosberg, while not recognizing limitations on Parliament, regarded this resolution as "the rudiment of what may become a new kind of constitutional convention" (p. 102). (Italics mine.) See R. W. Parsons, "Status of Parliament and Entrenched Clauses," *Cape Times*, March 16, 1951, p. 8.

23. "Dr. Malan on the Registration of Coloured Voters," *Weekly Newsletter*, No. 487 (April 2, 1949), p. 1.

24. *Ibid.*

25. Matheson, *op. cit.*, p. 9.

26. *Ibid.*

27. *Ibid.*

28. "Smuts on 'Entrenched Clauses,'" *Weekly Newsletter*, No. 478 (January 29, 1949), p. 2.

29. "The Doctrine of Apartheid," *Round Table*, XXXIX (December, 1948), 34.

30. See Preface, p. vii.

31. "Havenga States Afrikaner Party Policy," *Weekly Newsletter*, No. 470 (December 4, 1948), p. 1.

32. *Ibid.*, pp. 1–2.

33. Quoted *ibid.*, p. 2.

34. *Ibid.*, p. 2a.

35. *Ibid.*

36. *Ibid.*

37. *Ibid.*, p. 2b.

38. "Government Leaders Explain Legislative Programme," *Weekly Newsletter*, No. 524 (December 17, 1949), p. 1.

39. Henry John May, *The South African Constitution* (Cape Town and Johannesburg: Juta, 1949), pp. 17–18.

40. Since 1936 the Cape has been divided into two electoral districts from which the Natives elect two members of the Cape Provincial Council. Indians, as well as Coloreds, in the Cape who possess the qualifications for the parliamentary franchise vote on the common roll in provincial elections. Members of the provincial councils are required to be European. However, the Asiatic Land Tenure and Indian Representation Act of 1946 provided, in part, that Natal Indians would be represented by two members, who may be Indians, on the Natal Provincial Council. This is the first instance in which non-Europeans have been admitted to membership on higher legislative bodies in the Union. This provision has remained theoretical, however, since the provisions in that act for Indian representation in the House of Assembly were repealed in 1948.

41. "Government Leaders Explain Legislative Programme," *op. cit.*, p. 1.

42. "Union of South Africa. Debate in House of Assembly," *Journal of the Parliaments of the Commonwealth*, XXXI (June, 1950), 335.

43. "Dr. Malan and Mr. Havenga Reach Agreement," *Weekly Newsletter*, No. 567 (October 21, 1950), pp. 2–3.

44. The *Star*, February 13, 1951, as quoted in "The Coloured Franchise," *Race Relations News* (published by the South African Institute of Race Relations), XIII (March, 1951), 41.

45. There is considerable Colored hostility to the proposed Coloreds Representative Council. This is identical with Colored hostility toward the Colored Advisory Council set up by the government in 1943. The Colored Advisory Council consisted of twenty members appointed by the government and was to provide, as the Coloreds Representative Council is meant to provide, more adequate channels for airing grievances of the Coloreds and placing their case before the authorities. The creation of the Colored Advisory Council produced the deepest political division which has yet occurred among the Colored people. Its establishment was seen by the opposing forces to be the forerunner of intensified segregation. It was felt that the segregationist parties would use the council as a starting point for removal of the Coloreds from the common roll, residential segregation in the Cape between Europeans and Coloreds, and tighter restrictions generally. After the Nationalist party assumed power in 1948, the council, though it did useful work, was seized by political antipathy, and the members resigned in a body on January 6, 1949, on the issue of apartheid and removal of Coloreds from the common roll.

46. "Havenga States Afrikaner Party Policy," *op. cit.*, p. 1.

47. John Hatch, "Malan Sows the Wind," *New Statesman and Nation*, XLI (April 28, 1951), 472.

48. *Ibid.* For a more detailed presentation of Hertzog's opposition to Malan's Colored policy see "Faithlessness the Guiding Line," *South African Outlook*, LXXX (November 1, 1950), 165–67.

49. The South African Institute of Race Relations, without a color bar and with non-Europeans on its national councils, is affiliated with no political creed or political party. It is, however, affiliated with the larger municipalities, the English-speaking universities, churches, missions, and other organizations. The Institute was established in 1929 under grants by the Carnegie Corporation and the Phelps-Stokes Fund of New York.

In September, 1948, the Suid-Afrikaanse Buro vir Rasseaangeleenthede (the South African Bureau of Race Relations), commonly known as "SABRA," was formed. This is primarily an Afrikaner society devoted to the study of race relations. Its members include distinguished academicians and prominent Nationalist party members and cabinet officers. The bureau supports a policy of "total apartheid."

50. "The Coloured Franchise," *Race Relations News*, XIII (January, 1951), 8.

51. The *Star*, February 12, 1951, as quoted in "The Coloured Franchise," *Race Relations News*, XIII (March, 1951), 39. (Italics mine.)

52. *Die Transvaler*, February 13, 1951, as quoted *ibid.*, pp. 39–40. The Nationalists eventually relented on this point, however. During the second reading of the bill in the House of Assembly the government added amendments which provided that Colored voters in Natal would not be removed from the common roll and would continue to exercise their existing rights in parliamentary and provincial elections. While the original measure provided for a separate voters' roll for the Colored people of the Cape and Natal, these amendments stipulated that any European or non-European in Natal who is registered as a voter at the date when the bill becomes law will continue to be so registered as long as he retains his qualifications in terms of the Electoral Act and remains resident in the province.

53. *Ibid.*, p. 40.

54. *Ibid.*

55. *Ibid.*, p. 41.

56. *Ibid.*

57. Technically, the "new party" adopted the name "National party." This was not successful in the Union, however, and continued use of the terms "Nationalist party" and "HNP" was but a manifestation of political reality.

58. "Final Stages of Coloured Voters' Bill," *South Africa Reports, May 31, 1951* (Union of South African Government Information Office, New York), p. 3.

59. *Ibid.* The speaker had earlier rejected the contention that the proposed bill could only be considered by a joint sitting (unicamerally) of both houses of Parliament (see "Speaker's Ruling on Franchise Legislation in House of Assembly on April 11, 1951," *Special Bulletin* [Pretoria: Information Office]). For an analysis of the speaker's ruling in relation to the constitution see T. W. Price, "Speaker's Ruling Not Last Word on Vote Bill," *Cape Times*, May 8, 1951, p. 8.

60. For the full text of the ruling see "President Rules Senate Competent To Discuss Vote Bill," *Cape Times*, May 25, 1951, pp. 2, 5. For comment on the ruling see "President's Ruling," *Cape*

Times, May 25, 1951, p. 8. Senator G. Heaton Nicholls, leader of the Opposition in the Senate, took the step of giving notice of motion dissenting from the ruling of the president. This indicated that the mover did not agree with the president's ruling, and, while not necessarily a motion of no confidence, it is an unusual and serious step to take. There was no precedent for such an action in the Union Senate, and the device has been used only a few times in the House. The status of the president is not affected in any way. The Senate later rejected the motion.

61. The duties of the parliamentary draftsman are to see that all bills and their provisions contain proper legal bearing on existing legislation which such bills purport to amend, alter, or repeal. His advice is directed to the speaker of the House and the president of the Senate. There is no obligation on the part of the speaker or president to accept the opinion.

62. The full text of Mr. Piennaar's opinion laid before the Senate on May 18, 1951, appears in "Piennaar's Opinion on Vote Bill," *Cape Times,* May 19, 1951, pp. 1, 3. The speaker of the House had earlier expressed the view that the bill would be recognized by the courts as a valid and legally binding act (see "Union of South Africa. Representation of Non-European Bill," *Journal of the Parliaments of the Commonwealth,* XXXII [July, 1951], 341–47).

63. "S. A. Ex-Soldiers' Manifesto," *Cape Times,* May 16, 1951, p. 1.

64. "South Africa. Sailor *v.* Premier," *Time,* LVIII (July 9, 1951), 24. Active membership in the Torch Commando probably does not exceed 175,000 members. A significant statement has been issued by the National Executive of the Torch Commando concerning non-European membership: "In the same way as the framers of the Act of Union recognized that different local conditions determine different local policies, so does the W.V.T.C. Its constitution permits each region to decide its own policy on the question of non-European membership. As our chief weapon is the vote, the paramount factor differentiating conditions in one locality from those in another is the possession by the non-European of the franchise. In the light of this it is felt that at present no useful purpose could be served by the admission of non-Europeans as members, or the formation of non-European branches in those localities where the non-European cannot exercise the franchise. On the other hand, in those localities where non-Europeans such as the Cape Coloured in the Cape exercise the franchise, the National Executive approves the policy that separate branches may be formed" ("Torchmen Set Out on Union Tour for Recruits," *Sunday Times* [Johannesburg], October 14, 1951, p. 16).

65. *Ndlwana v. Hofmeyr,* 1937 A.D. 229.

66. Selected excerpts from pp. 22–23 of the full and certified text of the decision forwarded to the author by the Union of South Africa Government Information Office, New York. Professor D. V. Cowen, dean of the Faculty of Law, University of Cape Town, in strong disagreement with the conclusions reached by the government's law advisers and the views expressed by constitutional commentators W. Pollak, K.C., Advocate R. S. Welsh, Henry John May, and Dr. H. Verloren van Themaat, published an essay in 1951 in which he contended that, should the question of efficacy of the entrenched clauses come squarely before the Appeal Court, the Court need not and should not be fettered by the decision in *Ndlwana* v. *Hofmeyr*. Like the Court in its 1952 decision, he declared that the present efficacy of the entrenched clauses is in no way incompatible with the sovereign status of South Africa or with the sovereignty of the Union Parliament, and the Statute of Westminster left unaffected the manner and form of the legislating powers of the Union Parliament. See D. V. Cowen, *Parliamentary Sovereignty and the Entrenched Sections of the South Africa Act* (Cape Town: Juta & Co., 1951). This essay was relied on and quoted extensively by the leader of the Opposition during debate on the pending Separate Representation of Voters Bill.

67. "Appeal Court Declares Voters' Act Invalid," *South African News Cable*, March 20, 1952, pp. 83–84.

68. "Legislation To Ensure Parliament's Sovereignty," *South African News Cable*, March 22, 1952, p. 85.

69. "Warning to Malan Given by Veterans," *New York Times*, April 28, 1952, p. 8. Conversely, the Nationalists have been accused of forming a private army (*Skietkommando*). The Torch Commando is reported to be following a three-point plan of action to resist the government's moves: (1) fighting the government constitutionally by arousing the public through a series of nation-wide rallies in the hope of putting Dr. Malan on the road to defeat in the 1953 general election; (2) meeting unconstitutional action by unconstitutional means (these means have not been disclosed but are generally recognized to stop short of civil war—"unless the other side starts one"); and (3) resisting "any move by the Government against the Torch Commando" even if this means going underground.

70. "Government Attitude to Cape Coloured People," *Weekly Newsletter*, No. 463 (October 18, 1948), p. 7.

71. "Cape Coloured People May Appeal to U.N. against Segregation," *Weekly Newsletter*, No. 458 (September 13, 1948), 8.

72. Article II, Sec. 7, of the United Nations Charter provides: "Nothing contained in the present Charter shall authorise the

United Nations to intervene in matters which are essentially within the domestic jurisdiction of any state or shall require the members to submit such matters to settlement under the present Charter. . . ."

73. "Prime Minister Outlines Non-European Policy," *Weekly Newsletter*, No. 457 (September 6, 1948), p. 7.

74. *Ibid.*

75. *Ibid.*

76. "Union of South Africa, Native Legislation; 'Apartheid.'" *Journal of the Parliaments of the Empire*, XXIX (December, 1948), 641–42.

77. Known as the Mixed Marriages Act.

78. "Ban on Mixed Marriages," *Weekly Newsletter*, No. 494 (May 21, 1949), p. 2A.

79. *Ibid.*

80. "Registration for All Races in Union," *Weekly Newsletter*, No. 468 (November 20, 1948), p. 8.

81. The Immorality Act, passed in 1927, prohibits extramarital intercourse between Europeans and Non-Europeans.

82. "National Registration Bill," *Weekly Newsletter*, No. 536 (March 11, 1950), p. 3.

83. *Ibid.*

84. *Ibid.*, p. 4.

85. "Union of South Africa. Population Registration Bill," *Journal of the Parliaments of the Commonwealth*, XXXI (June, 1950), 339.

86. *Ibid.*, pp. 339–40.

87. "Population Registration Bill To Help Non-Europeans," *Weekly Newsletter*, No. 537 (March 18, 1950), p. 8.

88. "Union of South Africa. Population Registration Bill," *op. cit.*, pp. 341–42.

89. Hoernlé, *Race and Reason*, p. 67.

90. *Ibid.*

91. *Ibid.*, p. 68.

92. " 'Apartheid' on Cape Trains," *op. cit.*, p. 7.

93. "Cape Coloured People May Appeal to U.N. against Segregation," *op. cit.*, p. 8.

94. "New Coloured Council Supports Prime Minister's Policy," *Weekly Newsletter*, No. 464 (October 25, 1948), p. 7.

CHAPTER VI

1. "Prime Minister Addresses Natives," *Weekly Newsletter*, No. 465 (November 1, 1948), p. 7.

2. I. S. Lloyd, " 'Apartheid'—South Africa's New Native Policy," *Political Quarterly*, XX (April–June, 1949), 129.

3. Gerald W. Broomfield, *Colour Conflict, Race Relations in Africa* (London: Edinburgh House Press, 1934), p. 88.

4. *Ibid.*, p. 89.

5. *Ibid.*

6. *Ibid.*

7. "Statement of Policy," *Native Policy of the Union of South Africa: Statements by Dr. the Honourable E. G. Jansen, Minister of Native Affairs* (issued by the State Information Office, Pretoria, Union of South Africa), p. 4.

8. "Tribal Organization," *ibid.*, p. 8.

9. Lloyd, *op. cit.*, p. 129.

10. *Ibid.*

11. Broomfield, *op. cit.*, p. 89.

12. *Ibid.*

13. Dudley Kidd, *Kafir Socialism and the Dawn of Individualism: An Introduction to the Study of the Native Problem* (London: Adams & Charles Black, 1908), p. 46.

14. *Ibid.*, pp. 4–5.

15. I. Schapera, "Political Institutions," in *The Bantu-speaking Tribes of South Africa: An Ethnological Survey*, ed. I. Schapera (London: George Routledge & Sons, 1937), chap. viii, p. 173.

16. *Ibid.*

17. *Ibid.*

18. Kidd, *op. cit.*, p. 5.

19. *Ibid.*, p. 9.

20. *Ibid.*, p. 11.

21. Schapera, *op. cit.*, p. 174.

22. Thus the Nguni group comprises hundreds of tribes living in the Reserves between the Drakensburg escarpment and the sea, in the Cape Province, Natal, and the Transvaal. The Sotho group includes the Bantu in Basutoland and those living in Reserves in the western and portions of the northern Transvaal. The Shangana-Tonga group are found mostly in the northeastern Transvaal. Smaller groups are the Venda and the Lemba. (L. Marquard, *The Native in South Africa* [Johannesburg: Witwatersrand University Press, 1948], pp. 5–6).

23. Schapera, *op. cit.*, pp. 174–79.

24. Diedrich Westermann, *The African Today and Tomorrow* (rev. ed.; London: Oxford University Press [H. Milford], 1939), p. 164.

25. Schapera, *op. cit.*, pp. 181–83.

26. *Ibid.*, p. 184.

27. Kidd, *op. cit.*, p. 5.

28. *Ibid.*

29. *Ibid.*

30. *Ibid.*
31. Schapera, *op. cit.*, p. 184.
32. *Ibid.*, p. 185. Hoernlé states that the membership of a tribe is determined more by allegiance to a chief than by birth and that the unity of the tribe depends on the common loyalty of the tribesmen toward him. A popular chief will therefore gradually enlarge his tribe by accession of refugees from other tribes, while an unpopular chief will lose his adherents (A. Winifred Hoernlé, "Social Organization," in *The Bantu-speaking Tribes of South Africa: An Ethnological Survey*, ed. I. Schapera [London: George Routledge & Sons, 1937], chap. iv, pp. 68–69).
33. Schapera, *op. cit.*, pp. 185–87.
34. *Ibid.*, p. 187.
35. Kidd, *op. cit.*, p. 42.
36. *Ibid.*, pp. 44–45.
37. Westermann, *op. cit.*, p. 171.
38. *Ibid.*, pp. 166–67.
39. Native Administration Act (1927), Sec. 1. The powers of the supreme chief are found in the Natal Native Code of 1891. The relevant sections of this code are presented in Henry John May, *The South African Constitution* (Cape Town and Johannesburg: Juta, 1949), pp. 309–12.
40. *Ibid.*, pp. 335–36.
41. In other than purely Native cases, however, Natives in both civil and criminal matters are subject to the ordinary laws and courts of the land. Further details on the organization and functions of the Native courts are presented in *Official Yearbook of the Union and of Basutoland, Bechuanaland Protectorate and Swaziland* (Pretoria: Union Office of Census and Statistics, 1948), No. 24, pp. 426–28; H. J. Simons, "The Law and Its Administration," in *Handbook on Race Relations in South Africa*, ed. Ellen Hellmann (Cape Town, London, New York: Oxford University Press, 1949), chap. iv, pp. 41–108. See also May, *op. cit.*, pp. 336–37.
42. May, *op. cit.*, pp. 333–37.
43. "Minister Outlines Government Non-European Policy," *Weekly Newsletter*, No. 458 (September 13, 1948), p. 7.
44. Minister Appeals for Goodwill between Black and White," *Weekly Newsletter*, No. 572 (November 25, 1950), p. 9; "Minister Explains Apartheid to Native Council," *Weekly Newsletter*, No. 574 (December 9, 1950), p. 7.
45. "Bunga Spends £300,000 Annually on Native Services," *Weekly Newsletter*, No. 479 (February 12, 1949), p. 7; "Government Is Planning More Native Councils," *Weekly Newsletter*, No. 467 (November 15, 1948), p. 8; "Bunga Does Not Make Full Use of Its Powers," *Weekly Newsletter*, No. 494 (May 21, 1949), p. 7.

A particularly valuable Nationalist government publication on Native policy is the pamphlet entitled *Native Policy of the Union of South Africa: Statements by Dr. the Honourable E. G. Jansen, Minister of Native Affairs* (issued by the State Information Office, Pretoria, Union of South Africa).

46. "Plans for Developing Union's Native Reserves," *Weekly Newsletter*, No. 457 (September 6, 1948), p. 8.

47. Howard Rogers, *Native Administration in the Union of South Africa* (Johannesburg: University of the Witwatersrand Press, 1933), p. 185.

48. Lloyd, *op. cit.*, p. 131.

49. Ifor L. Evans, *Native Policy in Southern Africa: An Outline* (Cambridge: University Press, 1934), p. 37.

50. *Ibid.*

51. "Native in Pretoria To Be Strictly Controlled," *Weekly Newsletter*, No. 471 (December 11, 1948), p. 8.

52. *Ibid.*

53. "The Doctrine of Apartheid," *Round Table*, XXXIX (December, 1948), 33.

54. Broomfield, *op. cit.*, pp. 90–91.

55. *Ibid.*, p. 29.

56. *Ibid.*

57. Lloyd, *op. cit.*, p. 130.

58. The report of the Commission on Native Laws as quoted *ibid,*. p. 131.

59. Broomfield, *op. cit.*, p. 30.

60. *Ibid.*

61. *Ibid.*

62. "Proposed Abolition of Native Representation," *Weekly Newsletter*, No. 445 (August 23, 1948), p. 7.

63. Hoernlé as quoted in Broomfield, *op. cit.*, p. 91.

64. One morgen is equal to 2.1 acres.

65. Lloyd, *op. cit.*, p. 130.

66. *Ibid.*

67. "The Doctrine of Apartheid," *op. cit.*, p. 34.

68. "Secretary Outlines Plans for Developing Reserves," *Weekly Newsletter*, No. 529 (January 21, 1950), p. 7.

69. "Minister Outlines Plans for Native Reserves," *Weekly Newsletter*, No. 547 (May 27, 1950), p. 8.

70. "Secretary Outlines Plans for Developing Reserves," *op. cit.*, p. 7.

71. *Ibid.*, p. 8.

72. *Ibid.*

73. *Ibid.*, pp. 7–8.

74. Monica Hunter, *Reaction to Conquest: Effects of Contact*

with *Europeans on the Pondo of South Africa* (London: Oxford University Press [H. Milford], 1936), p. 69.

75. In the period from October 1, 1943, to September 30, 1944, cattle sold at auction sales organized by the Department of Native Affairs represented less than 1 per cent of the total cattle in the Reserves (Edward Roux, "Land and Agriculture in the Reserves," in *The Handbook on Race Relations in South Africa*, ed. Ellen Hellmann [Cape Town, London, New York: Oxford University Press, 1949], chap. vii, p. 182).

76. "Natives Refuse To Cooperate in O.F.S. Betterment Area," *Weekly Newsletter*, No. 557 (August 5, 1950), p. 9.

77. "Natives Again Begin To Overstock Ciskei," *Weekly Newsletter*, No. 525 (December 24, 1949), p. 4.

78. In 1950 the Department of Native Affairs found it essential to obtain more technical staff for its agricultural branch and to reallocate responsibilities to produce the speediest and most efficient results.

The Union is divided into five areas for purposes of agricultural administration, and the agricultural branch of the Department of Native Affairs is similarly divided. The direction and supervision of Native agricultural work are undertaken by a director. Chief agricultural officers have been appointed to administer such work in the Ciskei, Transkei, Natal, the western areas, and the northern areas. These officers work in collaboration with the chief Native commissioners of the various areas. In each district there are agricultural officers assisted by overseers and Native demonstrators. Under the new system it is hoped that the five areas will be better integrated not only for rehabilitation work but also to give mutual support to each other in time of drought by providing aid to the distressed area.

79. "Secretary Outlines Plans for Developing Reserves," *op. cit.*, p. 8.

80. "Minister Outlines Government Native Policy," *Weekly Newsletter*, No. 494 (May 21, 1949), p. 6.

81. *Ibid.*

82. See "The Black Man's Burden," *Time*, LIV (November 14, 1949), 33, for an account of Native opposition to the extension of the pass laws to Native women.

83. "Government To Press Ahead with Zwelitsha Township," *Weekly Newsletter*, No. 463 (October 18, 1948), p. 8.

84. "Labour Exchange for Natives," *Weekly Newsletter*, No. 482 (February 26, 1949), p. 8.

85. *Ibid.*

86. *Ibid.*

87. "Minister Suggests Service Contracts for Farm Natives," *Weekly Newsletter*, No. 466 (November 8, 1948), p. 8.

88. Of the Union's male Natives, 62.4 per cent have been employed in agriculture for a period of at least ten years, while 86.5 per cent of the females have been so employed. Natives thus form the bulk of the Union's farm labor force except in the western Cape, but even here the number and proportion of Native farm laborers are increasing. For the Colored people agriculture is likewise the principal occupation, 45 per cent of the male population being engaged in it. These figures are from the 1936 occupational census (the latest available) and appear in Sheila T. van der Horst, "Labour," in *Handbook on Race Relations in South Africa*, ed. Ellen Hellmann (Cape Town, London, New York: Oxford University Press, 1949), chap. v, pp. 113–14.

CHAPTER VII

1. "Industrialisation of Native Reserves Advocated," *Weekly Newsletter*, No. 448 (July 5, 1948), p. 6.
2. See "Professor on Afrikanders' Duty towards Natives," *Weekly Newsletter*, No. 472 (December 18, 1948), p. 7.
3. "Factories for Native Areas Suggested," *Weekly Newsletter*, No. 450 (July 19, 1948), p. 8.
4. "New Secretary for Native Affairs," *Weekly Newsletter*, No. 516 (October 22, 1949), p. 8.
5. "State Plan for Rehabilitating Reserves," *Weekly Newsletter*, No. 517 (October 29, 1949), p. 8.
6. "Minister Appeals for Goodwill between White and Black," *Weekly Newsletter*, No. 572 (November 25, 1950), p. 9.
7. This is not to be confused with the Natives Representative Council, which is described in the next chapter. The Native Affairs Commission, established under the Native Affairs Act, No. 23 of 1920, is an advisory body of three to five members appointed by the governor-general and presided over by the minister of Native affairs. The functions and duties of the commissioners include consideration of any matter relating to the general conduct of the administration of Native affairs or to legislation in so far as it may affect the Native population. Its functions are advisory, but adequate means are reserved to it of placing its views before the cabinet and Parliament if its recommendations are not accepted. Membership on the commission may be combined with membership in Parliament.
8. "Government May Form Industrial Development Corporation," *Weekly Newsletter*, No. 577 (January 6, 1951), p. 8.
9. *Ibid.*
10. *Ibid.*

11. "Minister Explains Apartheid to Native Council," *Weekly Newsletter*, No. 574 (December 9, 1950), p. 7.

12. *Ibid.*

13. *Ibid.*

14. "Commission Handicapped in Buying Land for Natives," *Weekly Newsletter*, No. 464 (October 25, 1948), p. 7.

15. G. P. Lestrade, "Some Aspects of the Economic Life of the South African Bantu," *South African Journal of Economics*, II (December, 1934), 427.

16. Ellison Kahn, "Whither Our War-Time Native Policy?" *South African Journal of Economics*, X (June, 1942), 132.

17. I. S. Lloyd, " 'Apartheid'—South Africa's New Native Policy," *Political Quarterly*, XX (April–June, 1949), 131.

18. *Ibid.*

19. Leslie Blackwell and Henry John May, *This Is South Africa* (Pietermaritzburg: Shuter & Shooter, 1947), pp. 140–41.

20. *Ibid.*

21. *Ibid.*, p. 141.

22. Gerald W. Broomfield, *Colour Conflict, Race Relations in Africa* (London: Edinburgh House Press, 1943), p. 91.

23. Lloyd, *op. cit.*, p. 129.

24. Evidence to the Commission on Native Laws by the Gold Producers Committee of the Transvaal Chamber of Mines as presented *ibid.*, p. 132.

25. *Ibid.*, pp. 131–32. Obviously there is a split within the Transvaal Chamber of Mines on the merits of the migratory labor system.

26. "Housing Plans," *Native Policy of the Union of South Africa: Statements by Dr. the Honourable E. G. Jansen, Minister of Native Affairs* (issued by the State Information Office, Pretoria, Union of South Africa), pp. 9–10.

CHAPTER VIII

1. "Proposed Abolition of Native Representation," *Weekly Newsletter*, No. 445 (August 23, 1948), p. 7.

2. Prior to 1936 the Cape Natives enjoyed the franchise along with the Coloreds and Europeans. In 1935 there were 10,628 Native voters scattered in some twenty constituencies and controlling ten seats. In 1936, however, the "entrenched clauses" relating to alteration of electoral privileges were made inoperative in the case of the Union Native. A measure passing the requisite joint sitting of both houses by the two-thirds majority stipulated in the South Africa Act removed the Cape Natives from the common roll and instead substituted communal representation, with three Euro-

pean members in the House of Assembly and four in the Senate indirectly elected by the Natives by means of four electoral colleges each representing an electoral area. In 1945 there were 24,084 Natives on the communal roll in the Cape. The increase in Native voters is due to lowered qualifications put into effect after communal representation was introduced.

3. "Nationalist Non-European Policy," *Weekly Newsletter*, No. 478 (January 29, 1949), p. 3.

4. "Native Representation May Be Issue at Provincial Elections," *Weekly Newsletter*, No. 460 (September 27, 1948), p. 6.

5. "Government To Press Ahead with Zwelitsha Township," *Weekly Newsletter*, No. 463 (October 18, 1948), p. 7.

6. J. S. Marais, "The Imposition and Nature of European Control," in *The Bantu-speaking Tribes of South Africa: An Ethnological Survey*, ed. I. Schapera (London: George Routledge & Sons, 1937), chap. xv, pp. 351–52.

7. *Ibid.*, p. 352.

8. Howard Rogers, *Native Administration in the Union of South Africa* (Johannesburg: University of the Witwatersrand Press, 1933), p. 58.

9. L. Marquard, *The Native in South Africa* (Johannesburg: Witwatersrand University Press, 1948), p. 19.

10. Marais, *op. cit.*, p. 353.

11. Rogers, *op. cit.*, p. 57.

12. Marquard, *op. cit.*, p. 20.

13. Walter Fitzgerald, *Africa: A Social, Economic and Political Geography of Its Major Regions* (London: Methuen, 1948), pp. 204–6.

14. Marquard, *op. cit.*, pp. 20–21.

15. For a detailed description of the various types of Native local government organs see Henry John May, *The South African Constitution* (Cape Town and Johannesburg: Juta & Co., 1949), chap. xiv: "Local Government of the Natives," pp. 325–38.

16. "Third Native General Council May Be Formed," *Weekly Newsletter*, No. 491 (April 30, 1949), p. 8.

17. "Minister Outlines Plans To Tackle Native Problem," *Weekly Newsletter*, No. 578 (January 13, 1951), p. 8.

18. Ifor L. Evans, *Native Policy in Southern Africa: An Outline* (Cambridge: At the University Press, 1934), p. 5.

19. *Ibid.*

20. Raymond Leslie Buell, *The Native Problem in Africa* (New York: Macmillan Co., 1928), I, 105–10.

21. Leonard Barnes, *Caliban in Africa* (Philadelphia: J. B. Lippincott, 1931), p. 219.

22. "Bunga Spends £300,000 Annually on Native Services," *Weekly Newsletter*, No. 479 (February 12, 1949), p. 7.

23. "Government Is Planning More Native Councils," *Weekly Newsletter*, No. 467 (November 15, 1948), p. 8.

24. "Minister Reviews Native Policy," *Weekly Newsletter*, No. 493 (May 14, 1949), p. 7.

25. "Tribal Organization," *Native Policy of the Union of South Africa: Statements by Dr. the Honourable E. G. Jansen, Minister of Native Affairs* (issued by the State Information Office, Pretoria, Union of South Africa), p. 8. (Italics mine.)

26. *Ibid.*

27. "Urban Life," *ibid.*, p. 9.

28. "Natives' Representative Council Adjourns," *Weekly Newsletter*, No. 475 (December 8, 1949), p. 7. See also "Government Is Planning More Native Councils," *op. cit.*, p. 8; "Natives' Representative Council Not To Meet," *Weekly Newsletter*, No. 527 (January 7, 1949), p. 4.

29. The body as set up consists of the secretary for Native affairs as chairman, six assessor members, being the six chief Native commissioners of the Union, and sixteen full members, all Natives, four of whom are nominated by the government and twelve of whom are elected from the four electoral districts which return the four senators representing all of the Union's Natives in the Senate.

30. The 1936 Land Act set up the trust as the authority, by means of parliamentary grants, to acquire land for Native occupation to be added to that already scheduled in the 1913 Natives Land Act.

31. Edgar H. Brookes, "Government and Administration," *Handbook on Race Relations in South Africa*, ed. Ellen Hellmann (Cape Town, London, New York: Oxford University Press, 1949), chap. iii, p. 31.

32. *Ibid.*

33. *Ibid.*

34. "Deficiencies of Natives' Representative Council," *Weekly Newsletter*, No. 445 (August 23, 1948), p. 8.

35. "Natives' Representative Council Adjourns," *Weekly Newsletter*, No. 475 (December 8, 1949), p. 7.

36. *Ibid.*

37. "Natives' Representative Council Adjourns," *Weekly Newsletter*, No. 575 (December 15, 1950), p. 8.

38. "Minister's Comments on Council's Decision," *Weekly Newsletter*, No. 575 (December 15, 1950), p. 8.

39. "Minister To Summon Natives' Council," *Weekly Newsletter*, No. 546 (May 20, 1950), p. 8.

40. "Government Is Planning More Native Councils," *op. cit.*, p. 8.

41. "Ciskei Bunga Asks Retention of Natives' Representative Council," *Weekly Newsletter*, No. 516 (October 22, 1949), p. 9.

42. "Minister Outlines Plans for Native Councils," _Weekly Newsletter,_ No. 550 (June 17, 1950), p. 8.
43. _Ibid._
44. May, _op. cit.,_ p. 325.
45. "Minister Appeals for Goodwill between Black and White," _Weekly Newsletter,_ No. 572 (November 25, 1950), p. 8.
46. "Tribal Organization," _op. cit.,_ p. 8.
47. Sir Charles Dundas, "Apartheid and the Union," _Nineteenth Century and After,_ CXLVIII (October, 1950), 229.
48. _Ibid._
49. "Tribal Organization," _op. cit.,_ p. 8.
50. Dundas, _op. cit.,_ p. 229.
51. May, _op. cit.,_ pp. 248–49.
52. "Union of South Africa. Privy Council Appeals Bill," _Journal of the Parliaments of the Commonwealth,_ XXXI (June, 1950), 324.
53. _Ibid._
54. _Ibid.,_ pp. 323–24.
55. "Minister Outlines Government Non-European Policy," _Weekly Newsletter,_ No. 458 (September 13, 1948), p. 6.
56. "Prime Minister Tells How Coloreds Will Benefit under Apartheid," _Weekly Newsletter,_ No. 469 (November 27, 1948), p. 9.
57. _Weekly Newsletter,_ No. 465 (August 30, 1948), p. 8.
58. "Proposed Legislation Affecting Urban Natives," _Weekly Newsletter,_ No. 525 (December 24, 1949), p. 4.
59. "Prime Minister Tells How Coloreds Will Benefit under Apartheid," _op. cit.,_ p. 9.
60. "Group Areas Bill Passed in Assembly," _Weekly Newsletter,_ No. 548 (June 3, 1950), p. 2.
61. "Union of South Africa. Group Areas Bill," _Journal of the Parliaments of the Commonwealth,_ XXXI (September, 1950), 585–86.
62. "Group Areas Bill Passed in Assembly," _op. cit.,_ p. 2.
63. "Group Areas Measure Amended," _Weekly Newsletter,_ No. 549 (June 10, 1950), p. 2.
64. "Union of South Africa. Group Areas Bill," _op. cit.,_ p. 593.
65. _Ibid.,_ p. 586.
66. "How Group Areas Act Will Be Applied," _Weekly Newsletter,_ No. 565 (October 7, 1950), p. 8.
67. "Use and Training of Native Builders," _Weekly Newsletter,_ No. 537 (March 8, 1950), p. 9; see also "Native Building Workers Bill Published," _Weekly Newsletter,_ No. 518 (November 5, 1949), p. 7.
68. "Unemployment Insurance Ceases for Africans," _South African Outlook,_ LXXX (February 1, 1950), 19–20.

69. "The Doctrine of Apartheid," *Round Table*, XXXIX (June, 1949), 212.

70. Gerald W. Broomfield, *Colour Conflict, Race Relations in Africa* (London: Edinburgh House Press, 1943), p. 97. Broomfield refers to Smuts's "Rhodes Lectures" as indicative of this early support of such a Native policy and to his *The Basis of Trusteeship* (1942) as indicative of his later opposition to it.

71. Broomfield, *op. cit.*, p. 97.

72. The two most prominent works in the Afrikaans language on the subject of apartheid are G. Cronjé, *Voogdyskap en Apartheid* (Pretoria: J. L. van Schaik, 1948), and G. Cronjé, William Nicol, and E. P. Groenwald, *Regverdige Rasseapartheid* (Stellenbosch: Christen Studentevereniging van Suid Afrika, 1947).

73. "Apartheid Opposed," *Weekly Newsletter*, No. 462 (October 11, 1948), p. 7.

74. "The Protest Day Fiasco," *South African Outlook*, LXXX (July 1, 1950), 101.

75. "Considerable Native Support for Apartheid Policy," *Weekly Newsletter*, No. 578 (January 13, 1951), p. 9.

76. "Native Teacher Asks for Fair Trial of Apartheid," *Weekly Newsletter*, No. 463 (October 18, 1948), p. 7.

CHAPTER IX

1. "Minister Outlines Cabinet Policy to Indians," *Weekly Newsletter*, No. 470 (December 4, 1948), p. 6.

2. Maurice Webb, "Indian Land Legislation," in *Handbook on Race Relations in South Africa*, ed. Ellen Hellmann (Cape Town, London, New York: Oxford University Press, 1949), chap. ix, p. 206.

3. *Ibid.*, pp. 206–13. This chapter provides a concise history of European land legislation directed against pre-Union and post-Union Indian land holdings from 1891 to the present day. See Bhaskar Appasamy, *Indians of South Africa* (Bombay: Padma Publications, 1943), for a history of anti-Indian land legislation in the Union written from the Indian point of view.

4. Appasamy, *op. cit.*, p. 46.

5. Webb, *op. cit.*, p. 208.

6. The act provides for nomination by the governor-general-in-council of a senator on the ground mainly of his thorough acquaintance by reason of his official experience or otherwise with the reasonable wants and wishes of Indians in the provinces of Natal and the Transvaal. In addition, one senator is, in terms of the Indian Representation Act, to be elected to represent the Indians of Natal and Transvaal. He, however, has to be directly elected by those

Indians possessing the qualifications laid down in the act: (1) Union nationality, (2) age of twenty-one, (3) Standard VI (or for the first year of registration Standard IV), and, lastly, possession of an income of not less than £84 per annum or immovable property to the value of not less than £250. Three members of the House of Assembly are to represent the Indians of Natal and the Transvaal under the 1946 Act.

7. In 1891 the Orange Free State enacted a law which prohibited Indian occupation or purchase of land within the republic. This law, together with the ban on the entry of Indians into the Orange Free State, has meant that virtually no Indians have entered the territory. The total number of Indians in the Orange Free State was fourteen according to the 1946 census, a decrease of fifteen since the previous census in 1936.

8. Webb, op. cit., p. 210.

9. See n. 6 above.

10. R. M. de Villiers, "Politics," in Handbook on Race Relations in South Africa, ed. Ellen Hellmann (Cape Town, London, New York: Oxford University Press, 1949), chap. xxi, p. 531.

11. Ibid.

12. "Minister Outlines Cabinet Policy to Indians," op. cit., p. 6.

13. Ibid.

14. "Government Bonus for Indians Leaving Union," Weekly Newsletter, No. 484 (March 12, 1949), p. 7. The practice of offering a cash bonus for voluntary repatriation is not new. The Cape Town Agreement of 1927 stipulated a schedule of cash bonuses for each member of the Indian family in addition to free passage. Between 1927 and 1940 a total of 15,855 Indians left the Union. From January 1, 1949, to December 1, 1949, a total of 165 Indians left South Africa under the Nationalists' bonus scheme.

15. The Smuts-Gandhi Agreement was a personal agreement between Gandhi, the acknowledged leader of the Indian community, and General Smuts, then minister of the interior. The agreement was the prelude to the Relief Act which conceded to the Indians some of their demands against previous restrictions. "Their was no finality about the settlement. Gandhi had warned Smuts that complete satisfaction could not be expected until full civic rights had been conceded to the Indian population. But Smuts had demanded that the Indians should accept what had been conceded to them as a complete settlement of the controversy" (Appasamy, op. cit., p. 29).

16. Ibid.

17. "Government To Abolish Family Allowances for Indians," Weekly Newsletter, No. 460 (September 27, 1948), p. 8.

18. For the complete figures furnished by the government see ibid.

19. "Prime Minister Outlines Policy towards Indians," *Weekly Newsletter*, No. 460 (September 27, 1948), p. 6.

20. "Government Policy towards Indians," *Weekly Newsletter*, No. 453 (August 9, 1948), p. 8.

21. "Asiatic Penetration in the Cape," *Weekly Newsletter*, No. 459 (September 20, 1948), p. 2.

22. *Ibid.*

23. In terms of this act, "any person or class of persons deemed by the Minister on economic grounds or on account of standard or habits of life to be unsuited to the requirements of the Union or any particular Province thereof" may be declared a prohibited immigrant. Although neither Indians nor Asiatics were specifically mentioned, one of the purposes of the act was undoubtedly designed to give the minister power to apply it to Indians. By this mechanism, free movement between provinces has been prohibited (Webb, *op. cit.*, p. 206).

24. Villiers, *op. cit.*, p. 533.

25. *Ibid.*, p. 532.

26. Appasamy, *op. cit.*, p. 10.

27. *Ibid.*, p. 86.

28. *Ibid.*, p. 92.

29. "Minister Says Indians Are Seeking To Control Africa," *Weekly Newsletter*, No. 465 (November 1, 1948), p. 8.

30. "Treatment of Indians in South Africa," *United Nations Bulletin*, VI (June 1, 1949), 576.

31. *Ibid.*

32. *Ibid.* Article 2(7) provides: "Nothing contained in the present Charter shall authorize the United Nations to intervene in matters which are essentially within the domestic jurisdiction of any state or shall require the members to submit such matters to settlement under the present Charter; but this principle shall not prejudice the application of enforcement measures under Chapter VII."

33. *Ibid.*

34. *Ibid.*

35. *Ibid.*, p. 578.

36. *Weekly Newsletter*, No. 463 (October 18, 1948), p. 1.

37. "Prime Minister Reports on London Conference," *Weekly Newsletter*, No. 493 (May 14, 1949), p. 1.

38. "India Withdraws from Round Table Conference," *Weekly Newsletter*, No. 549 (June 10, 1950), p. 2.

39. "Committees' Recommendations on Indian Question," *Weekly Newsletter*, No. 548 (June 3, 1950), pp. 2–3.

40. "African Indians versus Natives," *Commonweal*, L (May 6, 1949), 92.

41. "Treatment of Indians in South Africa," *op. cit.*, p. 581.

42. "African Indians versus Natives," *op. cit.*, p. 92.

43. "Minister Favours More Bus Services for Natives," *Weekly Newsletter*, No. 495 (May 28, 1949), p. 7.

44. "Indian Buses Boycotted by Natives," *Weekly Newsletter*, No. 501 (July 9, 1949), p. 7.

45. "Prime Minister Tells How Coloureds Will Benefit under Apartheid," *Weekly Newsletter*, No. 469 (November 27, 1948), p. 9.

46. "Newspaper Comments on Riot," *Weekly Newsletter*, No. 477 (January 22, 1949), p. 3.

47. *Ibid.*

48. "South Africa's Attitude to UNO," *Weekly Newsletter*, No. 457 (September 6, 1949), p. 2.

CHAPTER X

1. Hugh Ashton, "The High Commission Territories," in *Handbook on Race Relations in South Africa*, ed. Ellen Hellmann (Cape Town, London, New York: Oxford University Press, 1949), chap. xxxiv, pp. 721–22.

2. *Ibid.*, p. 708.

3. *Ibid.*

4. South Africa Act, Secs. 150 and 151.

5. See, in particular, Margery Perham and Lionel Curtis, *The Protectorates of South Africa: The Question of Their Transfer to the Union* (London: Oxford University Press [Humphrey Milford], 1935), for a presentation of opposing views.

6. Dr. Malan has stressed that this is not incompatible with continued membership in the Commonwealth. India is an example.

7. "Union of South Africa, External Affairs," *Journal of the Parliaments of the Commonwealth*, XXXI (June, 1950), 321.

8. "Bechuanaland. Dirty Trick," *Time*, LV (March 20, 1950), 24.

9. See *Weekly Newsletter* (State Information Office, Pretoria), No. 445 (June 14, 1948), p. 2, and Supplement; No. 479 (February 12, 1949), p. 2; and No. 481 (February 19, 1949), p. 3. Since 1919 South-West Africa has been administered by the Union of South Africa under the League of Nations mandate system. Though a legislative assembly was granted to South-West Africa, the Union Parliament had full power to make laws for this territory and the appellate division of the Union's supreme court was made the appeal court for South-West Africa.

10. The elections for the Legislative Assembly of South-West Africa were held at the same time. Of the eighteen seats in the Assembly, the Nationalists won fifteen. An electoral college, composed of six members, of the Union House of Assembly and the

eighteen members of the Legislative Assembly, elect two members by proportional representation to represent South-West Africa in the Senate; two other senators are nominated by the Union government. The table of election returns and the information as to the South-West Africa–Union electoral arrangement are taken from "Union of South Africa. House of Assembly," *Journal of the Parliaments of the Commonwealth*, XXXI (September, 1950), 574.

11. Of the remainder, 9,632 were German-speaking and 2,395 English-speaking.

12. T. Walter Wallbank, "Britain's New Program for the Colonies," *Current History*, XV (August, 1948), 84.

13. Certain of the recommendations of the Coussey Report were modified; for example, a unicameral rather than a bicameral legislature was adopted.

14. For further details see A. C. Russell, "The Gold Coast General Election, 1951," *Journal of African Administration*, III (April, 1951), 65–77; "Constitutional Reform in the Gold Coast: The Recommendations of the Coussey Committee," *Journal of African Administration*, II (January, 1950), 2–11; "Local Government Reform in the Gold Coast," *Journal of African Administration*, II (January, 1950), 35–44; "The Adaptation of English Local Government Principles to Colonial Territories," *Journal of African Administration*, II (October, 1950), 34–39.

15. R. E. Robinson, "Why 'Indirect Rule' Has Been Replaced by 'Local Government' in the Nomenclature of British Native Administration," *Journal of African Administration*, II (July, 1950), 14–15.

16. Rita Hinden (ed.), *Local Government and the Colonies* (London: George Allen & Unwin, 1950), pp. 91–92.

17. *Ibid.*, p. 92.

18. In 1948 a third of the Northern Rhodesian school children spoke Afrikaans as their home language. In Southern Rhodesia certain sections of the Afrikaner population are endeavoring to have Afrikaans recognized as the second official language of the colony. Immigrants from the Union form 30 per cent of Southern Rhodesia's white population. In Kenya, from the earliest days of white settlement, Afrikaners from South Africa and English whites formed a cohesive and solid white minority.

19. In Kenya there are five million Natives and about 30,000 whites; a ratio of nearly 170:1. In Northern Rhodesia there are 1,700,000 Natives and 36,000 whites; a ratio of 47:1. In Southern Rhodesia there are 1,900,000 Natives and 130,000 whites; a ratio of 15:1.

20. W. R. Crocker, *Self-government for the Colonies* (London: George Allen & Unwin, 1949), pp. 72–74.

21. Hinden, op. cit., p. 123.

22. "Southern Rhodesia. White Settlement in Africa," *Journal of the Parliaments of the Commonwealth*, XXXI (September, 1950), 633.

23. *Ibid.*

24. *Ibid.*

25. André Siegfried, *African Journey* (London: Jonathan Cape, 1950), pp. 136–37.

26. "Apartheid the Only Sound Policy," *Weekly Newsletter*, No. 558 (August 12, 1950), p. 9.

27. "Union of South Africa. External Affairs," *Journal of the Parliaments of the Empire*, XXIX (December, 1948), 636–37.

28. *Ibid.*, p. 639.

29. See Crocker, op. cit., p. 75; Siegfried, op. cit., p. 134.

30. Alexander Campbell, *Empire in Africa* (London: Victor Gollancz, 1944), p. 135.

CHAPTER XI

1. I. S. Lloyd, " 'Apartheid'—South Africa's New Native Policy," *Political Quarterly*, XX (April–June, 1949), 124.

CHAPTER XII

1. I. S. Lloyd, " 'Apartheid'—South Africa's New Native Policy," *Political Quarterly*, XX (April–June, 1949), 126.

2. *Ibid.*

3. "The Doctrine of Apartheid," *Round Table*, XXXIX (December, 1948), 32.

Bibliography

A. BOOKS

AFRICANUS. *Transvaal Boers*. London: Horace Marshall & Son, 1899.

APPASAMY, BHASKAR. *Indians of South Africa*. Bombay: Padma Publications, 1943.

ASHTON, HUGH. "The High Commission Territories," in ELLEN HELLMANN (ed.), *Handbook on Race Relations in South Africa*, chap. xxxiv, pp. 706–41. Cape Town, London, New York: Oxford University Press, 1949.

BARNES, LEONARD. *Caliban in Africa*. Philadelphia: J. B. Lippincott Co., 1931.

BARNOUW, ADRIAAN. *Language and Race Problems in South Africa*. The Hague: Martinus Nijoff, 1934.

BELL, FRED W. *The South African Conspiracy*. London: William Heinemann, 1900.

BLACKWELL, LESLIE, and MAY, HENRY JOHN. *This Is South Africa*. Pietermaritzburg: Shuter & Shooter, 1947.

BOVILL, JOHN H. *Natives under the Transvaal Flag*. London: Simpkin, Marshall, Hamilton, Kent & Co., 1900.

BRADY, ALEXANDER. *Democracy in the Dominions*. Toronto: University of Toronto Press, 1947.

BRAND, R. H. *The Union of South Africa*. Oxford: Clarendon Press, 1909.

BROOKES, EDGAR H. *The Colour Problems of South Africa*. Lovedale, South Africa: Lovedale Press; London: K. Paul, Trench, Trubner & Co., 1934.

———. "Government and Administration," in ELLEN HELLMANN (ed.), *Handbook on Race Relations in South Africa*, chap. iii, pp. 27–40. Cape Town, London, New York: Oxford University Press, 1949.

———. *The History of Native Policy in South Africa from 1830 to the Present Day*. Pretoria: J. L. van Schaik, 1927.

BROOMFIELD, GERALD W. *Colour Conflict, Race Relations in Africa*. London: Edinburgh House Press, 1943.

BROWNE, J. H. B. *South Africa: A Glance at Current Conditions*. London: Longmans, Green & Co., 1905.

BRYCE, JAMES. *Impressions of South Africa*. New York: Century Co., 1900.

BRYCE, JAMES, et al. *Briton and Boer: Both Sides of the African Question*. New York and London: Harper & Bros., 1900.

237

BUELL, RAYMOND LESLIE. *The Native Problem in Africa*. New York: Macmillan Co., 1928.

BUTLER, JOSEPHINE. *Native Races and the War*. London: Gay & Bird, 1900.

BUXTON, CHARLES R. *The Race Problem in Africa*. London: Hogarth Press, 1931.

CAMPBELL, ALEXANDER. *Empire in Africa*. London: Victor Gollancz, 1944.

COOK, P. A. W. "Non-European Education," in ELLEN HELLMANN (ed.), *Handbook on Race Relations in South Africa*, chap. xv, pp. 348–86. Cape Town, London, New York: Oxford University Press, 1949.

COWEN, D. V. *Parliamentary Sovereignty and the Entrenched Sections of the South Africa Act*. Cape Town: Juta & Co., 1951.

COX, OLIVER CROMWELL. *Caste, Class and Race: A Study in Social Dynamics*. Garden City, N.Y.: Doubleday, 1948.

CRIPPS, ARTHUR S. *An Africa for Africans*. London: Longmans, Green & Co., 1927.

CROCKER, W. R. *Self-government for the Colonies*. London: George Allen & Unwin, 1949.

CRONJÉ, G. *Voogdyskap en Apartheid*. Pretoria: van Schaik, 1948.

CRONJÉ, G.; NICOL, WILLIAM; and GROENWALD, E. P. *Regverdige Rasseapartheid*. Stellenbosch: Christen Studentevereniging van Suid Afrika, 1947.

DAWSON, WILLIAM H. *South Africa: People, Races and Problems*. London: Longmans, Green & Co., 1925.

DE WET, CHRISTIAN R. *Three Years' War*. New York: Charles Scribner's Sons, 1902.

EISELEN, W. M. "Christianity and the Religious Life of the Bantu," in I. SCHAPERA (ed.), *Western Civilization and the Natives of South Africa*, chap. iii, pp. 65–82. London: George Routledge & Sons, 1934.

EVANS, IFOR L. *Native Policy in Southern Africa: An Outline*. Cambridge: At the University Press, 1934.

FARRELLY, M. J. *The Settlement after the War in South Africa*. London: Macmillan & Co., 1900.

FISHER, W. E. *The Transvaal and the Boers*. London: Chapman & Hall, 1900.

FITZGERALD, WALTER. *Africa: A Social, Economic and Political Geography of Its Major Regions*. London: Methuen & Co., 1948.

FRIEDGUT, A. J. "The Non-European Press," in ELLEN HELLMANN (ed.), *Handbook on Race Relations in South Africa*, chap. xx, pp. 484–510. Cape Town, London, New York: Oxford University Press, 1949.

GEEN, M. S. *The Making of the Union of South Africa.* London, New York, Toronto: Longmans, Green & Co., 1947.

GIBBS, HENRY. *Twilight in South Africa.* London: Jarrolds, 1949.

GUYOT, YVES. *Boer Politics.* London: John Murray, 1900.

HAILEY, LORD. *An African Survey: A Study of Problems Arising in Africa South of the Sahara.* London, New York, Toronto: Oxford University Press, 1938.

HANCOCK, W. K. *Survey of British Commonwealth Affairs,* Vol. II, Part 2. London, New York, Toronto: Oxford University Press, 1942.

HATTERSLEY, A. F. *South Africa, 1652–1933.* London: Thornton, Butterworth, 1933.

HELLMANN, ELLEN. "Urban Areas," in ELLEN HELLMANN (ed.), *Handbook on Race Relations in South Africa,* chap. xi, pp. 229–74. Cape Town, London, New York: Oxford University Press, 1949.

HILLEGAS, HOWARD. *Oom Paul's People.* New York: D. Appleton & Co., 1900.

HINDEN, RITA (ed.). *Local Government and the Colonies.* London: George Allen & Unwin, 1950.

HOERNLÉ, A. WINIFRED. "Social Organization," in I. SCHAPERA (ed.), *The Bantu-speaking Tribes of South Africa: An Ethnological Survey,* pp. 67–94. London: George Routledge & Sons, 1937.

HOERNLÉ, R. F. A. *Race and Reason.* Johannesburg: Witwatersrand University Press, 1945.

HOFMEYR, JAN H. *South Africa.* New York: Charles Scribner's Sons, 1931.

HOOKER, LE ROY. *The Africanders.* Chicago and New York: Rand McNally & Co., 1900.

HUNTER, MONICA. *Reaction to Conquest: Effects of Contact with Europeans on Pondo of South Africa.* London: Oxford University Press (H. Milford), 1936.

KENNEDY, W. P. M., and SCHLOSBERG, H. J. *The Law and Custom of the South African Constitution.* London: Oxford University Press, 1935.

KEPPEL-JONES, ARTHUR M. "Land and Agriculture Outside the Reserves," in ELLEN HELLMANN (ed.), *Handbook on Race Relations in South Africa,* chap. viii, pp. 191–205. Cape Town, London, New York: Oxford University Press, 1949.

KIDD, DUDLEY. *Kafir Socialism and the Dawn of Individualism: An*

Introduction to the Study of the Native Problem. London: Adams & Charles Black, 1908.

KIRK, JOHN. *The Economic Aspects of Native Segregation in South Africa.* London: P. S. King & Son, 1929.

MACKENZIE, W. DOUGLAS. *South Africa, Its History, Heroes and Wars.* San Francisco: J. Dewing Co., 1899.

MCKERRON, M. E. *A History of Education in South Africa (1652–1932).* Pretoria: J. L. van Schaik, Ltd., 1934.

MACMILLAN, WILLIAM MILLER. *Africa Emergent: A Survey of Social, Political, and Economic Trends in British Africa.* London: Faber & Faber, 1938.

——. *Bantu, Boer and Briton: The Making of the South African Native Problem.* London: Faber & Gwyer, 1929.

MALHERBE, ERNEST GIDEON. *Education in South Africa (1652–1922).* Cape Town and Johannesburg: Juta & Co., 1925.

MARAIS, J. S. "The Imposition and Nature of European Control," in I. SCHAPERA (ed.), *The Bantu-speaking Tribes of South Africa: An Ethnological Survey,* chap. xv, pp. 333–55. London: George Routledge & Sons, 1937.

MARKHAM, V. R. *The South African Scene.* London: Smith, Elder & Co., 1913.

MARQUARD, L. *The Native in South Africa.* Johannesburg: Witwatersrand University Press, 1948.

MATHESON, ALASTAIR. *The Coloured People of the Cape.* London: Public Relations Office, South Africa House [1947?].

MAY, HENRY JOHN. *The South African Constitution.* Cape Town and Johannesburg: Juta & Co., 1949.

Meet the Indian in South Africa: A Pictorial Survey. Pretoria: State Information Office, [1950].

MOKITIMI, SETH. M. "African Religion," in ELLEN HELLMANN (ed.), *Handbook on Race Relations in South Africa,* chap. xxiii, pp. 556–72. Cape Town, London, New York: Oxford University Press, 1949.

NEVILLE, JOHN ORMAND. *Boer and Britisher in South Africa.* Chicago: Thompson & Thomas, 1900.

NEWTON, A. P., and BENIANS E. A. (eds.). *The Cambridge History of the British Empire,* Vol. VIII. New York: Macmillan Co.; Cambridge: Cambridge University Press, 1936.

NOON, JOHN A. *Labor Problems of Africa,* ed. H. A. WIESCHOFF. ("African Handbooks," No. 6.) Philadelphia: University of Pennsylvania Press, 1944.

Official Yearbook of the Union and of Basutoland, Bechuanaland Protectorate and Swaziland, No. 24. Pretoria: Union Office of Census and Statistics, 1948.

OLDHAM, J. H., and GIBSON, B. D. *The Remaking of Man in Africa*. London: Oxford University Press (H. Milford), 1931.

PERHAM, MARGERY, and CURTIS, LIONEL. *The Protectorates of South Africa: The Question of Their Transfer to the Union*. London: Oxford University Press (H. Milford), 1935.

PHILLIPS, RAY E. *The Bantu in the City*. Lovedale, South Africa: Lovedale Press, 1938.

ROBERTS, M., and TROLLIP, A. E. G. *The South African Opposition, 1939–1945*. London, Cape Town, and New York: Longmans, Green & Co., 1947.

ROGERS, HOWARD. *Native Administration in the Union of South Africa*. Johannesburg: University of the Witwatersrand Press, 1933.

ROUX, EDWARD. "Land and Agriculture in the Native Reserves," in ELLEN HELLMANN (ed.), *Handbook on Race Relations in South Africa*, chap. vii, pp. 171–90. Cape Town, London, New York: Oxford University Press, 1949.

SCHAPERA, I. "Political Institutions," in I. SCHAPERA (ed.), *The Bantu-speaking Tribes of South Africa: An Ethnological Survey*, chap. viii, pp. 173–95. London: George Routledge & Sons, 1937.

SIEGFRIED, ANDRÉ. *African Journey*. London: Jonathan Cape, 1950.

SILBURN, P. A. *South Africa, White and Black—or Brown?* London: George Allen & Unwin, 1927.

SIMONS, H. J. "The Law and Its Administration," in ELLEN HELLMANN (ed.), *Handbook on Race Relations in South Africa*, chap. iv, pp. 41–108. Cape Town, London, New York: Oxford University Press, 1949.

SMUTS, ADRIAAN J. *The Education of Adolescents in South Africa*. Cape Town and Johannesburg: Juta & Co., [1938].

SOUTH AFRICA. *A Selection of Articles*. London: South African Association, 1896.

Southwest Africa and the Union of South Africa: The History of a Mandate. New York: Union of South Africa Government Information Office, [1946].

SOWDEN, LEWIS. *The Union of South Africa*. Garden City, N.Y.: Doubleday, Doran & Co., 1943.

TINLEY, J. M. *The Native Labor Problem of South Africa*. Chapel Hill: University of North Carolina Press, 1942.

VAN DER HOOGT, C. W. *The Story of the Boers, Prepared under the Authority of the South African Republics*. N.p., 1900.

VAN DER HORST, SHEILA T. "Labour," in ELLEN HELLMANN (ed.), *Handbook on Race Relations in South Africa*, chap. v, pp. 109–57. Cape Town, London, New York: Oxford University Press, 1949.

VILLIERS, R. M. DE. "Politics," in ELLEN HELLMANN (ed.), Handbook on Race Relations in South Africa, chap. xxi, pp. 511–33. Cape Town, London, New York: Oxford University Press, 1949.

WEBB, MAURICE. "Indian Land Legislation," in ELLEN HELLMANN (ed.), Handbook on Race Relations in South Africa, chap. ix, pp. 206–13. Cape Town, London, New York: Oxford University Press, 1949.

WELLES, SUMNER (ed.). An Intelligent American's Guide to the Peace. New York: Dryden Press, 1945.

WESTERMANN, DIEDRICH. The African Today. London: Oxford University Press, 1934.

———. The African Today and Tomorrow. Rev. ed. London: Oxford University Press (H. Milford), 1939.

WILKINSON, SPENSER. British Policy in South Africa. London: Sampson Low, Marston & Co., 1899.

WILLIAMS, BASIL. Botha, Smuts and South Africa. London: Hodder & Stoughton, 1948.

WITHERS, HARTLEY. The English and Dutch in South Africa. London: Clement Wilson, 1896.

WOLTON, DOUGLAS G. Whither South Africa? London: Lawrence & Wishart, 1947.

B. ARTICLES

"Adaptation of English Local Government Principles to Colonial Territories, The," Journal of African Administration, II (October, 1950), 34–39.

"African Indians versus Natives," Commonweal, L (May 6, 1949), 92.

"Appeal Court Declares Separate Voters' Act Invalid," South Africa News Cable, March 20, 1952, pp. 83–84.

"Bechuanaland. Dirty Trick," Time, LV (March 20, 1950), 24.

"Black Man's Burden, The," Time, LIV (November 14, 1949), 33.

BLAXALL, A. W. "South Africa Belongs to Us," International Review of Missions, XXXVIII (July, 1949), 295–305.

BOOTH, NEWELL S. "The Ministry in Bantu Religion," International Review of Missions, XXXVI (July, 1937), 334–44.

"Church Opposition to 'Apartheid' Growing," Christian Century, LVI (November 16, 1949), 1348–49.

"Coloured Franchise, The," Race Relations News, XIII (January, 1951), 8–9.

"Coloured Franchise Bill," Race Relations News, XIII (March, 1951), 38–41.

"Constitutional Reform in the Gold Coast: The Recommendations of the Coussey Committee," *Journal of African Administration,* II (January, 1950), 2–11.

"Defiant South Africa," *Christian Century,* LXVI (September 28, 1949), 1126–28.

"Doctrine of Apartheid, The," *Round Table,* XXXIX (December, 1948), 32–35.

"Doctrine of Apartheid, The," *Round Table,* XXXIX (June, 1949), 208–13.

DUNDAS, SIR CHARLES. "Apartheid and the Union," *Nineteenth Century and After,* CXLVIII (October, 1950), 224–31.

"Dutch Churches Call for Root and Branch Separation, The," *South African Outlook,* LXXX (May 1, 1950), 68–69.

DVORIN, EUGENE P. "The Theory of Apartheid: Nationalist Racial Policy in the Union of South Africa," *Western Political Quarterly,* IV (March, 1951), 32–47.

"Eyes on South Africa," *Christian Century,* LXVI (May 4, 1949), 550–52.

"Faithlessness the Guiding Line," *South African Outlook,* LXXX (November 1, 1950), 165–67.

"Final Stages of Colored Voters' Bill," *South Africa Reports* (Union of South Africa Government Information Office, New York), May 31, 1951, pp. 2–3.

FLAVIN, MARTIN. "Durban Deep," *Harper's,* CXCVIII (April, 1949), 65–75.

Full and Certified Text of the Judgement of the Appellate Division of the Supreme Court of South Africa, Delivered on March 20, 1952, Declaring Invalid the Separate Representation of Voters Act (Act No. 46 of 1951).

"General Hertzog's Native Policy," *New Statesman,* XXXIII (June 8, 1929), 262–64.

GEYER, A. L. "South Africa in the World Crisis," *United Empire,* XLII (March–April, 1951), 81–85.

HATCH, JOHN. "Malan Sows the Wind," *New Statesman and Nation,* XLI (April 28, 1951), 471–72.

HINDEN, RITA. "The Dilemma That Racism Poses for Britain: Labour's Colonial Heritage," *Commentary,* XII (August, 1951), 151–56.

KAHN, ELLISON. "Whither Our War-Time Native Policy?" *South African Journal of Economics,* X (June, 1942), 126–52.

"Legislation To Ensure Parliament's Sovereignty," *South African News Cable,* March 22, 1952, p. 85.

LESTRADE, G. P. "Some Aspects of the Economic Life of the South African Bantu," *South African Journal of Economics*, II (December, 1934), 426–43.

LITVINOFF, BARNET. "The Dilemma That Racism Poses for Britian: Cocktail Party in East Africa," *Commentary*, XII (August, 1951), 156–60.

LLOYD, I. S. " 'Apartheid'—South Africa's New Native Policy," *Political Quarterly*, XX (April–June, 1949), 123–35.

"Local Government Reform in the Gold Coast," *Journal of African Administration*, II (January, 1950), 35–44.

MILLIN, SARAH GERTRUDE. "Fear in South Africa," *Foreign Affairs*, XXVIII (October, 1949), 102–3.

MOKITIMI, SETH M. "Apartheid and the Christian Spirit," *International Review of Missions*, XXXVIII (July, 1949), 276–79.

"Native Policy of the Union, 1910–1932, The," *Round Table*, XXII (June, 1932), 658–72.

NICOL, WILLIAM. "Why the Christian Council Failed," *South African Outlook*, LXXI (December 1, 1941), 251.

"Noted D.R. Church Scholar and Apartheid," *South African Outlook*, LXXX (January 1, 1950), 15.

OLIVIER, S. H. "General Hertzog's Eirencion to the Native," *New Statesman*, XXVIII (October 16, 1926), 8–9.

PATON, ALAN. "South Africa Today," *Sunday Compass Magazine*, III (October 21, 1951), 9, 11, 17; *ibid.*, October 28, 1951, pp. 11, 12, 17.

"Piennaar's Opinion on Vote Bill," *Cape Times*, May 19, 1951, pp. 1 and 3.

PRICE, T. W. "Speaker's Ruling Not Last Word on Vote Bill," *Cape Times*, May 8, 1951, p. 8.

"Protest Day Fiasco, The," *South African Outlook*, LXXX (July 1, 1950), 101–2.

"Representation of Non-European Coloured Franchise Bill," *Race Relations News*, XIII (April, 1951), 44–48.

ROBINSON, R. E. "Why 'Indirect Rule' Has Been Replaced by 'Local Government' in the Nomenclature of British Native Administration," *Journal of African Administration*, II (July, 1950), 12–15.

RUSSELL, A. C. "The Gold Coast General Election, 1951," *Journal of African Administration*, III (April, 1951), 65–77.

"S.A. Ex-Soldiers' Manifesto," *Cape Times*, May 16, 1951, p. 1.

SCOTT, H. S. "The Christian Churches and the Colour Bar," *International Review of Missions*, XXXI (July, 1942), 301–7.

SHEPHERD, ROBERT H. W., and GRANT, EDWARD W. "The Christian Council of South Africa," *International Review of Missions*, XXXIII (July, 1944), 258–66.

"South Africa. Sailor v. Premier," *Time*, LVIII (July 9, 1951), 24.

"South African Race Problem in the Light of General Hertzog's Proposed Legislation, The," *International Review of Missions*, XVI (April, 1927), 182–91.

"Southern Rhodesia. White Settlement in Africa," *Journal of the Parliaments of the Commonwealth*, XXXI (September, 1950), 633–37.

"Torchmen Set Out on Union Tour for Recruits," *Sunday Times* (Johannesburg), October 14, 1951, p. 16.

"Treatment of Indians in South Africa," *United Nations Bulletin*, VI (June 1, 1949), 576–81.

"Unemployment Insurance Ceases for Africans," *South African Outlook*, LXXX (February 1, 1950), 19–20.

"Union of South Africa. Debate in House of Assembly," *Journal of the Parliaments of the Commonwealth*, XXXI (June, 1950), 329–36.

"Union of South Africa. External Affairs," *Journal of the Parliaments of the Commonwealth*, XXI (June, 1950), 318–21.

"Union of South Africa. External Affairs," *Journal of the Parliaments of the Empire*, XXIX (December, 1948), 631–42.

"Union of South Africa. Group Areas Bill," *Journal of the Parliaments of the Commonwealth*, XXXI (September, 1950), 585–94.

"Union of South Africa. House of Assembly," *Journal of the Parliaments of the Commonwealth*, XXXI (September, 1950), 574.

"Union of South Africa. Native Legislation; Apartheid," *Journal of the Parliaments of the Empire*, XXIX (December, 1948), 641–42.

"Union of South Africa. Population Registration Bill," *Journal of the Parliaments of the Commonwealth*, XXXI (June, 1950), 336–43.

"Union of South Africa. Privy Council Appeals Bill," *Journal of the Parliaments of the Commonwealth*, XXXI (June, 1950), 322–26.

VANE, MICHAEL. "Restrictive Legislation in South Africa," *Quarterly Review*, CCLXXXIX (July, 1951), 304–17.

WALLBANK, WALTER T. "Britain's New Program for the Colonies," *Current History*, XV (August, 1948), 83–87, 104.

"Warning to Malan Given by Veterans," *New York Times*, April 28, 1952, p. 8.

Weekly Newsletter (State Information Office, Pretoria, Union of South Africa).

C. PAMPHLETS

GEYER, A. L. The Most Complex Multi-racial Problem in the World: Apartheid Seeks To Find a Synthesis of Valid Rights of Black and White. Address by the High Commissioner for the Union of South Africa. London: South Africa House, 1951.

JANSEN, DR. THE HONOURABLE E. G. Native Policy of the Union of South Africa: Statements by Dr. the Honourable E. G. Jansen, Minister of Native Affairs. Pretoria: State Information Office, Union of South Africa, [1950].

VERWOERD, H. F. "Apartheid Policy. Address by the Minister of Native Affairs." New York: Union of South Africa Government Information Office, [1950]. (Mimeographed.)

Date Due

MAY 2 3 '58		
OCT 2 8 '60		
MAR 1 7 '61		
PRINTED	IN U. S. A.	